Developmental
MANAGEMENT

TOTAL QUALITY LEARNING

𝕭

Developmental Management

General Editor: Ronnie Lessem

Charting the Corporate Mind
Charles Hampden-Turner*

Managing in the Information Society
Yoneji Masuda

Developmental Management
Ronnie Lessem

Foundations of Business
Ivan Alexander

Greening Business
John Davis

Ford on Management
Henry Ford*

Managing Your Self
Jagdish Parikh

Managing the Developing Organization
Bernard Lievegoed

Conceptual Toolmaking
Jerry Rhodes

Integrative Management
Pauline Graham

Executive Leadership
Elliott Jaques and Stephen D. Clement

Transcultural Management
Albert Koopman

The Great European Illusion
Alain Minc

The Rise of NEC
Koji Kobayashi

Total Quality Learning
Ronnie Lessem

* *For copyright reasons this edition is not available in the USA*

Developmental
MANAGEMENT

Total Quality
Learning

BUILDING A LEARNING
ORGANISATION

RONNIE LESSEM

First published 1991
Reprinted 1992
First published in paperback 1994

Blackwell Publishers
108 Cowley Road, Oxford, OX4 1JF, UK

238 Main Street
Cambridge, Massachusetts 02142, USA

British Library Cataloguing in Publication Data

A CIP catalogue record for this book is available from the British Library.

Library of Congress Cataloging in Publication Data

Lessem, Ronnie.
Total quality learning / Ronnie Lessem.
p.   cm.—(Developmental management)
Includes index.
ISBN 0–631–19306–5 (pbk.)
1. Management.   I. Title.   II. Series
HD31.L384   1994   658.4–dc20   90–40346
CIP

Typeset in 11 on 13 pt Ehrhardt
by Hope Services (Abingdon) Ltd.
Printed in Great Britain by
T.J. Press Ltd., Padstow, Cornwall

This book is printed on acid-free paper

Contents

Foreword

Ronnie Lessem's *Total Quality Learning* is an essential addition to the Developmental Management Series which he edits. As the designation implies, in management terms, the various series texts to date go well beyond the merely topical nature of so many recent books on management. *Total Quality Learning* is no exception to the already high standard of the series.

The book invites its readership to place themselves individually in a personal development mode – to learn about and grow their own managerial personas. The stress on the word 'learning' and its linkage with 'total quality' emphasizes the importance of individual initiative and that excellence is the objective. Of particular attraction to me is the breadth of vision implicit in the final part of the book. A vision of development is needed by all of us who purport to practice the profession of management.

Overall, not only will the book contribute to encouraging a personal sense of direction and focus for managers, but it will also assist materially with the road map.

Total Quality Learning is provocative, realistic and highly relevant. Importantly, I predict that it will remain valid, and thus endure. I sincerely commend it.

Sir Graham Day

Preface

This book on 'Total Quality Learning' (TQL) is the result, equally, of a sense of mission and of deep frustration, on two connected fronts. The missionary within me, dedicated to education in all walks of life, has firstly been captivated by the notion of the learning organization, ever since I came across it in the late 1970s. My deep sense of frustration is born out of the fact that so many otherwise thoughtful managers are paying no more than lip service to this powerful concept, and we management educators are to blame for failing to enrich their imaginations. Secondly, my soul has responded to the call of 'quality', as a business ethic for our time. Yet I am enormously frustrated by the narrowness of perspective, that is outside of Japan, surrounding the much-lauded TQM. Again I feel that I, as a member of the management educational fraternity, am to blame.

To relieve myself from the pain of yet unrealized ambition I therefore set out, three years ago, to do full justice to the concept of quality, in the context of learning. It was my good fortune that, at around the same time, my colleague at City University Business School, Professor Hugh Murray, had formed a learning consortium, in partnership with several progressive and internationally based organizations. The opportunity with which I was faced was that of bringing together individual and organizational learning, across the public and private arena. The university, together with the diverse institutions represented, had the chance of both learning for themselves and from one another. I jumped at the prospect.

Today some 200 learners, educators and coaches are intertwined within a learning community, based in London but extending into Europe and America. Engaged in knowledge, skill and self-development – as individuals and as organizations – we are transforming not only the learning environment, but also our institutions and our industries. The all-round quality that we are bringing to bear upon our learning enterprise is represented in the marriage between thought, feeling and action that this kind of educational activity involves. Moreover, as I have illustrated in this book, the outward manifestation of learning is in fact innovation.

A week before settling down to write this preface my heart missed several beats when I took the time and trouble to read Michael Porter's latest tome on *The Competitive Advantage of Nations*[1]: for, in describing the evolution of national economies from 'factor' to 'investment', and ultimately to 'innovation'-driven economies, he is in fact describing, from the perspective of this book, a cumulative learning experience.

In many ways, therefore, my mission is complementary to Porter's, for both of us – my initial training was as an economist – are concerned with the economic development of nations. I am oriented, however, towards the inner dynamics of development, that is within the individual manager and organization, while Porter is oriented towards the outer ones, surrounding the individual firm and the national economy. In effect I am more concerned with processes of learning and individuation, while Porter is concerned with those of innovation and wealth creation.

By virtue of such a concern with the inner dynamics of development, I have no choice but to start this book in ancient Greece, where the desire for mankind to 'know thyself' first emerged. In subsequently focusing on the interaction between the Greek concept of quality, virtue – or 'arete' – and learning, I venture further into Robert Pirsig's world of *Zen and the Art of Motorcycle Mainten-ance*,[2] the classic text on 'quality' in the 1970s. Between these rather wayward journeys I study the substance of management – self, skill and knowledge – and proceed to transform the whole subject, so that it might become a manifestation of learning, and of innovation.

By way of conclusion, I return to the theme of total quality learning, linking it with the emerging science of holography. It is my view, in the final analysis, that over the course of the next 25 years the learning organization will supplant the business enterprise as the critical entity within the national and international economy, if not within society as a whole. By implication, therefore, it will be the quality of our learning, as individuals and managers, and as organizations and societies, that will determine our overall development. To the extent

that such a prediction is even halfway right, I do hope that this book
will be of some service to you.

Ronnie Lessem
London, 1990

Notes

1 M. Porter, *The Competitive Advantage of Nations* (Macmillan, London, 1990).
2 R. Pirsig, *Zen and the Art of Motorcycle Maintenance* (Black Swan, 1989).

Acknowledgements

I first want to thank Professor Hugh Murray, at City University Business School, for creating the very foundations upon which 'Total Quality Learning' could be built, and Patti Davis and Jenny Steele for providing the communal ground in which seeds of learning could be planted. Secondly, I want to thank in particular Mary Coles, Brenda Malalehka and Dippy Sembhi at the London Borough of Ealing, Philipe Marmara at American Express, Charles Richardson at County Natwest Investment Bank, Martin Wheatley and Stanley Young at the International Stock Exchange, Peter Sirman at Sainsbury's, and Conrad Fernandez at Tektronix for taking to heart the learning organization. Thirdly, I want to thank once again Richard Burton for his courage in championing the series, and Geoffrey Palmer for his endurance in copy-editing the manuscript.

Ronnie Lessem

To all those participants on our Management MBA programme, who have worked with me on the concepts and applications underlying this book, over the course of three exciting years.

PART I

Total Learning

I

Introducing Total Quality Learning

Introduction

The Evolution of Management

In tracing the evolution of management over the past 50 years, you will find that history has repeated itself, albeit with some differences. Craftsmanship of traditional quality was displaced by mass production and marketing, which is now being replaced by intelligent manufacturing, of contemporary quality. Quality and learning have now displaced profitability and market share as the new managerial imperatives. Let me explain.

Just after the war, management science asserted itself as both mathematically based *operations* research and statistically based work study. No sooner were these analytically based advances made in Europe and America than they were rapidly imported into Japan, especially for purposes of quality control.

In the 1950s this production-led management science was supplanted in the West by rationally based approaches to management *control*. Capital budgeting and discounted cash flow techniques took pride of place over more prosaic methods of work study. These in turn were displaced in the early 1960s, particularly in America, by analytically based approaches to *marketing* management.

It was only in the late 1960s and early 1970s that this 'hard' and rational approach to management was fundamentally called into question by the behavioural scientists of the day. 'Soft' approaches to 'organization development' proliferated, as the management of *human* resources asserted its newly formed identity.

As recession bit, in the early 1980s, however, the 'number

crunchers' began to make their influence felt once again – but only up to a point. For in the postwar period there has been a fundamental shift in the balance of economic power, most particularly US towards Japan. Moreover, throughout that period, Japan has maintained unswervingly its primary orientation towards product and people. Influenced, at least in part, by the East, progressive management in the West has returned seemingly full circle to the operations function.

This simultaneous regression and progression has led, on the one hand, to total *quality* management (TQM), and on the other to the *learning* organization. In this book I shall be concerned with their fusion into 'total quality learning' or 'TQL'.

Total learning

The first great industrial revolution in nineteenth-century Europe, not to mention the scientific revolution that preceded it, was a gigantic Western exercise in learning. Yet it was not until the latter part of the twentieth century that the idea of a 'learning organization' gained prominence. The impetus for this has in fact come from the evolving production function rather than from the realms of human resource management.

In the early 1980s three professors at the Harvard Business School – Abernathy, Clark and Kantrow – in arguing the case for a renaissance in American manufacturing industry, claimed that: 'What is needed is a view of *production* as an enterprise of unlimited potential, an enterprise in which current arrangements are but the starting point for *continuous organizational learning* [emphasis added]'.[1] The theme that the late Bill Abernathy and his colleagues advanced has been more recently picked up by Harvard Professors Hayes, Clark and Weelright in their book on *Dynamic Manufacturing*. They say that the process of learning, from observation to problem-solving, involves a set of activities that they term the 'learning cycle'.[2] What has been learned, then, must be incorporated into the production system.

The problem with this approach is that it is devoid of feeling, and is therefore disconnected from 'quality' in the round, which involves such elements as unity, vividness, authority, economy, sensitivity, clarity, emphasis, flow, suspense, brilliance, precision, proportion and depth. What do such quality attributes have to do, then, with total quality management?

Quality management

TQM supposedly not only represents a successful marriage between product and people but also between tough-minded thinking and tender-hearted feeling. This may indeed be the case in Japan, but we in the West are far from achieving such a synthesis. In fact it seems that the greater our euphoria about quality the more we remove ourselves from its essence. It is therefore the aim of this book to recover the essence of 'quality', and to reveal how we might develop quality managers and organizations that draw on, and out of, a Western tradition.

Fortunately we can be helped along the way by the first American 'quality' philosopher, who took the management world by storm in the 1970s, only to lapse into virtual obscurity a decade or so later. Robert Pirsig's bestselling book had the unusual title *Zen and the Art of Motorcycle Maintenance*. His primary concern, long before TQM had become such a buzzword in Western management circles, was with quality: 'A person who sees *Quality* and feels it as he works *is a person who cares*. A person who cares about what he sees and does is a person who is bound to have some characteristics of Quality [emphasis added]'.[3]

Pirsig's definition of quality can be compared and contrasted with that of the contemporary American TQM authority, Philip Crosby: '*Quality means conformance*. When we talk about quality, we are really referring to the compliance of the product. Does it look like the advert? Does it conform to requirements? Will it do what the customer has been led to expect? [emphasis added]'.[4]

British Telecom, one of a group of large Europe-based multinationals who have banded together to help one another enhance their TQM, follows the Crosby approach in defining quality as: 'Meeting the Customers [agreed] requirements at lowest cost . . . first time, every time . . . British Telecom's goal is to achieve and sustain such Quality in everything it does'.[5] But if we were to ask how the Japanese have managed to transform the quality of their products, over the course of the past 30 years, we would have to reach beyond Crosby's grasp for an answer.

There are, in fact, two major factors. Firstly, the Japanese have been able to marry up Western mathematically and statistically based *technique*, with Eastern Buddhist and Confucian *philosophy*. To paraphrase Robert Pirsig,[6] the Buddha can just as easily be found in the gears of a motorcycle transmission as on a mountain top, or in the petals of a flower. Secondly, the Japanese have created veritable *learning* organizations, capable of adapting to change with extraordinary rapidity.

I will now pursue a line of thought, feeling and action whereby quality and learning are interlinked in the pursuit of a new management order: one which, while reaching forward into the information age, also reaches back to *ancient Greece*. For we in the West are neither Buddhists nor Confucians! The originators of learning in Western civilization, more than 2000 years ago, were the Greek Sophists: they focused on the cultivation of 'arete' which, as we shall soon see, was the equivalent of what is today called excellence.

Quality and Learning

Arete

Sophist rhetoric

The Sophists were probably the 'sages' in early Greek society: for about 70 years, until 380 BC, they were the sole source of higher education in the more advanced Greek cities. One of their most distinctive tenets was that virtue – arete, implying both success in life and the qualities needed to achieve such success – can be *taught*.

The implications of this belief were far-reaching, involving the rejection of the view that arete was acquired by birth (for example, by being born into a noble family) or purely by chance. In the Sophist's view, it was the result of known and controllable procedures.

To develop arete, the Sophists adopted the procedure of *rhetoric*: not merely as a method of public speaking, but rather as a means of putting into practice the wisdom one acquires in philosophy. In modern management parlance this may be referred to as turning vision into action: rhetoric involved not only the invention of a speech topic, but also the organization of the material, and the action involved in giving the oration.

Moreover, at least since the time of Plato, it has been common practice to suggest a relationship between rhetoric and democracy. For example, when the Roman philosopher Quintillian wrote his text on rhetoric for politicians to follow, it proved unsuited to an age of tyranny. It was only in the time of the Renaissance, therefore, that

Quintillian's *Institutes* came to be revered as the greatest educational treatise ever written.

Duty to oneself

Rhetoric, then, served as a means of developing character, or even a heroic outlook on life. What moved the Greek warrior to deeds of heroism, the classical scholar Professor Kitto wrote, was not a sense of duty as the Japanese would understand it – duty towards others: it was rather *duty towards oneself*.

Moreover, arete implies a respect for the wholeness or oneness of life, and a consequent dislike of specialization. It implies a contempt for efficiency; or rather a much higher ideal, an efficiency that exists not in one activity but in life itself: 'Quality! Virtue! That is what the Sophists were teaching. Before the Church of Reason. Before substance. Before form. Before mind and matter. Those first teachers of the Western world were teaching Quality, and the medium they had chosen was that of rhetoric'.[7]

Unfortunately, the Western world came under the influence of Aristotle, and reason and logic rather than virtue became the primary concerns: science and rationality, as we know them today, were given their founding charter. Arete was subsumed and rhetoric, once learning itself, reduced to the teaching of mannerisms and forms. Pirsig's solution to this unholy division of learning between the true (knowledge) and the good (virtue) is to combine these respectively 'classical' and 'romantic' approaches.

Quality in the Round

Classicism versus romanticism

Let us listen to Robert Pirsig: we take a handful of sand from the endless landscape of awareness around us and call that handful of sand the world. *Classical* understanding is concerned with the piles of sand and the basis for sorting and interrelating them. *Romantic* understanding is directed towards the handful of sand, before the sorting begins. Both are valid ways of looking at the world, although irreconcilable with each other.

The romantic mode is primarily inspirational, imaginative, creative and intuitive – feelings rather than facts predominate. 'Art', when it is opposed to 'science', is often romantic: it does not proceed by reason or laws, but by feeling, intuition and aesthetic conscience. The classical mode, by contrast, proceeds by reason and by laws.

The classical style is straightforward, unadorned, unemotional, economical and carefully proportioned. Its purpose is not to inspire emotionally but to bring order out of chaos, and to make the unknown known. While motorcycle riding (like learning and innovation) is romantic, motorcycle maintenance (like Crosby's version of TQM) is purely classical.

A fusion of classical and romantic quality, Pirsig suggests, can take place at a basic level within a practical working context. Skilled mechanics have patience, care and attentiveness to what they are doing; but, more than this, there is a kind of inner peace of mind that is not contrived but is derived from 'harmony' with the work in hand – work in which there is no leader and no follower.

The material and the craftsman's thoughts change together in a smooth, even progression until his mind is at rest at the exact instant the material is right. The same can be said, or should be said, for the 'craft' of management, pursued with quality in mind. Craftspeople, whether skilled artisans or managers, seldom follow a single line of instruction – they make decisions as they go along. That is why they become so absorbed and attentive. Their actions and the machine or organization with which they are working are in 'harmony'. The nature of the material or human resources at hand determines their thoughts and actions, which simultaneously change the nature of that material or those human resources.

The way to see what looks good, and to be at one with this goodness as the work proceeds, is to cultivate an inner quietness – a peace of mind – so that goodness, or arete, can shine through. This involves the absence of self-consciousness and complete identification with one's circumstances. The mountains of achievement are quality discovered in one direction only, and are relatively meaningless unless taken together with the ocean trenches of self-awareness – very different from self-consciousness – which result from inner peace of mind.

Quality in itself

Quality then, as Pirsig describes it, decreases subjectivity. It takes you out of yourself and makes you aware of the world around you. Quality is opposed to subjectivity:

If you want to build a factory, or fix a motorcycle, or set a nation right without getting stuck, then classical, structured, dualistic subject object knowledge, although necessary, is not enough. You have to have some feeling for the quality of the work. You have to have a sense of what's good. That is what carries you forward. This sense isn't just something you're born with, although you are born with it. It's also something you can develop.[8]

When you are not dominated by feelings of separateness from what you are working on, then you can be said to 'care' about what you are doing. You can then also see the inverse side of caring, quality itself:

The place to improve the world is first in one's own heart and head and hands, and then work outward from there. Other people can talk about how to expand the destiny of mankind. I just want to talk about how to fix a motorcycle. I think that what I have to say has more lasting value.[9]

A real understanding of quality, therefore, doesn't just serve the 'system' (quality means conformance), or even beat it or escape it. In fact it captures the 'system', tames it and puts it to work for your own personal use, while leaving you completely free to fulfil your inner destiny.

The fault with technology, as with management, is that it is not connected in any real way, in the West, with matters of the spirit and of the heart. And so, according to Pirsig, it often does blind, ugly things, for which it is hated. Yet quality, or its absence, resides neither in the subject nor the object. The real ugliness lies in the relationship between the people who produce the technology and the things they produce, which results in a similar relationship between the people who use the technology and the things they use. At the moment of pure quality there is no subject and there is no object – they are identical. Subjects and objects are produced by a later awareness.

It is impossible to run away from technology. The way to resolve the conflict between human values and technological needs, therefore, is to break down the barriers of dualistic thought that prevent a real understanding of what technology is – not an exploitation of nature, but a fusion of nature and the human spirit into a new synthesis that transcends both. 'The real cycle that you're working on', Pirsig says, 'is a cycle called yourself. The machine that appears to be out there and the person that appears to be in here are not two separate things. They grow towards Quality or fall away from Quality altogether'.[10]

Human beings are not the source of all things, then, as the subjective idealists and humanists would say. Nor are they passive observers of all things, as the objective idealists and materialists would believe. The quality that creates the world emerges as a *relationship* between people and their experiences. In other words, you are a participant, with other people and things, in both 'inner-directed' learning and also in 'outer-directed' innovation. We now turn from quality to learning.

The Age of the Smart Machine

From sentient craft to 'informated' activity

The evolution of management history, from a traditional to a contemporary operational context, has been powerfully captured by Shoshana Zuboff, Associate Professor at Harvard Business School, some 15 years after the writings of Robert Pirsig. In fact, in many ways, Zuboff has taken off from where Pirsig stopped. Whereas his predominant concern was with quality and technology, her preoccupation is with individual and organizational learning. Similarly, whereas Pirsig looked back to ancient Greece and to the role of the craftsman, Zuboff first looks back to such an age of craftsmanship and then forward to our emerging 'informated' age. Between the two lies the era of mechanization and automation.

Manufacturing activity, Zuboff tells us, has its roots in the work of the skilled craftsman, who may not have been intellectual but was certainly knowledgeable. He participated in a form of knowledge that had always defined the making of things:

It was knowledge that accrues to the *sentient* body in the course of its activity; knowledge inscribed in the labouring body – in hands, fingertips, wrists, nose, eyes, ear, skin, muscles, shoulders, arms and legs – as surely as it was inscribed in the brain. It was *knowledge filled with intimate detail and ambiance* – the colour and consistency of metal as it was thrust into the blazing fire, the smooth finish of clay as it gave up its moisture [emphasis added].[11]

Few of those who had such knowledge, Zuboff maintains, were able to explain, rationalize or articulate it. Such skills were learnt through observation, initiation and action rather than being taught, reflected upon or verbalized. In other words, learning was immediately reactive, responsive and interactive rather than distantly analytical or conceptual.

However, with the advent of mechanized mass production, such craft-based activity was successively gutted of the elements that made it skilful. In Pirsig's terms, production-line work in the twentieth century was stripped of all its romantic elements, the caring relationship between man and machine being thereby torn asunder. In effect, the world of romance was transferred from the shop floor to the scientific laboratory, both technically and managerially:

It was in this context, characterised by a new romance with science, a profound belief in progress, an urgent demand for coordination and efficiency in increasingly complex and large scale organizations, and a growing professionalisation of the managerial class, that . . . scientific management was born . . . American manager learnt that *the interior of the labour process had to be penetrated, explicated and rationalised* [emphasis added].[12]

The analytical mind, harbouring a classically based division of labour, took over from the sentient body, and was spurred on by the 'romance' of management science. Buried in the habit of each task, according to Zuboff, was a hidden truth, the 'one best way' to accomplish the work according to criteria of efficiency. Workers left to perform on their own would never achieve a 'scientifically' rigorous organization of their task. As a result *systematic analyses* were developed and thus information was expropriated to the ranks of management:

Fundamental to this approach was the notion that only a special class of men – formally educated, specially trained, able to reason scientifically – was fit to control this knowledge . . . The emphasis on the professional and scientific orientation of the manager lent force to the growing conviction that managers and workers were intrinsically different.[13]

A rigid separation was therefore enforced, under the aegis of management science, between sentient learning, with its physical and social associations, and analytically based learning, with its mental connotations. The whole orientation towards the MBA – duly and distantly schooled within the mentally bracing classroom, necessarily without the sentient workplace – followed automatically from this 'scientific' division of labour.

I remember with frightening clarity how, some 20 years ago, barely a year after graduating from Harvard Business School, I was asked to take over the management of my family clothing business. As I assumed my position as managing director, at the tender age of 26, our 56-year-old buyer came to me, asking me to 'feel the cloth' that was being used in our merchandise. I could feel nothing. My sentient body had lain dormant for all those years that I had been schooled – mentally but neither physically nor emotionally – to be a business administrator. I felt that I was a fraud. Perhaps, I then thought, I should have listened to my father, and started out from the packing room, gradually feeling my way into the business. The problem, of course, was that within the confines of colonial Africa, white managed black just as manager controlled worker, so that never the twain did meet. Once again I would have been cut off from my sentient world, reluctantly heeding what Zuboff terms the 'hierarchical faith'.

Each day, she says, workers and managers could see and feel those things that made them different from one another. This lived experience helped them to sustain the credibility of beliefs about who should command and who should obey. Within this technologically and socially 'automated' context, where Pirsig's classical world rules over the romantic, 'the rulers of efficiency that create the industrial division of labour seem to have the power of a natural phenomenon, of necessity itself'.[14]

The automated versus the 'informated' workplace

At this point Zuboff makes the critical distinction between the automated, mechanized workplace of yesteryear and the informated, 'intelligent technological' workplace of tomorrow. In effect, intelligent technology 'textualizes' the production process. When the text is made accessible to production operators, the essential and hierarchical logic of scientific management is undermined. For the first time technology returns to the workforce something that it once took away, but with a crucial difference. For whereas the craftsperson's knowledge had formerly been implicit in action, the *informating process* now makes this knowledge explicit: it holds up a mirror to the worker, reflecting what was known sensually before, but now in an explicit, analytical form. What we have then is a fusion of the romantic and the classical.

Most importantly, from the perspective taken in this book, Zuboff's 'informated organization' is not only a natural home for contemporary quality, but also a learning institution. One of its principal purposes is the expansion of knowledge: not knowledge for its own sake, as in academic pursuit, but knowledge that comes to reside at the core of what it means to be productive. Learning, then, is not something that requires time out from being engaged in productive activity; learning is the *heart* of productive activity – it is the new form of labour.

Automation, intrinsic to mass production, preserves what is already known and assumes that it knows best: it disregards the potential value that could be added in the living situation. Well aware of this, the Japanese are in the habit of 'stopping the line' where there is new learning to be gained. In contrast, conventional practice in the West has been to allow the assembly line to move relentlessly onwards, crushing any embryonic attempt on the part of the workers to learn from trial and error: '*The informating process takes learning as its pivotal experience*. The objective is to achieve the value that can be added from learning in the situation. Informating assumes that *making the organization more transparent will evoke valuable communal insight* [emphasis added]'.[15]

What we are beginning to see, then, in Zuboff just as in Pirsig, is a marriage between the true and the good, between knowledge and virtue.

Total learning – quality management

Zuboff's newly 'informated' world is one in which the classical and the romantic, knowledge and virtue, and thought and feeling combined with action, are all united in 'total learning – quality management'.

In a traditional and hierarchical organization employees are treated as being objectively measurable and, in return, they give of their bodies without giving of themselves. There is no quality to be seen anywhere. In a post-hierarchical, 'informated' organization this all changes. Work involves a collective effort to create and communicate meaning. Such interpretive processes as are required to function in such a learning environment depend, for their effectiveness, on the sharing of such meaning through inquiry and dialogue. This places a high premium on intuitive as well as analytical sources of understanding. Therefore classical, intellectually based skills of interpretation need to be interwoven with romantic, imaginatively based skills of creation, as is suggested by a process engineer at an 'informated' pulping mill at Cedar Bluff:

I think being successful here has a lot to do with imagination. You have to be able to imagine things that you have never seen, to visualize them. For example, when you see a dash on the computer screen, you need to be able to relate that to a thirty-five-foot-square-by-twenty-five foot high room full of pulp. I think it has a lot to do with creativity and the freedom to fantasize. Sometimes I wonder if this eventually turns the operator into something like an autistic child with a closed circuit on their own imagination instead of actual sensory input.[16]

In fact, Zuboff maintains that the 'informated' organization serves to reconnect rather than disconnect the worker from his sentient self because, she says, the demands of managing intricate relationships reintroduce the importance of the 'sentient body' and so provide a counterpoint to the classical rationality imposed by computerization. The body now functions, in fact, as a centre of human feeling rather than as a source of physical energy. As members work together their feelings become an important factor in the structuring of these intricate relationships. As a result 'acting on' is replaced by 'acting with', through which we return to Pirsig's theme of quality, and – as we shall progressively see – total learning can take place.

Conclusion

In the final analysis, then, we have re-entered Pirsig's world of quality, where subject and object come together in an atmosphere of mutual caring. We therefore find ourselves a long way from the narrowly based, hierarchical world. For Zuboff, as for Pirsig, mutual interaction between either people and things, or between people and people, replaces vertical interaction between worker and management:

Relationships will need to be fashioned and refashioned as part of the dynamism of social processes, like inquiry and dialogue, that mediate learning. Such relationships are more intricate because their character derives from the specifics of the situation that are always both pragmatic – what it takes to get the work done best – and psychological – what people need to sustain their motivation and commitment.[17]

The caring relationship, then, is intrinsic to both quality and to learning. The interweaving of thought, feeling and action becomes a precondition for both total learning and quality management. However, whereas learning is more evidently a process, quality is characteristically more of an outcome. Total learning is a means to a quality management end. To the extent, therefore, that TQM is divorced from individual or organizational learning, it can be seen as a prospectively rich end that is actually impoverished by a lack of means. Such a state of affairs can only result in frustrated ambitions.

The prime reason, therefore, why the Japanese have been successful with their version of TQM is because they have created their own brand of learning organization; which, as I have indicated, draws on their particular Buddhist and Confucian traditions, the philosophical keynotes of which are self-discipline, selflessness and the submission of the individual to the group.

By contrast, we in the West, drawing upon our Judeo-Christian and Greek traditions, need to create learning organizations in which *self-knowledge, self-realization* and the progressive *individuation* of our institutions become our own hallmark. In such learning organizations, we shall ultimately find, quality will be born out of nothing less than a *holographic* form of integration between the different 'learning fields' in which we work, between total learning and quality management.

In the course of this book, therefore, I first introduce the concept and context of the learning organization. Secondly, I trace paths to individual self-realization, for managers, that accord with it. Thirdly, I reconstitute the functions and skills of business and management, to foster the individuation of not only separate managers but also of integrated business institutions. Finally, I conclude by bringing the holographic metaphor into organizational play.

Notes

1 W. Abernathy, R. Clark and T. Kantrow, *The New Industrial Renaissance* (Harvard University Press, Harvard, 1983), p. 124.
2 H. Hayes, R. Clark and Weelright, *Dynamic Manufacturing* (Free Press, New York, 1988).
3 R. Pirsig, *Zen and the Art of Motorcycle Maintenance* (Black Swan, 1989), p. 271.
4 P. Crosby, *Quality is Free* (Mentor, 1979), p. 78.
5 S. Askew, Total quality management (unpublished manuscript, 1989), p. 10.
6 Pirsig, *Zen*, p. 281.
7 Pirsig, *Zen*, p. 374.
8 Pirsig, *Zen*, p. 280.
9 Pirsig, *Zen*, p. 293.
10 Pirsig, *Zen*, p. 321.

11 S. Zuboff, *In the Age of the Smart Machine* (Heinemann, London, 1988), p. 40.
12 Zuboff, *Age of the Smart Machine*, p. 230.
13 Zuboff, *Age of the Smart Machine*, p. 231.
14 Zuboff, *Age of the Smart Machine*, p. 240.
15 Zuboff, *Age of the Smart Machine*, p. 305.
16 Zuboff, *Age of the Smart Machine*, p. 86.
17 Zuboff, *Age of the Smart Machine*, p. 400.

2

Towards the Learning Organization

Introduction

Towards the New Management Order

In the mid-1980s Britain in particular, and Europe in general, began its search, not for excellence, but for a 'new management order'.[1] The onset of unprecedented rates of change, in both public and private enterprise, combined with the intensified competition – particularly from Japan – with the additional spur of 1992, has made European management sit up and rethink.

The new management order that we should be seeking is to be found within the emergent 'learning organization', the origins of which are now widely spread across the Atlantic, also reaching Japan. Europe has the chance, nevertheless, of playing a leading role in the development of this new order.

Our Management Heritage

Conventional management wisdom

As explained in chapter 1, ever since the proliferation of business schools, initially in America in the 1950s, efficient and effective management has become associated with the conventional business functions, both generalist and specialist in nature.

While such highly respected American business gurus as the corporate strategist, Igor Ansoff,[2] the management analyst, Peter Drucker,[3] and the doyen of marketing, Philip Kotler,[4] made their combined impact in the 1960s and 1970s, European business thinking was left out in the cold. Ironically, though, those very Americans who led the conventional management way were first-generation immigrants from central Europe.

The European fringe

In the UK in the 1970s, in fact, there were at least three management thinkers who had something significant to say. Professor Reg Revans,[5] who had an enormous influence on management education in Belgium, if not in the UK, advanced the case for action learning, whereby dynamic processes of management learning superseded the more static management functions. Revans was a Cambridge physicist and Olympic long jumper who became involved in management education via the British Coal Board; initially with the German economist, Fritz Schumacher, who became renowned in the Third World for his ideas on intermediate technology. In Europe and the US in the 1970s, he was also a leading influence in the reinstatement of small-scale enterprise.[6] However, Schumacher, whose most fundamental concern was with the rebalancing of freedom and order within the context of the whole person, failed to make real inroads into management education and development.

The same applied, also in the 1960s and 1970s, to a world-renowned operations researcher and computer scientist, Stafford Beer, when he entered the management arena. In his *Design for Freedom*,[7] he developed an approach to management that accommodated rather than 'attenuated' individual and cultural variety. Beer's attempt to introduce a computer-based democracy into organizational life, while initially adapted by President Allende in Chile, was never taken seriously in Europe or the US.

Revans, Schumacher and Stafford Beer have never been accommodated within the management mainstream. Their essentially European brand of management thinking has almost completely bypassed the marketing, operations, finance and human resource establishment. Their combined emphasis on processes of learning as opposed to functions of management has only been received by a fringe group of management educators and developers.

In fact, it is Charles Handy who has probably had the most influence on what may be called the 'British School'. In his book on *The Gods of Management*,[8] he focuses on the need for variety rather than uniformity in management style and organizational culture. Yet, interestingly enough, with the recent upsurge of interest in so-called 'corporate culture', his work has been totally overshadowed – this time by a new wave of American influence.

Whereas the management thinking of Revans, Beer and Schumacher has been exported to the four quarters of the globe, it has ironically never taken root within Europe as a whole. The stream of management thinking that has had a much more pervasive influence in Europe is the developmental approach that is generally associated with the Dutch organizational psychologist, Bernard Lievegoed.[9] Lievegoed, in fact, has drawn on the creative inspiration of the Austrian, Rudolph Steiner, who established 'anthroposophy' at the turn of the century. Steiner was an educator, philosopher, architect, agronomist, economist and scientist, whose concept of 'threefold man'[10] – thinking, feeling and willing – underpins our own approach to the learning organization. Moreover, for Lievegoed, the developing organization is in turn predominantly wilful (economic), thoughtful (technological) and emotional (social), as it learns and develops over time.

Processes of managerial and organizational learning, then, duly influenced by what we might term a British or Western European school of thought, and of management and organization development, influenced by a Central and Eastern European stream, are indigenous to Europe as a whole. And both of these related approaches are antithetical to the more narrow, analytical perspective taken by the Central European management thinkers who settled in America.

In search of excellence

Yet, ironically enough, in the 1980s it has been the Americans themselves who have most rigorously called into question the analytical approach adopted by their own management gurus. Led by the irrepressible Tom Peters, they have recently gone out *In Search of Excellence*[11] via autonomy, entrepreneurship and shared values. Overthrowing 'scientific management' they have heralded in an 'enterprise culture' that Western Europe has quickly adopted as its own.

To the extent that European managers have moved from American-style rational management back to entrepreneurial and cultural basics, they have once again turned their backs on their philosophical heritage. Revans, Schumacher, Stafford Beer or Charles Handy on the one hand, and Rudolph Steiner or Bernard Lievegoed on the other, have as much in common with Tom Peters as chalk with cheese.

Yet, interestingly enough, an alternative and integrated approach has been emerging in the past ten years, that, unlike the work of Tom Peters, crosses the divide between America and Europe.

Managerial Learning and Development

Societal Learning

The European context

As I have already indicated, it is no accident that the greatest management thinkers in the UK and Europe have focused their attention on processes of learning and development. In fact, the contemporary Italian industrialist and management philosopher, Aurelio Peccei, set up a learning project in the 1970s to deal with the whole question of societal learning. The central issue, for Peccei, was that of learning how to cope with increasing organizational and societal complexity – a matter dear to the hearts of Revans, Schumacher and Stafford Beer.

Understanding and learning

Tangles of mutually reinforcing old and new problems, too complex to be apprehended by the current analytical methods and too tough to be attacked by traditional policies and strategies, are clustering together, heedless of boundaries. There is a desperate need to break these vicious circles. . .

An entirely new enterprise is thus required. Focusing on people themselves, this new enterprise must be aimed at developing their latent innermost capability of understanding and learning, so that the march of events can eventually be brought under control.[12]

Peccei's perspective, at a societal level, is not far removed from that of Peter Bowen, a management consultant with the British retailers, W. H. Smith, at a commercial level. Bowen states that managers who have learnt to manage their own learning will be more competent and better at motivating and managing others; moreover, progressive businesses in the 1990s must be learning environments as well as commercial organizations.

No limits to learning

The requirements of managing in a changing environment are closely interlinked with processes of learning – that is, in a managerial context. In fact, according to Peccei, it is possible to read the history of humanity as a sustained effort to overcome complexity through increasingly refined and effective means, first of representing reality and then of acting upon it.

Developments in knowledge, technology, power, organization, norms of conduct and, above all, the creation of coherent mental constructs to represent the surrounding environment have resulted from the interplay between the challenge of complexity and the urge to master it:

Two basic ways to reduce complexity can be envisaged. The first is the attempt to simplify reality. Much of the work of science is aimed at formulating simple hypotheses and creating powerful concepts to increase our understanding. But this approach all too often entails the pitfall of slipping into 'reductionism' where simplifying concepts are reduced to over-simplifications.

The second strategy is to 'absorb' complexity by differentiating, restructuring and improving our means to cope with it. It is this process we have in mind when we speak of 'innovative' learning. Through such learning individuals, organisations and societies can develop the capacity to face new situations of growing complexity.[13]

Botkin, then, distinguishes between maintenance and innovative learning. We would associate the first with conventional, analytically based management and the second with the emerging, developmentally oriented approach.

Traditionally, societies and individuals have evolved a pattern of continuous 'maintenance learning', interrupted by short periods of innovation, stimulated by the shock of external events. Analytical approaches to business and management might be regarded in that 'maintenance' light, with Tom Peters providing his recent rude and basic disruption.

Maintenance learning

Maintenance learning is the acquisition of fixed outlooks, methods and rules for dealing with known and recurring situations. It enhances our problem-solving abilities – for problems that are given.

It is the type of learning designed to maintain an existing system; an established way of business, of management education or of life. Such learning is, and will continue to be, indispensable to the stability of society.

However – according to Botkin – for long-term survival, particularly through times of turbulence, change or discontinuity, another type of learning, that can bring change, renewal, restructuring and problem reformulation to individuals and to organizations, is even more essential.

Innovative learning

Innovative learning involves both anticipation and participation. Through 'anticipation', individuals or organizations consider trends and make plans, shielding institutions from the trauma of learning by shock: 'Through anticipatory learning the future may enter our lives as a friend, not as a burglar'. 'Participation' involves more than the formal sharing of decisions; it is an attitude characterized by co-operation, dialogue and empathy. It means not only keeping communications open but also constantly testing your operating rules and values against those of others. Without participation, anticipation becomes futile; and participation without anticipation can be misguided.

On the one hand, then, managers have to be able to enrich their contexts, keeping up with the rapid appearance of new situations. On the other, they must communicate the variety of contexts through ongoing dialogue with other individuals. The one is pointless without the other.

Cultivating understanding in isolation can lead to reliance on self-defeating, quickly obsolescent, local truth, and ignoring the contexts of others usually runs the danger of narrowmindedness and a false sense of security. Whereas anticipation encourages solidarity in time, participation creates solidarity in space.

Organizational Learning: The Evolution of Production

Production as learning

The Italian Aurelio Peccei, the American Jim Botkin, and their Moroccan and Romanian colleagues, Mahdi Elmandjra and Mircea

Malitza, were soon succeeded by other management thinkers. In fact, a group of academics at Harvard Business School led the way, interestingly enough from an operations management perspective:

What is needed is a view of production as an enterprise of unlimited potential, an enterprise in which current arrangements are but the starting point for continuous organisational learning.[14]

It is interesting that this evolutionary management perspective should have emerged from the field of operations or production management, often considered the cinderella of business disciplines. Obviously, though, the link between manufacturing processes and information technology has established the developmental thrust. For as Abernathy and his HBS colleagues have argued, 'only when grafted onto a production system dedicated to on-going learning and communication can new technologies realise their potential as competitive weapons'.[15]

Alternating paths

Whereas Abernathy, writing in the early 1980s, still operated within the context of a competitive ethos, his colleague at HBS, Robert Reich, in his *The Next American Frontier*[16] had shifted his ground towards co-operation. As a political scientist reflecting upon America's national destiny. Reich called for a shift in emphasis from 'hands' (his first path) to 'brains' (his second path) and, correspondingly, from competition to co-operation:

The first path – towards stable mass production – relies on cutting labour costs and leaping in to wholly new product lines as old ones are played out. For managers this path has meant undertaking (or threatening) massive layoffs, moving (or threatening to move) to lower wage states and countries, parcelling out work to lower cost suppliers, automating to cut total employment, and diversifying into radically different goods and services. For workers this has meant defending existing jobs and seeking protection from foreign competition.

The second path – towards collective entrepreneurship – involves increasing labour value. For managers this path means continuously retraining employees for more complex tasks, automating in ways that cut routine tasks and enhance worker flexibility and creativity, diffusing responsibility for innovation, taking seriously labour's concern for job security. This path involves a closer and more permanent relationship with other parties that have a stake in the firm.[17]

For Reich, then, the wealth of society has come ever more to depend on the value added by the power of thought. As the world economy has grown more integrated, brains have become, for him, the determinants of international advantage. Modern machinery, technologies and money are increasingly footloose; the only factors of production that remain unique to a nation are the minds of its citizens (how they are utilized and interconnected). Conceptual value added then becomes the prime source of a nation's standard of living.

A new learning capability

In that respect Reich's colleague at HBS, Shoshana Zuboff, would be in total agreement. Zuboff, as we saw in the last chapter, has called for a new management language. She wants us to move away from military metaphors to metaphors of learning, exploration, discovery and experimentation. Technology, as a production manager reveals, is on her side:

In 1953 we put operation and control as close together as possible. We did a lot of localising, so that when you made a change you could watch the change, actually see the motor starting up. With the evolution of computer technology, you centralise controls and move away from the central physical process. If you don't have an understanding of what is happening and how all the pieces interact it is more difficult. You need a new learning capability, because when you operate with the computer, you can't see what is happening. There is a difference in the mental and conceptual capabilities you need. You have to do things in your mind.[18]

The dictates of a 'learning environment', then, rather than those of 'imperative control', now shape the evolving organization in which Zuboff anticipates that managers and workers will be operating. She describes such an organization as 'informated' rather than merely automated:

The informated organisation is a learning institution, and one of its principal purposes is the expansion of knowledge – not knowledge for its own sake (as in academic pursuit) but knowledge that comes to reside at the core of what it means to be productive. Learning is not something that requires time out from being engaged in productive activity; learning is the heart of productive activity; learning is the new form of labour.[19]

The Evolution of Management

The new realities

While Reich and Zuboff in the US have been establishing themselves as a new management breed, identifying themselves more closely with learning and co-operation than with management and competition, two members of the old guard – Drucker in the US and Handy in the UK – have recently renewed their own management thinking.

For Peter Drucker, the new realities mark a shift from a mechanical world view, in which analysis of the component parts was all important, to a biological approach to management, in which it is the perception of the whole that is critical. Moreover, whereas matter is the basic mechanistic building block, information is the basic, biological element.

The new information centre

Information, Drucker says, is data endowed with relevance and purpose. Converting data into information thus requires knowledge. In the information-based organization, then, knowledge will lie at the base, in the minds of specialists who do different work and who direct themselves, working together as a team. Since information knows no boundaries – departmentally, organizationally or nationally – it will also serve to form the basis for newly interactive communities of people:

The city may become an information centre (news, data, words), the place from which information radiates, rather than a centre for work. It might resemble the medieval cathedral where the peasants from the countryside congregated once or twice a year at the great feast days; in between it stood empty except for its learned clerics and its cathedral school.[20]

According to Drucker, in the nineteenth century there were two competing models of society: one foresaw a society composed of small independents; the other found its clearest expression in the Marxian prophesy of a society of Proletarian masses – neither has become a reality.

The reality today, at least in the industrialized nations, is a society of knowledge employees, who are neither exploited or exploiting, who individually are capitalists but who own the means of production only collectively through their pension funds, who are subordinates but are also often bosses themselves. Knowledge has now become the real capital of the developed economy. Knowledge workers know that their knowledge gives them freedom to move. The institution they work for is not primary: their knowledge, their craft is. It is immaterial for computer specialists whether they work for a department store, a university or a hospital. What matters to them – other than pay – is that the equipment is 'state of the art' and the assignment challenging. That kind of rationale applies to the financial analyst or to the personnel manager alike.

The Age of Unreason

In an evolutionary sense, Drucker therefore says, management has developed from 'working harder' to 'working smarter'. Accounting, for example, has evolved from bookkeeping to analysis and control. Marketing has evolved as a result of applying management concepts to distribution and to selling. Every one of these managerial innovations represents the application of knowledge to work, the substitution of system and information for guesswork, brawn and toil. In fact the shift from the mechanical to the biological universe will eventually require a new 'philosophical synthesis'.[21]

Charles Handy might argue that he has produced such a synthesis. Handy's argument is that we live in an age of 'discontinuous change' (borrowing from Drucker), and that in order to cope with this, as managers, we have to be able to learn faster than the rate of change (borrowing from Revans). Learning is therefore a central part of coping in 'The Age of Unreason'.

Handy then provides us with his 'wheel of learning' (see figure 2.1). Such learning starts with a question, a problem to be solved, a challenge to be met. Questions need possible answers, speculations, ideas or theory. Ideas or theories can never be enough: they have to be tested in reality. Some will work while others will not, and until you know why – the final stage of reflection – you will not have learnt.

The learning organization, for Handy, therefore has five major attributes:

- It has a formal way of asking questions, seeking out theories, testing them and reflecting on them. The wheel of learning cannot be left to chance, or to the chairman thinking in a bathtub.

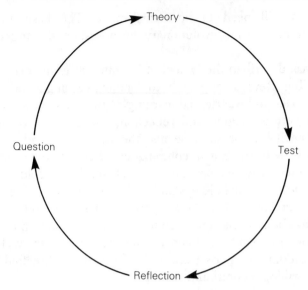

Figure 2.1   The wheel of learning.[22]

- It is properly selfish, clear about its role, its future and its goals, and is determined to reach them.
- It is constantly re-framing the world and its part in it. Quality circles, at their best, are an example of such recurrent re-framing.
- It cultivates negative capability, in that disappointment and mistakes are accommodated as part of the learning whole.
- Finally, it is a caring organization, in that it wants everyone to learn, and it bends over backwards to make that obvious.

So far so good, but not good enough! In effect, whereas Drucker and Handy on the one hand, and Reich and Zuboff on the other, point the way towards a new philosophical, economic and managerial synthesis, we are still left with some way to go towards the knowledge-based, learning organization that is so central to all their designs. To help us progress further, we turn to an Anglo-Indian organizational psychologist, Kevin Kingsland.

Learning and Innovation

The Personality Spectrum

To the extent that an enterprise is converted from an economic or administrative entity into a fully fledged learning organization so all of its functions will need to be transformed. The basis for this transformation, for our evolutionary purposes, is the process of learning.

Handy has described the 'wheel of learning' in terms that closely resemble Reg Revans' approach to 'action learning', and David Kolb's approach to 'experiential learning'.[23] In each case there is an alternation between action and reflection, and between doing and thinking. Inevitably, or so it seems, the Americans and Western Europeans view learning as a combination of cognitive and behavioural processes. Affective processes are left out in the cold.

The psychologist Kevin Kingsland, a Westerner who has been very much influenced by the East[24] – he spent a formative period of his life in India – has built up his approach to learning and innovation out of a combination of cognitive, affective and behavioural activity. This is similar to Rudolph Steiner's 1920s vision of man as a threefold being – thinking, willing (action) and feeling.

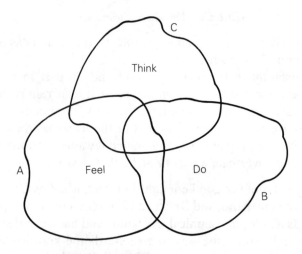

Figure 2.2   The personality spectrum.

Kingsland's personality spectrum, as can be seen in figure 2.2, is constructed using the overlapping sets created out of what I have called 'the three wise men of psychology'.[25]

In table 2.1 I have related the different combinations of cognition (C) or thinking, of affectation (A) or feeling, and of behaviour (B) or doing, to both personal and managerial functions. A high proportion of a given attribute is indicated by a capital letter (C, A, B) and a small

Table 2.1 The spectrum of personality and management

Combination	Personality attribute	Management style	Colour
CAB	Imaginative	Innovative manager	Violet
CAb	Insightful	Developmental manager	Indigo
CaB	Authoritative	Analytical manager	Blue
cAB	Wilful	Enterprising manager	Green
Cab	Flexible	Manager of change	Yellow
cAb	Sociable	People manager	Orange
caB	Energetic	Action manager	Red

proportion by a small letter (c,a,b). Each of the seven resulting combinations is designated a colour, for ease of memory if not for other, more significant reasons.

Modes of Learning

What does this all imply, then, for the learning organization? As I have already indicated, within the learning organization management roles and functions are transformed, so that they become extensions of learning. But how can we typecast learning?

Jim Botkin and his colleagues, in their learning society, differentiated between 'participative' and 'anticipative' learning. Kevin Kingsland, in similar vein, has distinguished between a 'horizontal' and a 'vertical' spectrum. The horizontal spectrum applies to learning roles in which different individual learners participate. The vertical spectrum prescribes functions or processes of learning or anticipation, and creativity or innovation. This is illustrated in table 2.2.

Whereas the learning process is inner-directed, or introverted, the

Table 2.2 Learning and innovation

Horizontal roles	Vertical processes		Colour
Learning style	Learning process	Innovation process	
Inspirer	Imagine	Envision	Violet
Harmonizer	Foresee	Enable	Indigo
Organizer	Conceptualize	Organize	Blue
Energizer	Grasp	Exploit	Green
Experimenter	Explore	Experiment	Yellow
Animator	Respond	Involve	Orange
Doer	React	Enact	Red

innovation process is outer-directed, or extraverted. At the same time 'inspirers', for example, learn through exercising their powers of imagination and take a lead in innovating, through their ability to transform people, things or situations.

Conclusion

As you can now see, there is much more to so-called 'learning organization' than readily meets the eye. Although Reich, Zuboff, Drucker and Handy have set the stage for the knowledge-based, or learning organization, they have not followed the argument through. That is what we shall be doing hereafter. In the next chapter, I want to investigate the processes of learning and innovation more closely.

Notes

1 The Charter Group Initiative, Presentation by CNED (London, November 1987).
2 I. Ansoff, *Corporate Strategy* (McGraw-Hill, New York, 1964).
3 P. Drucker, *Management* (Pan, London, 1970).
4 P. Kotler, *Marketing Management* (Prentice-Hall, Englewood Cliffs, NJ, 1965).
5 R. Revans, *Action Learning* (Blond Briggs, London, 1980).
6 E. F. Schumacher, *Small is Beautiful* (Abacus, London, 1963).
7 S. Beer, *Design for Freedom* (John Wiley, New York, 1974).
8 C. Handy, *The Gods of Management* (Sovereign, London, 1978).
9 B. Lievegoed, *The Developing Organisation* (Blackwell, Oxford, 1982).
10 R. Steiner, *The Philosophy of Freedom* (Pharos Books, London, 1979).
11 T. Peters and R. Waterman, *In Search of Excellence* (Harper & Row, New York, 1982).
12 J. Botkin, M. Elmandjea and M. Malitza, *No Limits to Learning* (Pergamon, Oxford, 1979), p. 17.
13 Botkin *et al.*, *No Limits to Learning*, p. 42.
14 W. Abernathy, R. Hayes and H. Kantrow, *The Renaissance of American Manufacturing* (Basic Books, New York, 1983), p. 124.
15 Abernathy *et al.*, *Renaissance*, p. 125.
16 R. Reich, *The Next American Frontier* (Penguin, London, 1982).
17 R. Reich, *Tales of a New America* (Random House, New York, 1987), p. 147.
18 S. Zuboff, *In the Age of the Smart Machine* (Heinemann, London, 1988), p. 71.
19 S. Zuboff, *Age of the Smart Machine*, p. 375.
20 P. Drucker, *The New Realities* (Harper & Row, New York, 1989), p. 259.

21 P. Drucker, *New Realities*, p. 264.
22 R. Revans, *The ABC of Action Learning* (Chartwell Brett, Kent, UK, 1987).
23 D. Kolb, *Experiential Learning* (Prentice Hall, Englewood Cliffs, NJ, 1986).
24 K. Kingsland, *The Personality Spectrum* (self published, 1986).
25 R. Lessem, *Developmental Management* (Basil Blackwell, Oxford, 1990).

3

Learning and Innovation

Introduction

The Departure and the Return

As I have indicated in the previous chapter, learning and innovation – in a managerial context – represent, each in their turn, an inward, reflective and an outward, active journey for either the individual manager or for the managed organization. Both journeys encompass the full range of either the individual or the organizational personality (see figure 3.1).

Individual and Organizational Learning

As a manager you may acquire social skills developmentally (learning) and apply them transformatively (innovation). Similarly, an entire

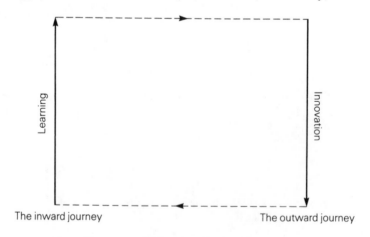

Figure 3.1 The departure and the return.

organization may progressively renew – as a learning organization – its family spirit, and gradually transform – as an innovative company – its client relationships from remote to intimate connections.

Whereas individually centred management training is oriented towards personal growth and development, organizationally centred management development is geared towards business growth and development. Similarly, whereas personal transformation is self-directed, organizational transformation is corporate in its focus. In the final analysis, though, one is merely the other writ large.

The Grain of Learning

Both learning and innovation, development and transformation, may take place *with* the grain – a relatively painless process – and *across* the grain – which is relatively painful. As will become evident in chapter 4, each of you has a predominating learning style. For example, as a 'deliberator', your style will be predominantly conceptual. In picking up one management concept after another, even in progressively higher degrees of complexity, you will be 'learning *with* the grain'. Thus you might progress from (conceptually) basic bookkeeping to management accounting.

Conversely, to the extent that you are able to ascend the entire ladder of learning, or to descend the complete ladder of innovation, you will be required to learn *across* the grain. This requires stepping outside your predominating style of learning, or of innovating, and into a less well-worn groove.

Most of you, by virtue of experience in life and in management, will be able to function productively in two or three different learning modes. Moreover, to the extent that you are either introverted or extraverted, so you will feel more comfortable learning, inwardly, or innovating, outwardly. In order to step outside these characteristic modes and into new ones, you will require a combination of inner will and outer circumstance. The journey into the unknown, from a well-worn groove into unexplored learning territory, will inevitably be physically, emotionally and mentally arduous.

Learning: the Inward Journey

The inward journey begins with your five senses and culminates in your creative imagination. Along the way, you build up your

Figure 3.2   The journey of learning and development.

developmentental repertoire, as shown in figure 3.2. You begin then, by reacting physically.

React Physically

As an individual

Total learning, that is when you are literally starting from scratch, begins with an inward and sensual reaction, that sets your adrenaline flowing. For example, you start out on your financially oriented business journey by being so floored by numbers (the effect is literally painful) that you have a physical urge to do something about it, for fear of being left way behind your much more numerate colleagues.

As an organization

Organizational learning begins when, threatened with extinction, whether at birth, or at a point of imminent takeover, the whole organism reacts instinctively, pulling out all the stops, drawing on and out of its fighting spirit – the more finely honed by touch, taste, smell, sight and sound, the better.

Respond Socially

As an individual

Once you are physically under way, but unaware of which way to turn, you become completely dependent on knowledgeable others, responding enthusiastically to their every instruction. For example, in the financial context, you put out 'help me' signals to every available accountant, until such time as you find one or more who will take you protectively under their wing. You become an enthusiastic apprentice, on the lookout for practical, specific instructions – not for 'heady' techniques.

As an organization

As the organization learns so it develops a feel for its people and product, both inside and outside, by dint of willing exposure. To the extent that it learns across the grain, physical reactions are accompanied by social responses; instead of being lean and mean the organization becomes warm and welcoming, of both people and things. The hard and aggressive qualities, acquired in the active struggle for survival, are counterbalanced by soft and receptive qualities, acquired in the process of bonding together, as both a community of people and a 'craftsman's' guild.

Explore Mentally

As an individual

As a would-be accountant you will have painstakingly learnt to do basic books before wanting to intellectually explore the financial subject matter in greater technical detail. At this point, once you have acquired at first hand the everyday bookkeeping language – some concrete feel for the area of knowledge, self or skill – you are ready mentally to move on. It is in fact at this point that intellectual curiosity can, and should get the better of you, as you begin to explore abstract financial techniques. You now seek out alternative books and courses, and avoid instruction by rote.

As an organization

Armed with direct experience of its community within, and of its industry without, the organization is ready to move on. To the extent that is willing to learn – across the grain – so the craft-based community will need to develop into a technology-based institution. This step, from a people-centred organization to a knowledge-centred one, is traumatic. Parochial values have to be cast aside and universal ones put in their place. Yet, to the extent that the organization wants to retain that 'family feeling', the two modes of learning and development will need to co-exist. Having lost its old way, as a social community valuing people and things, it will have to find its new way, as a learning community of interacting 'human and machine intelligences'.

Wilfully Grasp

As an individual

Once you have acquired the basic know-how – whatever it may be related to – you are ready to put it to use more purposefully. At this intermediate stage of managerial learning, as for example a would-be accountant, you begin wilfully to turn your thoughts, feelings and actions towards solving your own financially based problems. Management accounting now becomes a tool to be grasped to suit your own individual purposes. Any courses you go on, or articles you read, have to be customized to suit your own managerial requirements.

As an organization

As an organization you now have the instinctive aggressiveness, the communal responsiveness and the technology-based know-how to take on all-comers. However, you are yet to acquire the corporate will to win, the emotionally laden desire to exploit situations to your own advantage, and the kind of corporate power and influence that will beat all of the competition. The learning orientation required is acquisitive and intentional, physical and emotional, a combination of raw aggression and focused intent. To develop your organization in that wilful learning light you need to establish a culture and reward system through which individual and corporate egos are aligned.

Conceptualize Analytically

As an individual

Once you have played about with particular routines, and acquired a firm grasp of their specific and alternative applications, you are ready to appreciate the overall concepts of, say, management accounting, or influencing skill, or entrepreneurial management – whatever the case may be. In fact, if you are exposed to concepts before you have acquired a personally and situationally specific set of circumstances in which to apply them, they will be rendered largely sterile. A course on accounts will be of limited learning value if, on the one hand, you have no business to account for and, on the other, you are unfamiliar with basic books.

As an organization

The overtly competitive organization, accommodating overtly competitive individuals, will get so far and no further, because at a certain point the desire to learn is counteracted, rather than reinforced, by the will to win. Self-centred intrapreneurs begin to cancel out one another's efforts. Learning is inhibited by an unwillingness to share information, for fear of one group being overtaken by the other. A quantum leap in outlook is required if this confrontational, and highly personalized learning mode, is to be outgrown and replaced by a more cohesive and relatively depersonalized one. Such a learning leap represents a move across the organizational grain, from a person-centred enterprise to an organization-centred bureaucracy.

Foresee with Insight

As an individual

Concepts can only be fully understood in context. It requires a particular brand of insight to appreciate the significance of, for example, the management of change in Japan as opposed to that in the US. It takes foresight, born out of a combination of in-depth intelligence and broad experience, to manage in cross-cultural settings.

Moreover, such insight does not arrive all of a sudden. It emerges after you have passed through the other stages over an extended period of time. And the same learning process applies equally to managing a financial function as to managing across cultures.

As an organization

Bureaucracies are notorious for insulating themselves from their all too often changing environments. Concepts of management or of organization, of centralization or of decentralization, are conventionally static and narrowly prescribed, rather than dynamic and evolutionary in nature.

Organizations which consciously evolve, continually renewing themselves, have the foresight to anticipate the future. Through continually interacting with the world around them they progressively extend their boundaries of operation, through merger rather than takeover, through interfusion rather than expropriation. The organization thereby assumes a form which is molecular rather than hierarchical, organic rather than mechanistic. In fact, significant organizational learning is required – across the grain – if the institution is to overcome the restrictions of rigidly defined time and space.

Imagine Creatively

As an individual

The ultimate point in managerial learning, whether as a strategic planner or as a skilled motivator, is to be able to imagine yourself – as in the form of a motion picture – assimilating the knowledge or acquiring the skill. Such a capacity to imagine, to the full, represents the culmination of the process of learning. It is well known that champion skiers and great musicians, alike, can practice their art in their mind's eye. However, this only becomes possible once they have opened themselves cognitively, affectively and behaviourally to their particular pursuit.

As an organization

The manager's imagination, individually centred, can be likened to the corporate image, organizationally centred. Once the institution has neared the end of its inward journey it will have accumulated the necessary thoughts, feelings and behaviours which – when combined creatively – project its self-image. In other words, that image should project the full extent of what the institution knows, is and does.

The creative leap of learning from an evolutionary awareness to full-scale image projection demands a marrying up of thought and feeling with action. For image conveys not only the organization's inner being, or aspect, but also its outer doing, or impact. Image integrates past, present and future – inspirationally – invoking positive thought, feeling and action in others.

Innovation: the Outward Journey

Up to this point all the emphasis has been on the inward journey of learning; that is, the cumulative development of individual and organizational competence. It has involved the thoughtful assimilation of management knowledge, and professionally based know-how; the active acquistion of managerial skill, and organizational capacity; and the felt realization of yourself as an evolved manager and your organization as an evolved institution. But this learning and development is yet to make its desired impact – in terms of profit or market share, social service or community development.

We now turn to the outward journey; that is, to cumulative innovation, through the transformation of competence (see figure 3.3).

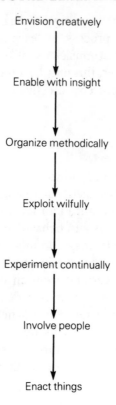

Figure 3.3   The journey of innovation and transformation.

Envision Creatively

As an individual

Whereas creative (or inventive) managers imagine the internal effect of their accumulated learning, they envision the external impact of their innovations. Their focus is extraverted and outer directed rather than introverted and inner directed. So, for example, they picture the marketplace being transformed by their innovative technology, or their creative approach to consumer retailing. The vision they subsequently project encapsulates the thoughts, feelings and actions of their transformed customers. Such a vision transports others, in inspirational colours, towards a new and promised land.

As an organization

An organization infused with vision is collectively inspired. People's individual purposes are aligned with those of the organization, and vice versa. Moreover, the business' purpose is aligned with that of society at large – technologically and ecologically, economically and culturally. The solution of environmental problems, for example relating to global warming or to the progressive destruction of the rain forests, are high up on the visionary's strategic agenda, albeit in a commercial context.

The spirit of the organization and its environment, then, rather than 'men, money, materials and machines' is envisaged as its most potent resource. It is the on-going transformation of that spirit into new matter, and of that matter back into new spirit, which is therefore senior management's reason for being. Whereas the former represents innovation or transformation – turning dreams into reality – the latter represents learning or development.

Enable with Insight

As an individual

No matter how brilliant the individual manager's vision may be it will fail to inspire others if they cannot access it. It is the function of an enabling technology, of an enabling organization, or of enabling finance, to provide the context in which the gap between vision and potential can be recognized and also bridged. Similarly, it is in particular the developmentally oriented manager – deploying listening, facilitating, team-building and joint venturing skills – who has a part to play in this enabling process.

In transforming yourself from being a visionary into playing the role of an enabler you are moving across the innovating grain. For as you move from a predominantly active to a primarily receptive outlook on innovation, you let go of envisaged action and, instead, adopt enabling insight.

As an organization

The enabling organization has the task of establishing a commercial and social context through which the potential created by the vision can be actualized. Both internal and external environments need to be made receptive to the innovative thrust of a new technology or method of social organization. New linkages have to be established once the old ones have broken down in the face of the disruptively, innovative force.

Through the enabling organization people and products, businesses and markets are developed to fulfil their potential. People, products and roles evolve rather than being mobilized, immobilized or demobilized. Physical or human energy is recognized and harnessed rather than being created, channelled or destroyed. Product families replace product lines; integrated systems displace separated products and services.

Organize Methodically

As an individual

Visionaries and enablers are rare managerial breeds, at least in Europe and the US. Both find great difficulty in transforming themselves into organizers – it goes against the pragmatic grain. The conventionally based principles of management – planning, organizing, directing and control – are all methodically contained within this watertight compartment.

Such analytically based management principles are required to channel potential, but only after it has been created, recognized and tapped. The conventionally and analytically based business functions – operations and marketing, finance and human resource management – serve that methodical end, as do the skills of organizing and directing, and the analytical manager, from an individual albeit impersonal perspective.

As an organization

A wealth of human, product or market potential can easily be squandered if it is not channelled, organizationally and strategically. Rules and procedures, policies and programmes, management by objectives and specialization by function all have their proper place, in the natural order of things.

An analytical approach to strategy and to structure thus creates method out of madness – bearing in mind that madness needs to precede method in the natural order of innovative things – before another kind of madness bursts onto the managerial scene.

Exploit Wilfully

As an individual

The entrepreneur wilfully, and often ruthlessly, exploits products and markets, if not also people, in pursuing his competitive managerial and strategic ends. Such entrepreneurs or intrapreneurs are the champions, the 'winners', the gamesmen or the raw 'jungle fighters' who bring in the resources in cash or in kind. Creative scientists often rely on such enterprising managers to champion their products in the same way as analytically based executives often rely on an entrepreneurially inclined sales force to 'make a killing' in the marketplace.

Moving from analytical into enterprising management, once again, involves you in crossing the innovative grain. The proverbial tension between operations and sales, and between finance and marketing, arises out of these contradictory styles of management. Skill in influencing people now predominates over organizing, or even creative skills.

As an organization

In urging us to go 'back to basics', Tom Peters has invited us to transform bureacuratic organizations into enterprising ones. This is indeed a necessary part of the innovative whole, but only a part. In fact, on the outward journey from vision to action, enterprise comes halfway through, and only after the creative, enabling and bureaucratic phases along the organizational way.

'Enterprise culture', vividly depicted in wheeler-dealing, and characteristically measured in profitable sales, is the order of our Anglo-American business day. It comes naturally to the sales force and to new business ventures. It represents capitalism at its sharpest cutting edge. Without the competitive spirit, the urge to commercially conquer, where would free enterprise be?

Experiment Continually

As an individual

It was the doyen of 'action learning' in the UK, Professor Reg Revans, who claimed that learning must be greater than the rate of change if the individual manager is to survive in today's business world. In fact 'the management of change' is probably the buzzword of our day, in British management circles if not around the entire globe.

Revans, and his colleague at MIT, David Kolb, have taken the scientific method and applied it to the process of management. For Kolb, managers' learning styles are determined by their relative preference for one of the four cyclic components of scientific method, active experimentation (test), concrete experience (audit), reflective observation (survey) and conceptualization (hypothesis): the management of change, and the capacity and inclination to adapt, is related to the managers' ability to continually move around the methodological cycle.

As an organization

The thinking organization is able to adapt its systems and its methods at the drop of a hat. In Edward de Bono's terms it has built in mechanisms for thinking laterally and, in Tom Peter's terms, it is full of 'ad hocery', favouring experimentation over deliberation.

It is important to note, though, that this generative capacity is positioned towards the end of the outward journey. The capacity to envision, the enabling function, the conventional organizational order and the enterprise culture, all precede situational flexibility along the road to innovation. In other words, thought devoid of feeling or action has its organizational part to play, but it is a limited one in the transformational hierarchy.

Involve People

As an individual

The people manager, or what I have called the 'animateur', is that socially skilled manager who is the genuine 'people person' within the human resource management fold. Such an individual, or such a social part of your managerial being, is the one best able to carry other people along the outward and innovative journey.

All too often none of the other managerial characters cited thus far has the warmth of personality that is necessary to care for employees or customers at this stage of the journey. It requires a softness of approach, and a degree of comfort with the world of feelings, that is characteristically lacking amongst organizers and entrepreneurs, visionaries and change agents alike. The pain involved for such managers in moving across the innovating grain, from the worlds of thought and action to a world of pure feeing, can be too great for them to bear. However, as we shall see in chapter 6, if they are willing to develop through midlife, such a personal transformation is there for the taking.

As an organization

No enduring organizational transformation can take place without provision of the social glue that can bind a new community together, once it has been recreated out of the old. Moreover, without a display of genuine caring for those people who have been lost along the wayside, the depressed spirit of those who remain will drag the organization down. For spirit, like energy, cannot be created or destroyed. It can only be transformed from one state to another.

With the renewed interest of the management establishment in 'corporate culture', the role of animateur has come back into the limelight. For, as the American culture gurus, Deal and Kennedy,[1] have told us, a healthily growing organization needs not only its heroes but also its priests and its storytellers, its gossips and its whisperers, each playing a well orchestrated part in the people-managed whole.

Enact Things

As an individual

At the end of the managerial day, any process of technological innovation or organizational transformation requires a physical and tangible outcome. Action managers make it their business to make things happen. In fact, genuine visionaries have a strong action streak within them whereby they have a relentless desire to turn vision into action. Their blindspots, therefore, are much more likely to be within the enabling, organizational, enterprising or people realms.

As an organization

In converting a far-sighted vision into everyday action, an organization engaged in continual learning and transformation will be actualizing itself completely. In so doing it will be employing a full set of knowledge-, skill- and character-based competencies. The urge to actualize, at this culminating end of things, will be stimulated by a sense of absolute urgency, a bias for continuous action and a spirit of physically based adventure.

Conclusion

These inward and outward journeys have been presented thus far as linear 'up and down' processes, in which never the twain do meet. Of course this is an artificial model of reality, presented at least in part for the sake of simplification. In fact there is much in the way of sideways movement linking the departure with the return (see figure 3.4). At the same time, given the haphazard nature of actual management situations, the hierarchical character of development and transformation will be constantly subverted by 'real life'.

It is still true to say, however, that there are distinct steps along the way to the manager's Damascus. If learner–managers fail to react physically to their management surroundings, for example, they will forever lack an instinctive sense of immediacy in what they do. Similarly, if they lack warmth and gregariousness they will inevitably have problems in carrying other people along with them.

In the next chapter then, you will be exposed to the 'learning fields' in which management development and transformation takes place. However, before moving on you are invited to consider your own individual and organizational learning, as well as your innovation skills, by answering the self-assessment questions that follow.

Note

1 T. Deal and A. Kennedy, *Corporate Cultures* (Penguin, London, 1987).

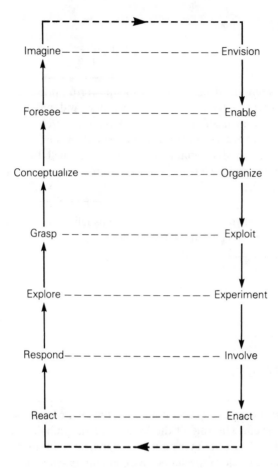

Figure 3.4 The cycle of learning and innovation.

Learning and Innovation: Self-assessment

Complete the four sets of questions on learning and innovation, individual and organizational – the preambles apply to *both* – below. Boxes are provided for you to insert your answers.

Individual Learning

React – the Call to Adventure

If learning is not an adventure it loses its powerful, primordial appeal. The 'call to adventure', then, represents the first and physical step towards managerial or organizational learning. Moreover, such a 'call' only arises when learner–managers or organizations keep themselves on physical alert – sniffing around for what's going on, touching base with the troops, listening to the office grapevine, looking out for trouble, and seeing for themselves who is doing what.

How do you keep yourself physically and sensually – in terms of managerial touch, smell, taste, sight and sound – alert?

```



```

Respond – Making Social Connections

Learning can never take place, both for individual managers and organizations, in isolation. The role of the 'coach', then, symbolizes the supportive role to be played by a 'mother figure', a supportive educator, or a protective mentor; while the role of the supportive community symbolizes the nurturing role to be played by a supportive customer or supplier, or a protective industrial, communal or professional association. Without a social context into which learning can be placed it becomes depersonalized and sterile. If you fail to respond to people who inevitably cross your learning path – and to society in general – your journey will have been in vain.

How do you attract to you people who will enhance your managerial learning?

```



```

Adapt – Learning from Experience

The 'road of trials' involves processes of trial and error, whereby learner–managers and organizations adapt to situations in which they find themselves, thereby learning from their experiences. This is the period of mental alertness and of intellectual discovery that is so much a part of growing up, managerially and organizationally. This is the youthful phase built into the learning process before you, or your institution, consolidate in an adult way. Any task you or your organization tackle, therefore, should lend itself to such exploration and adaption before commitment to a particular line of thought or action.

How (for example, through travel, short courses, books, people or flexible work assignments) do you keep experiencing/exploring?

Expose Yourself to Emotional Risk

Whatever ideas you or your organization pick up, intellectually, courage is needed to put both them and yourself, or itself, to the test. In the process you may become a different person, or your organization a different entity, disassembled and reassembled as a result of all the emotional wrangles and risk-laden activities. In fact, in order to significantly enhance managerial and organizational learning in an area which has previously been weak, such a risk-taking process is inevitable.

How do you continually expose yourself to psychologically and emotionally risk-laden situations?

Conceptualize Your Managerial Work, Systematically

As your newly acquired management or organizational prowess becomes physically, socially and mentally integrated, so the need arises to relate the job to your organization, or the organization to its environment. This ability to conceptualize, to analyse the parts and to relate the parts to the whole, as well as to relate theory to practice and practice to theory, serves to integrate your management role; or to integrate your organization with its people, as well as with the outside world.

Conceptualization is enhanced when you investigate the different elements contained within your job or your unit, and the way in which a particular function, like marketing, relates to the whole. Similarly, for example, marketing in theory becomes integrated in practice when you are habitually called upon to market your product or service, as part of your overall management role or your unit's overall function.

How do you continually conceptualize your work, both in its parts and as a whole?

Develop Insight – Penetrating to the Source

You may have integrated your job or your unit with yourself and your organization, without gaining any fundamental insight into its meaning and significance for you, the organization and the environment. For example, you or your unit may have developed problem-solving skills, without much appreciation for their timing and context, particularly within different cultural settings. Such understanding requires depth of individual, organizational and societal insight.

The insight is developed through a capacity to listen and respond, a power to observe, a willingness to be humbled, and an ability and inclination to link like with unlike, actual with potential, in yourself, in your unit and through others. It involves seeing meaning and context in all things.

How do you develop your powers of insight?

Imagine – Enhancing your Originality

True originality in the process of learning – whether as an individual or an organization – is only displayed when you are able to imagine yourself or your unit as something unique. While champion skiers and great musicians are renowned for regularly 'practising' their skill 'in their mind's eye', managers are yet to be recognized as such.

Thus, for example, you imagine yourself or your unit inspiring people through a particular brand of imagery that is uniquely your own. Metaphors of sailing, if you are a keen sailor (or of remote control, if you are an electronics buff), might be juxtaposed with a particular brand of management, drawn out of your creative imagination to convey a sense of momentum and direction.

How do you exercise your managerial imagination?

Organizational Learning

You will now also need to place your own individual learning in the context of your unit's organizational learning.

React – the Call to Adventure

How does your unit keep itself physically and sensually – in terms of touch, smell, taste, sight and sound – collectively alert?

```
┌─────────────────────────────────────────────────────────────────────┐
│                                                                       │
│                                                                       │
│                                                                       │
│                                                                       │
└─────────────────────────────────────────────────────────────────────┘
```

Respond – Making Societal Connections

How do you attract to you communities that will enhance your organizational learning?

```
┌─────────────────────────────────────────────────────────────────────┐
│                                                                       │
│                                                                       │
│                                                                       │
│                                                                       │
└─────────────────────────────────────────────────────────────────────┘
```

Adapt – Learning from Organizational Experience

How does your organization maintain its exploratory stance and institutional experimentation?

```
┌─────────────────────────────────────────────────────────────────────┐
│                                                                       │
│                                                                       │
│                                                                       │
│                                                                       │
└─────────────────────────────────────────────────────────────────────┘
```

Expose the Organization to Risk

How does your institution continually expose itself to commercially, technologically and culturally or socially risk-laden situations?

```
┌─────────────────────────────────────────────────────────────────────┐
│                                                                       │
│                                                                       │
│                                                                       │
└─────────────────────────────────────────────────────────────────────┘
```

Conceptualize the Organizational Activity, Systematically

How do you continually conceptualize your unit's activities, both in part and as a whole?

Develop Insight – Penetrating to the Organization's Source

How do you develop your powers of insight?

Imagine – Enhancing your Organizational Originality

How do you draw out your people's and your organization's origins, and consequent originality?

In the final analysis, though, organizational learning is only a means to an end; that is, continuing organizational transformation.

Individual Transformation

In order to place your managerial function in the context of your role, respond to each of the seven questions that follow. You are not expected to answer any further questions now, although they are relevant to your job in the future.

Purpose – Creating Your Vision

What is your far-reaching mission in your job?

Context – Recognizing Need

What market and/or organizational potential do you hope you to be realizing?

Defining Your Role

What definable core functions are you carrying out?

Committing Your Self

What's in your job for you personally?

Change – Experiment with Alternatives

How are you continually learning and growing in your job?

Involving People

How do you effect shared values whereby people will co-operate with you in your role?

Action – Implementing Your Role

How do you keep your people's energy level from waning?

Organizational Transformation

Ask your coach to fill in this departmental or divisional inventory; you may also want your chief executive to fill in a copy questionnaire for the organization as a whole.

Purpose – Creating Your Organizational Vision

What is the far-reaching mission of your part of the organization?

```
┌─────────────────────────────────────────────┐
│                                               │
│                                               │
│                                               │
│                                               │
└─────────────────────────────────────────────┘
```

Context – Recognizing Need

What market or organizational potential is your unit realizing?

```
┌─────────────────────────────────────────────┐
│                                               │
│                                               │
│                                               │
│                                               │
└─────────────────────────────────────────────┘
```

Defining Your Unit's Role

What definable core function is your unit carrying out?

```
┌─────────────────────────────────────────────┐
│                                               │
│                                               │
│                                               │
│                                               │
└─────────────────────────────────────────────┘
```

Self – Committing Your Unit

What special effort, and reward, is associated with your unit, individually?

```
┌─────────────────────────────────────────────┐
│                                               │
│                                               │
│                                               │
│                                               │
└─────────────────────────────────────────────┘
```

Change – Experiment with Alternatives

How is your unit continually learning and growing?

```



```

Involving People in, and with Your Unit

How does your unit effect shared values, whereby people co-operate with each other?

```



```

Action – Implementing the Skill

How are people's energy levels kept from waning?

```



```

4

Creating Learning Fields

Introduction

In this chapter I want to sketch out the total learning field which managers inhabit, inclusive of the learning organization into which we have all – perhaps unknowingly – entered. In effect, as you shall see, the learning field is a reflection of the learning organization. Before proceeding, however, I want to reinforce the significance of the learning organization for our time:

> The nineteenth century was the age of the entrepreneur, the self-made man. In the twentieth century the rational executive took command. Thoughtful business administration took over from action-centred business entrepreneurship. The bureaucratic organization took over from the pioneering enterprise. The twenty-first century, as I see it, will become the era of the learning organization. Such a learning organization will need to accommodate thoughts, feelings and actions.

In the context of society at large the education sector encapsulates thought (cognitive), the social services represents feeling (affective), and the commercial sector action (behavioural). Obviously, these three typecast identities represent predominating tendencies rather than complete fields; each of the cognitive, affective and behavioural elements necessarily overlap. However, what is significant for our purposes here is that only the simultaneous development of all three forms of institution will enable the learning organization to fully evolve.

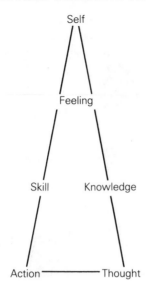

Figure 4.1 The field of competence.

The Learning Field

The Whole Learner

The whole learner is one who thinks, who feels and acts. Thought corresponds most closely with management *knowledge*; feeling accords with your*self* as a manager; and action corresponds with managerial *skill* (see figure 4.1).

The Whole Society

The three sectors

In society at large the educational sector encapsulates the knowledge domain; the public, and especially social, services are directly connected with the person; and, finally, the active commercial sector – in managerial terms – is the most prolifically skilled (see figure 4.2).

The threefold commonwealth

For the social philosopher Rudolph Steiner in the 1920s, there were three distinct elements within society. In the first, *economic* one,

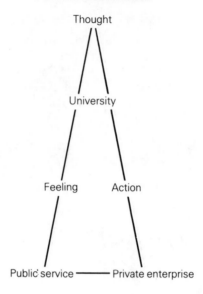

Figure 4.2   The field of learning.

people further the interests of the community through their work, activities and achievements: in this field human will, and hence action, predominates. In the second, socio-*political* field, people need to live at peace with one another, and hence feeling for one's fellow man or woman is of primary importance. In the third, *cultural* field, the production of values arises, by dint of individual capacity, talent and ability: here thought predominates.

In fact, as indicated in figure 4.3, the combination of the three – cognitive (thought), affective (feeling) and behavioural processes (action) – results in seven different styles of learning, or fields within the learning organization.

The Learning Organization

A learning organization in which all seven kinds of individual are able to fully participate will have a similar number of 'learning fields' associated with it. These will represent different combinations of knowledge, skill and self-development. The full combination involves the following:

• An *activity field* of disorganized chaos out of which *survival skills* are born, in the context of the 'adventure playground' in which *reactive learning* takes place.

- A *communal field* of social interaction and group celebration, nurturing activity and public service, out of which *selflessness* is born, and through which *responsive learning* takes place.
- A field of on-going technological, economic and organizational *adaptation*, out of which technical, professional and management *knowledge* is born, and through which *experimental learning* takes place.
- A *proactive field* set within a whirlpool of commercial wheeling and dealing, through which the individual manager *asserts him or herself and applies managerial skills*, providing a vehicle for the educational and commercial challenges that *energized learners* seek.
- A *functional field* in the major areas of marketing and operations, personnel and finance, business strategy and organizational behaviour, information and human resource management, through which *management knowledge is applied and skills implemented*, that

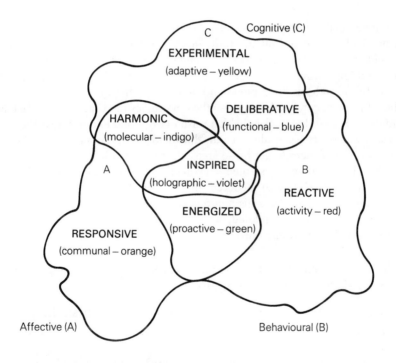

Figure 4.3 The spectrum of learning.

lend themselves to *deliberative learning* through pre-planned modules of instruction.

- A *molecular field* of personal, organizational, commercial and societal *harmony*, in which *self-discovery and insight into management* takes place, and through which the *harmonic learner* consciously develops him- or herself.
- A *holographic field* of personal, technological or organizational *creativity*, in which *self-realization* is attained alongside knowledge and skill development, as *inspired learners* grow through their own creative actions.

Let us now consider each of these in turn, summarizing both management and learning within each one.

The Reactive Field (Red)

Ready, Fire, Aim

Dean responded immediately to the security guard's call when he heard that a fire had broken out on the third floor. Having instantly called the fire brigade he commandeered his right-hand man, Kenichi, and told him to get the building cleared of people forthwith. At this point Kenichi, forever watchful of both his boss' mood and office procedure, brought in Claudia, the office manager, to advise her on the physical layout. Claudia immediately stopped Dean in his tracks – which wasn't easy – and told him that the fire hazard was restricted to the second, third and fourth floors only. So Dean told the two of them to get those areas cleared instantly.

Dean had become accustomed to taking the lead in times of crisis. He was a reactive manager who believed in working hard and playing hard. 'Learning from doing' was his motto, so that he was very sceptical of those 'boffin characters' who fiddled, with new technologies or fancy financial instruments, while Rome burned!

The activity field within the reactive learner's organization, and the survival skills gained within it, involve:

- individual and organizational activities that are physically visible and demonstrable at all times in all places for maximum sensory impact
- work and training activities which stimulate the learner's physical strength, stamina, dexterity and courage

- a bias for action, coupled with a sense of urgency, and the offer of immediate and practically useful instruction
- learning by wandering about – that is by touch, taste, sight, hearing, smell and, generally, physical contact
- an action orientation, typified by lots of trials, speed and immediacy of response and a 'work hard, play hard' culture
- coaching and education from individuals who can set immediate and physically demanding challenges for skill development

In summary, this action-based orientation, in which practical skills are to be acquired and applied, contains a hive of physical activities. The communal field is similarly down to earth, but yet different, in that it is more people-oriented.

The Communal Field (Orange)

People First

Much to her surprise, Katerina was given the job of customer services manager for her Japanese-owned manufacturing company, based in Spain. For the past seven years, while admittedly she had become the life and soul of her department, she had not assumed any managerial responsibility. Not used to being in the limelight, in that sense, she was reluctant to take on the job of leading a team of six people, several of whom were older than herself.

In fact she was only willing to do it because Akio, with whom she had become very friendly, was willing to be her guide and mentor. He had been with the company for 25 years, and was totally immersed within it – he personified its deepest values. Finally, Katerina was also fortunate to have, as the personnel manager on her team, an Indian woman married to a Spaniard, who could pick up the deeper nuances of Japanese-style management and integrate them into Spanish culture. Between the three of them, they were able to serve their employees and their customers very well.

Such people managers, and responsive learners within a communal learning field, therefore become involved in:

- an on-going, informal exchange of feelings between people, as staff or clients, learners or supervisors, in small groups
- absorbing a rich tapestry of myth and ritual, ceremony and storyline, including tales of creation and resurrection, crisis and resolution

- submission to a heroic cast of characters who personify the values of the organization, be it as staff or line, customers or suppliers, workers or managers
- the establishment, maintenance, communication and perpetuation of shared values, in person and in print, to which people feel they belong
- group activities, of both a working and educational nature, which make up the learning community's family life
- taking pride in the product or service, showing sympathy and exercising care in the course of learning and managing
- coaching and educating from 'people' people, who encourage individuals and groups to undertake communal activities and expect quality craftsmanship

Action-based and communal activities ground the organization, while knowledge-based ones help it to navigate a path through uneven and unknown terrain.

The Adaptive Field (Yellow)

Change or Die

Anikie, as team leader for an interactive video project based in Sweden, was a natural when it came to mentally juggling balls in the air. This was the seventh company she had joined in the past five years, since graduating from college both as a graphic artist and a computer scientist. Similarly, she had encouraged her team members to go on short courses, pick up new ideas and network with interesting people and organizations in their line of business.

Not only did Anikie have a network of professionals to deal with, across all manner of technological and sociological disciplines, but she had to adapt very rapidly to the changing demands of her geographically dispersed clients. Being something of a business and social chameleon herself, therefore, she was amazed at the coolness of Satoru, her Japanese sidekick.

Somehow he managed to take the continual technological and commercial changes much more philosophically than she did, sounding out with his Buddhist 'philosophy of Mu'. Fortunately, the team's financial controller, Klaus, was one of those very tolerant but solid citizens who was able to mediate between free spirited Anikie, spiritually minded Satoru, and the everyday business needs of their globally dispersed clients.

Such experimental learners, and the knowledge field within which they thrive, take part *in* and *with*:

- networked activities, linking departments and organizations, together with short- and medium-term monitoring and upgrading systems
- intelligent and interactive machines to generate and process information about people, money and things
- appropriate information (both in print and on line) and expertise of all kinds in professional and managerial fields
- project teams and *ad hoc* groups, that can be quickly formed and disbanded in response to changing circumstances
- individual, commercial and organizational experimentation involving the appropriate use of technical and social networks
- educators and coaches who encourage on-going learning and experimentation, provide access to information, and give continuing feedback on individual progress
- extensive learning facilities, including library sources and resource banks, varied and stimulating training programmes and interactive learning laboratories

While experimental learning ensures that the organization remains adaptable, energized learning carries with it the emotional commitment that enables the organization to both ride the difficulties and exploit the opportunities that come its way.

The Proactive Field (Green)

Energized Learner

J.R. had come up the hard way. Having left school at 17, and having started up two businesses of his own before joining this Texas-based oil company, he would inevitably rush in where others feared to tread. As chief 'honcho' for his company's acquisitions team he combined a wild streak with uncanny business instincts. As a team leader he was not only a hard taskmaster but he led from the front.

In the process, of course, he inevitably ruffled a lot of feathers, internally and externally. But, then again, he was only able to learn from his own mistakes. For J.R., work and life was eminently dramatic, emotionally draining and involved a continual battle of wits between him and his environment. When the chips were down, personally and commercially, his antennae were most finely tuned, ready to negotiate his way out of trouble. For that reason he benefitted far more from a nervy role play, a tension-filled business biography or from a nail-biting business game than from a dry management text or formal set of lectures. Substantive learning, for J.R., inevitably involved him in some kind of emotional catharsis!

The proactive field, for such an energized learner within a learning organization, therefore involves:

- educationally and *commercially* challenging projects involving the successful identification and exploitation of business opportunities
- popularization of the inventions that research and development have come up with, duly ensuring that such products or services can be made to appeal to the marketplace
- deals, involving profitable combinations of people from both within and without the learning organization
- calculated risks, that involve venturing into such unknown business and learning territory as can offer room for commercial and psychological manoeuvre
- acquiring, defending and expanding a power base – in the course of managerial and business development – through which personal influence and autonomy is enhanced
- selling themselves, their products and services to an ever-increasing range of customers
- being coached, educated and mentored in ways which are both emotionally and behaviourally challenging, including tough business games and dramatic role plays

Wheeler–dealer entrepreneurs, in fact, while seeking to assert themselves as opportunists, must work hand in glove with methodical analysts who take responsibility for the planning, organization and control of physical, financial and human resources.

The Functional Field (Blue)

The Well-Oiled Machine

Erich Klein, as finance director for a medium-sized manufacturing company based in Leipzig, was a master at keeping things under control. Having graduated from a respectable university, as a mechanical engineer, he then trained to become an accountant and thereafter, staying within the same firm for 20 years, gradually progressed up the promotional ladder.

Klein now ran a tight ship, in the accounts operation. Information from the production department, and from sales and distribution, was processed like clockwork – physical (input) data being turned into financial (output) reports. Knowledge of resource procurement, allocation and divestment was therefore built up cumulatively and methodically. Erich recruited well-qualified staff and trained them, formally and authoritatively, so that they could advance in knowledge, performance and status. The working environment was formal, courteous and predictable. Learning, like promotion, occurred in discrete and predictable lumps.

The functional field within the learning organization, and for the methodical or deliberative learner, therefore incorporates:

- formal training programmes covering each of the functional areas of knowledge, as well as their business and organizational integration
- the planning, organization and control of the training activities as a whole, including recruitment and staff education
- the delineation of formal organizational structures, specifying roles and responsibilities, programme instruction and supervision
- the establishment of specialized departments and divisions, each with clear boundaries and responsibility limits
- the installation of formal planning and control procedures to monitor and correct deviations between desired and actual performance
- clarification of lines of communication, both vertically and horizontally, to ensure that resources are procured and allocated efficiently and effectively
- coaching and training that is authoritative, depersonalized, role- and rule-based, and oriented towards the application of specialized expertise in specific practice

Efficiency and effectiveness is associated with such methodical management and learning; however, it inevitably falls short when a more profound form of learning is required. For such we need to turn to the harmonic learner, and the molecular learning field.

The Molecular Field (Indigo)

Unity in Diversity

When Hi-Tek (UK) and Italtek of Bologna joined forces, the selection of team leader to set up the joint venture was crucial. Rinaldo Barzzini was appointed because of his track record in bringing together people from different cultural backgrounds into a harmonious team. Rinaldo ran the company's industrial design group, so that not only did he have the aesthetic sensitivity of a designer, but he had also blended together a team of Italians, British, French and Germans, and all with artistic temperaments to boot! In fact, although Rinaldo had trained as a product designer in Italy, he had spent most of his working life in Germany, Spain and most recently Thailand.

At the same time, Rinaldo was not a typically commercial man, so Nelli, their recent Czech recruit, was brought in from export sales to lend an entrepreneurial hand. Finally, and fortunately, they had the good sense to bring Roberto, their Mexican marketing manager, who had enough geniality in him to stretch around the team three times, not to mention the fact that he spoke seven languages.

The most appropriate learning field for harmonic learners, acquiring and applying new insights, and partaking in the evolving commercial and organizational field, involves:

- a recognition of where the product, market, people and organization stand in the course of their evolution, together with an indication of how such evolution can be furthered
- conscious development, not only of themselves but also of both tangible and intangible resources by catalytic intervention
- focusing on areas of mutual benefit between individuals, departments, divisions, businesses and countries
- securing synergy between significant organizations – including customers and suppliers, divisions and distributors – with which the institution is connected
- identifying and setting up joint ventures – locally, nationally and internationally – to stimulate product, market and organizational development
- receiving empathetic coaching and deep and profound education, oriented towards worthwhile and significant activities

- progressively merging member and group, individual and organization, organization and environment, to the extent that narrowly based personal, functional or commercial identities are outgrown and new, more significant identities formed

The ultimate identity of an organization, though, is contained within its nucleus, or creative vision.

The Holographic Field (Violet)

From Vision to Action

Ivan was unique: not only was he an inventor in his own right but he was a boundless source of inspiration to others. As a research scientist he had been responsible for three major innovations in the pharmaceutics industry. What few people realized, however, is that he was totally dependent on two colleagues who had followed him from Russia to Israel and then to the US, over the course of seven years. While Ivan had the brilliant flashes of inspiration it was Fritz, with his meticulous attention to detail, who turned Ivan's ideas into workable concepts.

In fact, neither Ivan nor Fritz would have achieved very much without Simone, who was half French and half Vietnamese. She had a particular knack of intuitively recognizing which of Ivan's ideas were potentially marketable, and then of enticing Fritz to pursue them further. Between the three of them, then, they were able to advance from vision to action.

The inspired learner, through his or her work-based activities, reaches for self-actualization, and/or fuels organizational transformation by:

- uncovering both personal and organizational historical origins and destiny
- projecting a powerful image to the world, one which captures the imaginations of people within and without
- imparting fundamental values, ones which are closely in touch with the originator as a person, with the society of his or her heritage and residence, and with the underlying need that the product is serving
- reaching down to the underlying product or service, in its most profound sense

- engineering the physical transformation of the environment in which the organization is set, for the benefit of mankind
- receiving coaching and education from originators in their field, which serves to transform the individual's self-image
- continuing the work of innovation, of both a technical and social nature

Conclusion

Should any individual or organizational members either misrepresent themselves, or fail altogether to participate, then the learning field will be limited in one way or another. Moreover, all the institutions and individuals become part of an interdependent and 'learningful' organism *inside* the learning organization as a whole. Such 'learning-fulness' encompasses self-, skill and knowledge development.

We begin, then, with self.

PART II

Transforming Your Managerial Self

5

Identifying Your Learning Style

Introduction

Managing to Learn

You have now seen that there are seven kinds of learning fields, each of which, as will be revealed in this chapter, generate a different learning style. The learning style inventory at the end of this chapter will help you discover what kind of learner–manager you are.

As you uncover these styles you need to remember that, as with the seven managers (see chapter 6), you do have access to all seven of the alternatives. It is only that one, or perhaps two of these styles, will dominate your path to managerial learning. Of course, as you grow and develop, your style will deepen and broaden: starting from strength, consolidating on your natural learning style, and then moving out into weakness.

The Learning Styles

The seven learning styles, as indicated in table 5.1, directly correspond with the seven kinds of manager you will meet. They arise, in fact, out of the horizontal learning roles identified in chapter 2. We shall be investigating each style in turn, identifying their respective attributes, orientations, strengths and weaknesses. We start with the more commonplace or better established learner–managers, the reactor (action manager), the responder (people manager) and the deliberator (analytical manager). It is important to note, of course, that each style has its negative as well as its positive elements. In fact, the more you round out as a learner–manager, the stronger the positive features.

Table 5.1   Learning styles

Field	Learner	Manager	'Colour'
Reactive	Reactive learner	Action manager	Red
Communal	Responsive learner	People manager	Orange
Adaptive	Experimental learner	Manager of change	Yellow
Proactive	Energized learner	Enterprising manager	Green
Functional	Deliberative learner	Analytical manager	Blue
Molecular	Harmonic learner	Developmental manager	Indigo
Holographic	Inspired learner	Innovative manager	Violet

In rounding out as a learner, you work yourself through the full learning cycle, which incorporates all the learning elements, from reaction to inspiration (see figure 5.1). Any step missed along the way will result in a deficiency. For example, if you 'deliberate' on matters of strategy without having the opportunity to 'react' to a strategic opportunity, your learning will remain overly theoretical. In fact, the cycle is not a neat and tidy one. You may enter into it from any one of seven points, and then reach out, successively or simultaneously, to the other six.

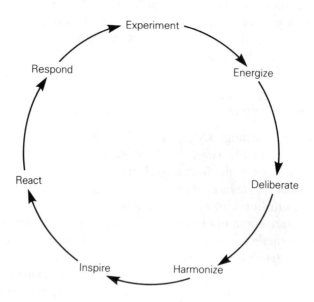

Figure 5.1   The learning cycle.

Styles of Learning

The Approaches to Learning

Established

Reactors believe explicitly in 'ready, fire, aim': they want to do something first, and learn from the consequences of their actions afterwards. Theory divorced from practice is meaningless, and frustrating for them. Sitting in classrooms, out of the thick of things, makes reactors restless and fidgety. They learn from doing, relying on crises to draw a novel reaction out of them. They respect people who are action-oriented and prefer practical tips on management to 'airy-fairy' concepts. As a result they run the danger of not seeing the wood for the trees, and rushing blindly into things.

Responders are 'people people'. Learning in isolation from other people is painful for them. Teaching materials which convey information in isolation from a social or practical context are inaccessible to them. Managerial learning, for responders, is a craft to be worked on practically, rather than a science to be worked out theoretically. It requires regular practice and specific applications: it can also lead to undue parochialism. A form of apprenticeship is preferable to purely classroom-based learning. For that reason the warmth of personality and the seasoned ability of any coach or educator are both crucial to the responder's development. Finally, like the Japanese, the responder aims for group rather than individual achievement.

Deliberators want to follow a methodical approach to both learning and management. They think problems through in a logical, step-by-step manner, assimilating disparate facts into coherent, established theories. Being good analysers they are keen to follow established models, principles and techniques. They also tend to be perfectionists who will not be content until they have fitted people and things into a neat and tidy framework: as such they can become narrow and pedantic. Status, authority, accreditation and formal promotion – finally – are an important part of their managerial and educational expectations.

Emergent

The four emergent approaches – becoming better recognized as enterprise and change, development and innovation gain in importance – are those of the energizer, the experimenter, the harmonizer and the inspirer.

Energizers respond to learning situations which are emotionally charged. Therefore, learning materials must be not only personally relevant but also emotionally stimulating. Energizers need to be emotionally spurred into achievement, operating within a competitive environment, both in the classroom and at work. In fact, such learners can become excessively competitive, and self-centred, thus inhibiting any group-oriented learning. Learning situations, for them, must carry tangible rewards, of both a personal and financial nature, and educators need to be 'heavyweights' in their field. Finally, opportunities must be provided for the energizers to make an emotional impact by spurring them on to achieve.

Experimenters want to involve themselves in new learning experiences: they are open-minded, flexible in their approach, and seek out a variety of activities, projects and learning materials. They are willing to try just about anything once, as an experiment, but will quickly tire from repeated exposure to the same kind of learning experience. As soon as the excitement generated from one activity or experience has ebbed they look out for the next one. Experimenters are therefore particularly susceptible to the latest fashion and fad in management education. In the final analysis they seek out stimulating, and argumentative coaches and educators, constantly looking for fresh ideas and for intellectual challenges.

Harmonizers want to fulfil their own learning potential, together with the potential of other people around them. They want to harmonize the different business functions and academic disciplines with which they have become involved, and also to balance out theory and practice so that neither predominates. They think in terms of wholes rather than parts, and need to combine thought and feeling in their learning activities. Harmonizers therefore require a rich and complex pattern of activities and experiences, of concepts and methods, of cultures and structures in their management development. They look for breadth and depth, in their coaches and educators, so much so that they run the risk of glossing over everyday reality in their lofty pursuits.

For *inspired* learners, learning is simultaneous with creativity: it needs to engage them totally to the extent that it becomes absolutely compelling. They need to be surrounded by inspiring people, while having the opportunity to inspire others, in their turn. Original ideas, and creative managers, artists or scientists, are necessary to their learning. Product, market or organizational innovations are the outcomes they would expect of themselves. Through their projects and programmes, therefore, they would expect to uncover highly unconventional ground, reaching profoundly into the origins of people or things, cultures or institutions. In their search for 'the holy grail', however, they might venture wildly off the beaten learning track.

The Learning Needs

We now need to examine, more specifically, the learning requirements that these different learner–managers have, in the context of a training and development programme.

The *reactive* learner is the 'action man', or woman, for whom action and learning are inextricably linked:

• Will there be lots of opportunities to do things?
• Will there be plenty practical tips and techniques?
• Shall I be tackling 'real' problems?
• Shall I be with people who want to make things happen?

The *responsive* learner is the people person, for whom people, social groups and learning are inextricably linked:

• Will the course be enjoyable?
• Will it be based on 'real' people and things?
• Will we all be encouraged to help each other?
• Will the educators and coaches be down to earth people?
• Will we be with nice people?

The *deliberative* learner is the analytical person, for whom theory and practice must inevitably be linked:

• Shall I be able to question the programme's assumptions?
• Will the programme's objectives be clear?
• Will the concepts and techniques stretch my mind?

- Will the teaching approach, and the instructors involved, be respected and respectable?
- Shall I be with managers of the same status as myself?

The *energized* learner is the emotionally turned on (or off) person, for whom realism and relevance hold pride of place, so that management education and personal achievement must link up:

- Will the programme be relevant to me?
- Will there be room for me to manoeuvre?
- Will I be personally and emotionally stretched?
- Shall I be exposed to the kind of experts who know what they are talking about because they've done it themselves?
- How will I be evaluated against my colleagues?

The *experimental* learner is the bright spark, for whom management education must be mentally stimulating:

- Shall I be learning something new?
- Will there be a wide variety of learning activities?
- Will it be okay to let my hair down?
- Shall I be tackling some interesting problems?
- Will there be a fun group of people to spark ideas off?

The *harmonized* learner is the deeply reflective person, for whom management in particular, and life as a whole, are inextricably interlinked:

- Shall I be learning something meaningful and worthwhile?
- Will we be studying subjects and situations in depth?
- Shall I be able to develop my full potential?
- Will we be exposed to a wide range of cross-cultural, inter-organizational and multidisciplinary contexts?
- Shall I be able to establish some significant relationships with people on the programme?

The *inspired* learner is the highly creative person, for whom management education and creative action must be the same:

- Will the course be completely unique?
- Shall I be exposed to the actual originators in their field?
- Will the programme stretch my imagination?
- Will the instructors be innovators in their own right?
- Shall I be with creative people?

The Learning Capacities

As well as having differing needs, of course, the seven learners have different capacities, both positive and negative. These are set out systematically below.

Reactive learners are first off the mark and last to see where they are going!

They are go-getters	*but* They leap before they look
They make things happen	They lack patience
They get straight to the point	They are intolerant of ambiguity
They cope with crises	They need crises to stimulate them

Responsive learners are attracted by down to earth people and things, and put off by 'airy fairy' concepts and ideas:

They are helpful to others	*but* They are dependent on others
They are practical and realistic	They lack imagination
They work well in a group	They cannot stand isolation
They create a good atmosphere	They are oversensitive to feedback

Deliberative learners are systematic and methodical, on the one hand, but can be pedantic and overcautious, on the other:

They are logical, 'vertical' thinkers	*but* They are unable to think 'laterally'
They are rational and objective	They cannot tolerate uncertainty
They are good at asking probing questions	They are intolerant of feelings
They are disciplined in approach	They are full of shoulds, oughts and musts

Energized learners are fully committed to improving their own managerial performance, but often at the expense of others:

They take the initiative	*but* They have a single-track mind
They motivate others to learn	They dominate others
They resolve crises	They are oblivious to feelings
They respond to opportunities	They manipulate people/ situations

Experimental learners are always willing to have a go, but seldom able to stick with things all the way:

They are flexible and open-minded	*but*	They like change for its own sake
They are happy to try something new		They get bored with implementation
They like being exposed to differences		They provoke unnecessary controversy
They optimistically accommodate change		They lack staying power

Harmonized learners are good at emotionally and intellectually recognizing potential, but are often much less adept at actively harnessing it:

They develop others	*but*	They fail to assert themselves
They recognize potential		They fail to exploit potential
They are good listeners		They are woolly thinkers
They enhance synergy		They ignore everyday reality

Finally, *inspired* learners reach for the stars, but might be living in cloud cuckoo land!

Their approach is innovative	*but*	They are 'daydreamers'
They have original ideas		They pursue originality for itself
They are able to inspire others		They can suppress opposition
They create potential		They fail to recognize potential

As we can see then, every learning style has both its strengths and its weaknesses. For that reason it is always advantageous, though not always easy, to move from one style into another. Weakness, in fact, is born out of one-sidedness.

Consolidating Upon Strengths

Appropriate Learning

In most cases, then, you will initially benefit as a learner–manager from consolidating on your strengths. As a result you will learn more from some kinds of learning situations than from others. It is therefore important that you deliberately seek out the appropriate situations from which you learn the most; and avoid inappropriate ones from which you learn the least. We start, once more, with the 'reactive' learner.

For the reactive learner

Appropriate learning involves:

- activities that involve hands-on management
- your own actions, as well as those of other managers who you respect for their actions rather than for their words
- the sort of management books that offer short and sharp tips
- adventure training programmes, where you can draw managerial lessons out of physically stressful situations
- a mentor who is always on the go, and books written by such 'go-getters'
- a coach or educator who can set you immediate challenges to which you can physically react

Inappropriate learning involves:

- learning activities of a purely intellectual nature
- an exchange of words, divorced from action
- deskbound activities, devoid of any physical challenge or movement
- classroom-based learning
- a mentor who is more thoughtful and reflective than behavioural and active
- a coach and educator who invite you to reflect rather than to act
- a purely theoretical project

The learning situation changes when you move from the reactive to the responsive, from the realm of action to that of people.

For the responsive learner

Appropriate learning involves:

- activities that involve on-going contact with people in groups
- educational activities that are fun
- people's needs – as colleagues, customers, superiors or subordinates – to which you can respond
- the sort of management books that are written in a popular and readable style

- teaching materials that involve you in concrete experience with people and things
- a mentor who is a people person and management books that are enjoyable to read, about real-life managers
- a coach or educator who puts out 'help me' signals to which you can respond
- people-centred projects

Inappropriate learning involves:

- a task that you undertake on your own
- educational activities that are a hard grind
- dry management texts
- lifeless teaching materials
- a mentor who is impersonal
- a coach or educator who encourages you only to use your head
- a depersonalized project

As you move from the standpoint of responder to that of deliberator so you turn from people to organization, from the social to the analytical.

For the deliberative learner

Appropriate learning involves:

- established management theories, drawing on concepts and models that have been tried and tested
- methodical analysis linking theory and practice
- probing the basic assumptions underlying the theory
- established management texts, with adjacent case studies
- distance-learning packages which can be worked through systematically on one's own
- a mentor who has a high status within the organization
- a coach or educator who is an authority in his or her field
- an organizationally acceptable, and methodologically rigorous project

Inappropriate learning involves:

- speculative ideas which have not stood the test of time and repeated application

- participation in situations explicitly involving the expression of emotions and feelings
- unstructured learning situations associated with a lot of uncertainty and ambiguity
- leading-edge ideas which have no evident validity, or practical application
- a hotchpotch of incoherent and inconsistent techniques, and applications, principles and practices
- a mentor who is a lateral thinker
- a coach or educator who bucks authority
- an impractical project

As you move on from being an established and deliberative learner to being an emergent and energized one, you move from method and organization to initiative and enterprise.

For the energized learner

Appropriate learning involves:

- relevant experiences, problems or opportunities
- personally challenging and interpersonally competitive educational activities, also involving commercial risk-taking
- dramatic learning situations that involve you in manoeuvring your way towards personal gain
- management books and role plays that involve crises and breakthroughs
- learning materials that serve to demonstrate achievement, on book, tape or video
- a mentor who is an influential manager
- an educator or coach who can spur you on, personally and emotionally, towards educational and managerial success
- personally challenging, and financially rewarding projects

Inappropriate learning involves:

- passive reflections on situations and concepts that have no immediate relevance
- ivory tower academics
- learning situations on which you are unable to make a personal impact
- management texts or packages that are heavily conceptual

- depersonalized learning materials that emphasize impersonal organization and de-emphasize personal judgment
- a mentor who is not a success in his or her own right
- a coach or educator who is a typical bureaucrat or academic
- an irrelevant project

In moving from being an energized learner to being an experimental one you move from emotionally to intellectually challenging terrain.

For the experimental learner

Appropriate learning involves:

- new experiences, problems or opportunities
- brief and varied educational activities, such as role plays, business games and group tasks
- a diversity of 'chop and change' activities, involving a continuing interplay of work- and learning-based activities
- management books and articles that are interactive
- a stimulating range of multimedia-based learning materials
- a mentor who is intellectually stimulating
- a coach or educator who will bounce ideas off you
- experimental, thought-provoking projects

Inappropriate learning involves:

- passive learning: listening to long lectures, monologues and prolonged explanations of things
- learning situations from which you are required to be removed, and not participate
- formal learning, following a single and preset curriculum
- lengthy management texts with a uniformity of content and style
- a single learning medium, such as reading books
- a mentor who is cautious and 'laid back'
- a coach or educator who is methodical and even pedantic in his or her approach
- a routine project

As you move on from routine to harmonized learning so the emphasis shifts from flexible perception to developmental insight.

For the harmonized learner

Appropriate 'discovery' learning involves:

- significant and meaningful learning experiences, that reach deep into your individual and social psyche
- learning contexts which allow the time and space for you to develop your own managerial insights
- depth and breadth of learning stimuli, drawing upon a wide range of cultural, managerial and organizational situations
- management texts written by profound thinkers in the field
- learning material that draws out the intimate feelings as well as the deep thoughts of the managers concerned
- a mentor who is a deep person
- a coach or educator who encourages you to reflect on ideas and experiences
- organizationally significant and personally worthwhile projects

Inappropriate 'discovery' learning involves:

- superficial, *ad hoc* exposure to people and situations
- a rapid sequence of learning experiences which allow no room for prolonged introspection
- a restricted and limited focus
- lightweight management thinkers and superficial case material
- popular management writers
- a mentor who is dispassionate about his or her work
- a coach or educator who wants to keep interaction light and bright
- a superficial project

As you progress from discovery-based to inspired learner so the emphasis shifts from gradually developing insight to radically transforming imagination.

For the inspired learner

Appropriate learning involves:

- total immersion in an illuminating, inspirational and productive work situation
- your own creative action
- exposure to originators in their field from all walks of life

- management books written by business and social visionaries such as Robert Owen and Henry Ford
- learning materials that compellingly represent the thoughts, feelings and actions of master managers
- a mentor who is himself or herself an innovator in their field
- a coach or educator who can draw out your originality
- a personally and organizationally unique project

Inappropriate learning involves:

- learning of a casual, intermittent nature
- the methodical teaching of others
- mundane learning experiences
- books written by accredited, mainstream authorities
- dry texts, devoid of feeling and action
- a pedestrian mentor
- a mediocre coach or educator, who heeds prevailing academic and managerial norms
- a conventional project

As you can see, then, one person's meat is the other person's poison. For that reason learners require individual facilitators (coaches or educators) who are able to match their distinctive learning requirements.

Supervising for Individualized Learning

In consolidating your learning you will learn most, at least at the outset, from those educators, coaches or mentors who are able to reinforce your natural inclinations. Subsequently, as you gain learning stride and momentum, you may well need to work with a facilitator who will reinforce a learning style that comes unnaturally to you. The important thing is to be able to consciously choose between the alternatives set out below.

The reactive supervisor/action manager:

- challenges you to 'get on with it'
- sets examples by his or her own actions
- points out your weaknesses, provoking you to do something about it
- encourages you to jump in at the deep end
- generates a climate of adventure

Is this challenging, action oriented, adventurous person for you, or would you prefer a less threatening coach?

The responsive supervisor/people manager:

- makes you feel at home
- sets learning targets with which you feel comfortable
- encourages you to work with a group of fellow learners
- ensures that you keep your feet firmly on the ground
- provides a communal learning environment

Is this homely, comfortable and encouraging coach for you, or do you prefer a more stimulating alternative?

The deliberative supervisor/analytical manager:

- guides you through accredited, established training programmes
- encourages you to relate theory to practice
- demonstrates the validity and practicability of any management concepts with which you are working
- shows you how to construct or demolish an argument through powers of logic
- sets high standards for you

Is this conventional, logical and practical person for you, or do you prefer a more stirring supervisor as an alternative?

The energized supervisor/enterprising manager:

- challenges you to achieve, setting you targets well beyond your immediate comfort zone
- exposes you to threatening situations in which you will sink or swim
- probes into your weaknesses, and challenges you to overcome them
- shows you the managerial ropes, especially when it comes to manoeuvring your way through tricky commercial waters
- keeps you on your toes, even to the point of bullying you to 'give it a go'

Is this brow-beating, even threatening, but undoubtedly wiley and resilient supervisor for you, or would you prefer a more intellectually stimulating alternative?

The experimental supervisor/manager of change:

- generates opportunities for you to acquire new skills
- gives you a positive lead towards short-term learning targets
- exposes you to novel and varied learning situations

- encourages you to experiment
- responds flexibly to your learning needs, as and when they arise, thus refusing to plan too far ahead

Is this novel, stimulating, flexible and varied approach for you or would you prefer a more intimate and profound form of supervision? The harmonic supervisor/developmental manager:

- enables you to discover your potential
- encourages you to draw out your strengths
- identifies opportunities for you to develop learning opportunities out of your job
- uncovers a balanced portfolio of learning activities
- encourage you to share your 'deep self' with him/her

Is this insightful, enabling and intimate style of supervision for you, or would you prefer someone more radical and imaginative? The inspired supervisor/innovative manager:

- encourages you to dream, and to turn that dream into a reality
- stimulates your imagination, through the use of powerful imagery
- sets an innovative example through his or her creative actions
- encourages you to transform your workplace into whatever you individually desire
- instils you with 'religious' zeal

Learning to Overcome Weakness

Finally, there are particular self-development activities that you can undertake to strengthen those aspects of your learning which are currently weak.

Strengthen Your Reactive Style

- Get into the habit of doing things 'just for the hell of it'. Change the layout of your office furniture, for example, or change your style of writing.
- Locate yourself, in times of mini-crisis, in a central position, whereas you might normally be inclined to take a backseat role. When someone has an accident be the first to offer your help. If two dogs get into a fight be the person to separate them.

- When colleagues react without thinking, prevent yourself from reacting negatively to their 'wayward' behaviour. Practise responding, for example, by saying 'I like your impulsiveness' or 'You're quick on your feet'.
- Gain yourself a newly acquired reputation for being someone who 'makes things happen', by deliberately acting on that physically active part of your management style. Take up more physical exercise, that is if you're not doing so already, such as jogging or weight training.

Alternatively, you may be satisfied with your speed and force of reaction and wish to become more socially responsive.

Strengthen Your Responsive Style

- Practise expressing your feelings at times when you would not normally have time to do so. Warmly compliment people for even modest achievements. Express your dismay when things go wrong – openly, and with heartfelt sympathy for those who suffer the ill consequences.
- Attend parties that you would have otherwise chosen to give a miss. Comment on people's appearance, warmly and favourably. Look out for anyone who is feeling ill at ease, and come to their rescue, by befriending them.
- Find out about the birthdays of those working with and for you: send them greetings and arrange festivities. Put fresh plants in your office and consciously make your working environment more pleasant.
- Dress less formally and wear warm colours. Stroll into your employees' workplace and have a friendly chat. Ensure you call everyone by their first names, and make the effort to remember what all their first names are.

Alternatively, you may be satisfied with your responsiveness to people, and wish to strengthen your ability and inclination to systematically organize people, information and things.

Strengthen your Deliberator Style

- Read something 'heavy' and thought-provoking – perhaps philosophy or even aspects of the theory of relativity – for at least 30 minutes every day. Tackle one of the more thoughtful management writers. Whatever you decide to read, make the effort to summarize the contents afterwards.

- Practise spotting inconsistencies and weaknesses. Go through reports, highlighting missing points in the argument. Analyse organization charts to discover overlaps and conflicts. Regularly compare and contrast the views of fellow managers who have opposing views on things.
- Practise asking probing questions. Refuse to be fobbed off with platitudes or with vague answers. Find out precisely why things have turned out the way they have, or why one department is so much more effective than another.
- Practise setting up things so that they are more likely to turn out as you might have predicted. Invent new procedures to cope with specific problems. Structure your own department in ways that increase productivity.

Alternatively, you may be satisfied with your powers of deliberation and wish to become more energized and energizing.

Strengthen Your Energizing Style

- Expose yourself to learning situations that involve you in uncomfortable predicaments, in which you will have to improvize and manoeuvre. Offer expertise when you don't have it. Practise committing yourself to projects and situations that you find somewhat unnerving. Turn a discussion into a negotiation, when you might not ordinarily have done so. Watch other people doing deals and observe in detail not only how they do it but also what makes them tick.
- Practise selling yourself in situations where your natural approach would be lower key. Accept speaking assignments at times where you would normally have declined because you lack the appropriate expertise. Put yourself out and about more.
- Get into the habit of motivating people, enthusing and energizing them through your emotionally based conviction. Watch the way that entrepreneurial people around you wind people up.

Alternatively, you may be satisfied with your ability to energize yourself and others and wish to strengthen your experimental learning style.

Strengthen Your Experimental Style

- Do something new, that is something you have never done before, once a week. Hitch a lift to work, visit a part of the organization you have never had any desire to see, go jogging at lunchtime (if you don't already), read a newspaper that has views diametrically opposed to your own from cover to cover.
- Practise initiating conversations with strangers. Select people at random from your internal telephone directory and go and visit them. At large gatherings, open a conversation with a wide and diverse range of people there. In your spare time go door to door canvassing for a cause of your choice.
- Deliberately fragment your day by chopping and changing activities at random intervals, say every half hour, for example, if you have spent 30 minutes occupied mentally, switch to something mechanical or physical.
- Practise thinking aloud, and on your feet. Set yourself a problem, and bounce ideas off a colleague (see if, between you, 50 ideas can be generated in ten minutes). Give an impromptu five minute speech to your staff.

Alternatively, if you are satisfied with your ability to experiment you may wish to strengthen your harmonic style.

Strengthen Your Harmonic Style

- Practise observing people and things, individuals and groups, marketplaces and whole societies, for prolonged periods. Study people's thoughts, feelings and actions. Observe tone and gesture, listen to the quality of the language used, reflect on the influence of culture on behaviour.
- Take time out to meditate for ten minutes a day, completely emptying your mind of any thoughts or internal chatter. Meditate upon an object, an image or an idea.
- Get into the habit of spending time on your own, preferably in the company of nature. Take solitary walks in the countryside, and harmonize your thoughts and activities with those of the natural environment around you.
- Listen and watch out for the hidden potential in people and in situations. Exercise your intuition in foreseeing how things will

turn out. Attach significance to coincidental events and 'tune in' to the way of the Universe, to the eternal stream of life.

Alternatively, if you are satisfied with your harmonic powers, you may wish to strengthen your inspired learning style.

Strengthen Your Inspirer Style

- Read the biographies of past and present visionaries such as Robert Owen, Henry Ford, Albert Einstein and Martin Luther King. Find out where their originality sprang from, and how it was subsequently manifested.
- Observe, through the media, the innovators of the day, in any walk of life, be it art or fashion, business or politics, science or technology. Watch their style. Listen to the words they use. Try and imitate their approaches on a small scale.
- Practise using metaphor, yourself, in the same way as the great orators, such as Martin Luther King and Jesse Jackson, are able to do. Begin to adopt a similar gesture and tone.
- Start to compliment other people around you on their originality. Get used to seeing such creative geniuses in a positive rather than negative light, without distancing yourself. In fact, purposefully build them into your own working group.

Alternatively, if you feel satisfied with the extent to which you are able to sustain inspiration in your learning you may wish to strengthen any of the other learning styles.

Conclusion

In the final analysis, and as indicated in table 5.2, a management and organization development programme that caters for the full variety of learning styles needs to incorporate a wide range of learning options, and management styles to which we now turn in chapter 6.

Learning Style Inventory: Self-assessment

To identify the learning style to which you naturally incline, fill in the inventory that follows. In fact, that role will be closely attuned to both your management and team role.

Table 5.2 Learning styles and programme features

Style	Feature				
	Project focus	Coaching abilities	Learning materials	Learning medium	Learning mode
Reactor	Action-centred	Energetic, practical	Practical tips	Adventure training	Action learning
Responder	People-centred	Sociable, skilled	Popular writings	Group learning	Apprentice-ship
Deliberator	Organiza-tion-centred	Respected, respectable	Business texts	Integral learning package	Formal course
Energizer	Business-centred	Dynamic, challenging	'Success' books	Dramatiza-tions and role plays	Challenge and response
Experimenter	Project-centred	Enthusiastic, bright	Leading-edge thinkers	Menu of learning resources	Problem-solving
Harmonizer	Environ-ment-centred	Sensitive, insightful	Profound thinkers	Multi-media experience	Discovery learning
Inspirer	Vision-centred	Imaginative, charismatic	Business originators	Master classes	Creative action

There are eight sets of statements, numbered 1 to 8. For each set, rank each statement (a) to (g) from 1 to 7 in turn. A ranking of 1 suggests that statement is absolutely you, and 7 indicates the opposite. Avoid any equal rankings.

After you have ranked yourself on all eight sets of statements, turn to the end for details of how to interpret your scores.

1   Score

    (a) I'm a hands-on learner.

    (b) The projects that really grab me are the unique ones, particularly those which transform people or things.

    (c) The sort of mentor I respect will inevitably be a deep person.

    (d) I respect a boss who is authoritative.

    (e) I am most likely to learn from relevant concepts, experiences or techniques.

    (f) I usually seek out someone I can bounce my ideas off.

    (g) I learn best through other people that I like.

2   Score
(a) I respect other people for their actions rather than
    their words.
(b) The sort of boss I value is the one who can draw out
    my individuality.
(c) I learn the most when I'm working with people who
    encourage me to reflect on my ideas and experiences.
(d) Any project I undertake I will take rigorously, step
    by step.
(d) I relish those learning experiences which are per-
    sonally challenging and commercially risky.
(f) The sorts of projects which excite me are thought-
    provoking ones.
(g) Learning should be enjoyable, at least as far as I am
    concerned.

3   Score
(a) The management books I prefer are those business
    biographies which tell things as they really are.
(b) I have the greatest respect for such business creators
    as Steve Jobs or the original Olivetti, who had
    compelling imaginations.
(c) The sorts of managers I learn the most from are
    profound people.
(d) I learn about a subject methodically.
(e) I love to be challenged.
(f) I prefer the sorts of management games or videos
    which are interactive.
(g) Projects which suit me are geared around people
    who are nice.

4   Score
(a) Of all the training programmes on the market the
    outward bound courses, and adventure training,
    make most sense to me.
(b) If I read a book on management it will be written by
    a visionary such as Henry Ford or Robert Owen.
(c) I learn the most from meaningful managerial and
    organizational experiences that draw out the whole
    of me.
(d) I am very partial to case studies.
(e) The sort of mentor who is worth his or her salt is the
    one who is influential in his or her right.
(f) If I am to have someone to guide me I would want
    such a person to be intellectually stimulating.

(g) Teaching materials that work for me have to be grounded in concrete experiences.

5

(a) My favourite managers have been those who 'manage by wandering about'; that is, always being on the go, making things happen.

(b) I expose myself to the real originators in the field of management.

(c) I can learn the most when I have the time and space to reflect on any insights I have come up with.

(d) When investigating a subject I ask probing questions, testing the underlying assumptions.

(e) I favour those sorts of learning materials, preferably on audiotape or video, that demonstrate business mastery.

(f) I relish a multi-media approach to education.

(g) The sorts of management books that appeal to me are the popular easily readable ones such as *The One Minute Manager*.

6

(a) The sort of manager I most respect, as a boss, is the one who sets me immediate and tough challenges.

(b) I learn the most through my own creative actions.

(c) I seek out a wide range of learning situations, preferably each of a fair degree of intensity, from within and without management.

(d) I am keen on self-study packages which I can work through systematically and thoroughly.

(e) Dramatic learning situations, in which there is plenty of room for manoeuvre, are just for me.

(f) I learn most from new experiences, problems or opportunities.

(g) The sort of boss I respect will be a people person.

7

(a) Projects which really get me going are all about action.

(b) I learn the most when I'm totally immersed in what I'm doing.

(c) When I really am learning I have to be able to feel as well think about the situation or material.

(d) If I am to have a mentor he or she needs to be someone of authority within my organization.

(e) I learn best through a role play or simulation which is dramatic.

(f) I seek out brief and varied learning situations such as role plays, business games and group exercises.

(g) I like to work for someone who is prepared to put out, from time to time, 'help me' signals.

8   Score

(a) I hate being tied down to sitting in a classroom for too long.

(b) The only real function of a lecturer, as far as I am concerned is to inspire me.

(c) When I tackle a project I always try to get to the heart of the matter.

(d) A good trainer, for my purposes, is a clear and objective communicator.

(e) I learn best from my own successes and failures.

(f) Learning is what work is all about for me.

(g) Within a study group I hate to stand out in case someone rejects me.

Scoring Procedure

You are now ready to interpret your responses. The learning styles to be scored are as follows:

Colour	Learning style	Management style
Red	Reactive	Action
Orange	Responsive	People
Yellow	Experimental	Change
Green	Energized	Enterprise
Blue	Deliberative	Analysis
Indigo	Harmonic	Development
Violet	Inspired	Innovation

You will find the scoring sheet below. Each of the numbered rows (1 to 8) refers to a statement set. Enter your scores next to the letter corresponding to the statement; that is, the score for statement (a) will be entered in the column containing an 'a'. At a glance you will see your predominant styles in the total line (lowest score = dominant style).

Learning style inventory scoring sheet

Set	Red score	Violet score	Indigo score	Blue score	Green score	Yellow score	Orange score
1	a	b	c	d	e	f	g
2	a	b	c	d	e	f	g
3	a	b	c	d	e	f	g
4	a	b	c	d	e	f	g
5	a	b	c	d	e	f	g
6	a	b	c	d	e	f	g
7	a	b	c	d	e	f	g
8	a	b	c	d	e	f	g
Totals							

6

Developing Yourself as a Manager

Introduction

The focus in this chapter is on self-development, including both self-discovery (individual learning) and self-realization (personalized innovation).

Your management style is not necessarily closely correlated with your learning style – described in chapter 5. At the same time, as and if you grow and develop as a manager, you have the chance to evolve, and to involve the total learning field – already described in chapter 4. Finally, certain skills, as well as particular members of the cast of knowledgeable characters, are correlated with certain managers – both established and emergent (see chapters 7 and 10).

The Process of Development

Development Paths

There are seven paths of manager self-development:

- the analytical manager ('deliberator') maps out a promotion path
- the action manager ('reactor') carves out a path of action
- the people manager ('responder') follows a path of service and friendship
- the manager of change ('experimenter') pursues a path of constant change
- the enterprising manager ('energizer') negotiates a path of enterprise

- the developmental manager ('harmonizer') becomes involved in a path of evolution
- the innovative manager ('inspirer') engages in a path of creative innovation

All managers, if they grow and develop over the course of their careers, evolve through distinct phases. Psychologically speaking, the growth phases of childhood are physical, social and intellectual. Those of adulthood involve exploration, consolidation, self-renewal and finally maturation.

Self-development and Maturation

Youth, when you are in your twenties, is a time for experimentation and for daring – whether physical, social, commercial or intellectual in nature. It is the age of enterprise and experimentation.

As you enter young adulthood, you need to become more organized in your activities and relationships. It is at this stage, in your thirties, that your path becomes clearly visible. This is the time for consolidation and organization.

In midlife, if you are to successfully pass through the proverbial crisis (early forties) you need to tap hitherto hidden powers within yourself. This requires you to reflect on the wider meaning of life and work. As you open out to yourself and to others in your forties, you enter the age of renewal and conscious development.

In the evening of your life, believe it or not, you can be at your most creative. For maturity, in your fifties and beyond, is the time to actualize yourself and your business vision. It is the age of 'individuation' and of personal and organizational maturation (transformation).

You Have the Choice

Self and manager development, unfortunately, is not inevitable. Many companies and individuals lose their way and fail to evolve: they start out in a particular path and then get stuck, and potential remains, at least temporarily, unfulfilled. That is where you have a free choice, in a sense. You cannot help but, through your personality and circumstances, follow a particular kind of path – but how far you get and in what particular way you get there is very much up to you.

In your late teens, or thereabouts, you stop growing physically. But you should never stop growing mentally and emotionally – in fact if you do so you fail to realize yourself. Each stage of your development represents a kind of simultaneous death and rebirth. For example, in the transition from youth to adulthood, you might relinquish a degree of recklessness and welcome a degree of sobriety.

In Management You Require Both Stability and Change

In stable periods you find an interim niche for yourself, and during transitional phases you begin to question that very stability – life never stands still. No matter how satisfactory your current position might be, in time you begin to see its flaws. For example, in your thirties you may become increasingly dissatisfied with what you had previously experienced as a life of fun and adventure; and that very dissatisfaction paves the way for your future development.

A 'decision' to stay put, within a particular career position, may not be a positive decision at all. It may stem from a sense of resignation, inertia, passive acquiescence or even genuine despair – and can mark the beginning of a long-term commercial or personal decline unless you choose to arrest it. Transition needs to be positively anticipated.

Development is Stimulated by Both Challenge and Support

In the process of development, as you have by now gathered, you need to be willing to venture into the unknown – you will have to risk change and loss. At the same time, though, you require friends and colleagues to act as the haven in the wilderness. It is simply unbearable to imagine confronting a major challenge all alone. By listening, by caring, by playing you back to yourself, such real friends support your better instincts.

In a sense, these two forces – of challenge and support – are like parental stereotypes. Father is the pull into the unknown; mother is the known, the touchstone. In balance and harmony they provide the perfect ground for growth, which, of course, takes place in stages.

Anticipating Self-realization

To positively anticipate change you need to have an image of what such change may represent. For example, you need to hold a positive mental picture of 'an effective manager' before you move on from being a trainee.

Secondly, you must be prepared to let go of an outlived identity; that is, to let it die. Old fears, of being 'tied down' for instance, need to be re-examined in the light of new possibilities that may arise. Therefore you separate from your old self and become attached to a new one. The same process applies to a change in activity as to a change in relationship.

Thirdly, having plunged into new territory, you expand yourself. In the process your senses are enlivened and your insights quicken. In fact, having dared to get your feet wet in a fresh stream you may be swept along in a fresh current of events. You may even feel, for a time, dangerously out of control.

Finally, and after the hurly burly of expansion, comes a more restful period. You find the time and the inclination to digest the change and to incorporate its meaning into your philosophy of life.

So you begin to take genuine pleasure in your newly found position, until such a time as dissatisfaction once more sets in. At this point the cycle must repeat itself as you start to anticipate the next major change.

Stages of Manager Self-development

In summary then, as an individual manager, you not only have seven different paths of self-development available to you, but each one unfolds in stages. Although these divisions are not clear-cut they can serve as useful indicators (see table 6.1).

Paths of Development

Each of the paths of manager self-realization, stretching over an adult lifespan, takes on a different complexion. We begin with the path of action.

The Path of Action

Are you an action manager?

● Always on the go: you work long hours, and travel to far flung places – you have lots of staying power.

Table 6.1   Stages of development

Youth (20s)	Young adulthood (30s)	Midlife (40s)	Maturity (50s)	'Colour'
Trainee manager	Analytical manager	Executive	Leadership spirit	Blue
'Action man'	Action manager	Activator	Spirit of adventure	Red
People person	People manager	Animator	Spirit of community	Orange
Troubleshooter	Manager of change	Change agent	Spirit of freedom	Yellow
Salesman	Enterprising manager	Corporate architect	Spirit of adventure	Green
Scientist/ artist	Developmental manager	Enabler	Spirit of development	Indigo
Inventor	Innovative manager	Visionary	Spirit of creativity	Violet

- Working hard and playing hard: you balance emotional and intellectual with physical activity – you put in lots of effort.
- Fit and healthy: you exercise regularly, in your work or in your leisure – you are full of energy.
- You move people: you make a physical impact and galvanize people around you into activity.
- Embodying the spirit of adventure: you are recognized as a wandering spirit – you are an explorer.

Becoming an action manager

In realizing your physical self, you will constantly seek out physical movement. You look for physically challenging situations. Your path will be bodily or geographically identified with physical landmarks. Hard work and hard knocks are taken in your stride. Learning, divorced from action, has no meaning and makes no impact. You are at home in operations or sales, emergency services or disaster relief, where there is plenty scope for action and reaction.

Should you grow and develop in this physical direction:

- in your youth you are always on the go as an 'action man or woman'
- as you enter adulthood, you have the commonsense to turn your raw energy into structured form as an 'action manager'
- you have the breadth of outlook in midlife to combine your energy with other people's as an 'activator', like a Richard Branson

- ultimately, your restless spirit turns you into a symbol of adventure with a powerful and physically based mission in life, embodying the 'spirit of adventure'

The learning you undergo will require plenty of physical action upon which to base your reflections, and physical landmarks to reflect your progress.
Alternatively, are you less action-driven and more people oriented?

The Social Path

Are you a people manager?

- Operating informally, making personal contacts: you establish a strongly cohesive, informal organization – creating ways and means of keeping in constant touch.
- Establishing rituals and ceremonies, uniting people: you hold 'revivalist' meetings, especially for sales people – you establish rituals to protect staff from fear of the unknown.
- Establishing a 'family feeling': you ensure that needs of individuals serve those of the whole – you become like a mother to your organizational children.
- Activating people's social lives: you provide access to an active and creative group life – you widen people's horizons.
- Creating a corporate culture, thereby sharing values: you create heroes who pass on your primary corporate values – you make sure that formative corporate legends live on.

Becoming a people manager

In realizing your social self, you will first seek out a familiar circle to which to belong. Your own development cannot be separated from that of particular groups to which you have become attached. People-oriented social service, in the public or private sector, comes naturally to you.

You learn by associating yourself with progressively broader-based circles of people; in sales, in operations, in personnel, in health or community work. You grow by building your own communities, by exercising your skills as a people person. Each community formed, locally or internationally, economically or socially, represents a landmark along your path of development.

If you grow and develop in this social direction:

- in your youth you are a carefree 'craftsman' or 'people person', finding it easy to get on with people and things that give you joy
- in adulthood you consolidate your knowledge of your people or service, turning your enthusiasm for either into that of a 'people manager', whether as a production person, in social/health services or as a salesman with vitality
- in midlife you round out the social base of your activity, enabling many others to enjoy you as an 'animateur'
- in maturity you draw out your mission in life as you animate an enterprise or embody the 'spirit of community'

The learning you undergo, finally, will require a close involvement with people and things from which to draw your learning, and with social landmarks to reflect your progress.

Alternatively, are you less people-oriented and more stimulated by change?

The Path of Change

Are you a manager of change?

- Adaptable professional: having in depth knowledge and experience in your field, and displaying greater loyalty to your profession than to your organization.
- Troubleshooting: rapidly identifying opportunities for change, and coming up with alternative courses of action to exploit them.
- Experimenting with change: continually forming temporary project groupings, and solving on-going problems in interdisciplinary teams.
- Planning for change: constructing long-term plans with built-in contingencies, and monitoring changes and adapting your plans accordingly.
- Embodying the spirit of change: being respected as a free thinker, and embodying the organization's cause.

Becoming a manager of change

In the course of becoming a change agent you will naturally seek out a path of learning and change. You will be likely to travel, to read a lot and to go on courses in order to find things out. A course, a book or a project serves as a landmark in your intellectual development. You like to be constantly on the move, but in order to be stretched mentally rather than physically or emotionally.

The path of change leads you into project-based activity in a wide range of fields in which knowledge-based work and self-expression are at a premium. These range from market research and public relations to design and advertising, to training and consultancy, to technical and social research and to computer programming and systems analysis. You will typically be professionally qualified.

Should you grow and develop along this intellectually challenging path:

- youthful self-expressiveness leads you into confrontation with the establishment, as a 'troublemaker or troubleshooter'
- in adulthood you turn from active but undirected opposition into becoming a more deliberate 'manager of change'
- in midlife you might become a more broadly based catalyst or 'agent of change', to help other people free themselves from oppression
- in maturity, as you fully realize yourself, you turn your function into a firmly based cause embodying 'the spirit of freedom'

The learning you undergo will finally need to be both varied and mentally stimulating, with ideas generated and changes made being the landmarks to reflect your progress.

Alternatively, are you less of a rebel and more like an enterprising manager?

The Path of Enterprise

Are you an enterprising manager?

- A marginal operator: you are marginal to the establishment – you seek to find your niche rather than to fill a role.
- A risk-taker: you believe that the future will turn out in your favour – you enjoy taking calculated risks.
- An opportunist: you see the creation of customers as fundamental to you – you expand outwards, like an amoeba, and then fill the spaces.
- A wheeler–dealer: by negotiating you create a system of exchange

and transaction – by scheming you create profitable combinations, out of people.

- An achiever: you bring your desired future into being – you are competitive, determined and persistent.

Becoming an enterprising manager

In becoming an enterprising manager, you pursue a path that is circuitous rather than direct. You love to overcome obstacles and to take calculated and emotionally thrilling risks. Your life and workstyle is dramatic, full of ups and downs and of mistakes from which to learn. In fact you only learn by taking an initiative and by facing the consequences of your decisions. In your work you need tangible feedback and incentives, and progressively larger territories to conquer. Each new territory acquired, each battle won, is a landmark or milestone on your dramatic journey.

Your home territory is sales and enterprise, of any kind as long as you can make money, and/or 'make waves' out of it – you love doing deals. You conventionally lack formal qualifications.

If, then, you grow and develop along this wilful path:

- in your youth you need to have the courage to sell your unqualified self and your unaccredited merchandise in the marketplace, as a 'market trader' or 'salesman'.
- then, in adulthood, you need the organizational ability to handle a growing enterprise as an 'enterprising manager'
- in midlife, you will initiate the development of associations of individual business enterprises and of whole industries, so that you become what we might call a 'corporate architect'
- ultimately, in the depths of your mature being, you may be moved to become an 'enterprising spirit' in the wider community

The learning you undergo will need to be both personally dramatic and organizationally relevant, with commercial landmarks to reflect your progress.

Alternatively, are you less enterprising and more analytical?

The Path of Promotion

Are you an analytical manager?

- Your direction is clear-cut: clear objectives have been set at all levels – they are internally consistent and collectively exhaustive.
- You have a competitive strategy: your mission is clearly and fully articulated – you have filled a gap in the market.
- Your management activities are clearly differentiated: you plan, organize, direct and control operations efficiently – you link up with other organizational departments effectively.
- Your communications are effective: authority and responsibility is purposefully delegated – horizontal and vertical communications operate effectively.
- You serve society: you serve your customers/the public efficiently and with integrity – you make a recognized contribution to the community at large.

Becoming an analytical manager

In realizing your organizational self, you will be following a linear path of promotion, from the lower to higher end of an organization. You will rise through the hierarchy in a series of progressive steps and accomplish your work in a similarly ordered way. You will undertake formal training and make good use of authoritative information whenever you need it. Certified qualifications as well as positions with progressively elevated responsibilities are signs of progress along your pre-planned journey.

The path of promotion leads you into positions of authority within business, government, education or in the voluntary sector. You become uniquely qualified to run anything, anywhere, once you grasp the managerial principles of planning, organization and control, and are able to apply them in progressively more complex and demanding situations.

Should you develop along this path:

- your outgoing youthful nature is geared towards getting things done efficiently as a junior manager, personal assistant or 'trainee manager' working for a small group of people
- in adulthood you subsequently apply your brainpower to achieving

effectiveness as a more experienced functional and 'analytical manager' in charge of a larger department within an organization

- as you open yourself in midlife to a broadly based notion of service you become a more generalist 'executive', responsible to and for a wide range of interested parties
- your inner spirit, when awakened in maturity, might merge with conventionally ordered religious beliefs, as in the case with a 'leader' such as Lord Sieff (Jewish), embracing a 'spirit of order'

The learning you develop will need to be formally accredited and practically realistic, with both theoretical and applied knowledge forming the landmarks for your progress.

Alternatively, are you less of a conventional executive and more of a developmental manager?

The Development Path

Are you a developmental manager?

- You are a harmonizer: you have a talent for invoking consensus – you focus on areas of mutual benefit.
- You recognize potential for development: you release potential by opening up hidden, connected pathways – you help people and enterprises to fulfil their potential.
- You are a link person: you are moored by many interlocking lines of connection – you build up alliances, as well as networks of mutual support.
- You uncover the flow of energy: you focus energy's quality, velocity, vitality and direction – you release such energy flows intuitively.
- You are in touch with evolution: you can recognize the individual's level of evolution, and you embody the spirit of development within your institution.

Becoming a developmental manager

In consciously developing yourself, you will follow a path that is neither linear nor bounded. It is diagonal and associative, picking up threads along the way and weaving them into a distinctive physical, psychological or economic pattern. Because of this sweeping movement, you are obliged to move outside of the bounds of any particular family or organization. Significant ideas, incidents or experiences serve to broaden your own understanding of your work and life.

The path of development leads you either into art or science, architecture or design, or into psychology or counselling, business, economic and social development.

Should you develop further from this point:

- in your youth you need to have the initiative to stand up against conventional wisdom, as an 'artist' or 'scientist', because of your outraged sensitivity against human or environmental ugliness
- then, in adulthood, you need to consolidate, as a 'developmental manager', through product, service, organization or business development
- in midlife you need the breadth of knowledge and insight of an 'enabler' to harness the potential of people, products or whole environments across a broad range of organizations
- then in maturity you need the spirit to design or to engineer social, economic or 'cultural development' across a whole society

The learning you undergo will need to be both significant and worthwhile to you and the organization, with fundamental insights and development forming the landmarks for your progress.

Alternatively, and finally, are you less developmental and rather more of an innovative manager?

The Creative Path

Are you an innovative manager?

- Having the courage to dream: you have the courage to tap powerful, subconscious images – you remain close to nature and to the spirit of your nation.
- Envisaging the future: you are connected with the distant past and the full present – a little corner of the infinite has been revealed to you.
- Imparting fundamental values: you express your vision in a language of uplift and idealism – you raise your organization's emotional and spiritual plane.
- You are impassioned: you experience pain and ecstasy through your work – you love what you do, as an all-embracing obsession.

- You are a master: you have conquered yourself – you are like the conductor of an orchestra.

Becoming an innovative manager

In realizing your imaginative self you will be following the path of a spiral! Over time your central idea spirals upwards and outward. Marks of progress are represented by flashes of inspiration and by scientific or design breakthroughs. As an innovator you also stand on the shoulders of giants, needing deep and firm foundations for your ventures into the complete unknown. The path of creativity leads out from the pure arts and sciences, shaping technologies and environments.

Should you grow and develop in this direction:

- in youth you need the courage to present yourself as an 'inventor' to a world that inevitably is not ready for you, and to suffer all the blows from cynics and sceptics around you
- in adulthood you need the self-discipline and structure of mind to build an organization around your inventiveness so that you can become an 'innovative manager'
- in midlife you need to broaden your inventiveness to include social and organizational, as well as product innovations – you will be engaged as a 'visionary'
- in maturity, through reaching down to the roots of your inspiration, you should be creating a new world around you that touches you on all walks of life – your 'spirit of creativity' will lead to physical transformation

The learning you undergo will need to involve original ideas and activities, with creative breakthroughs constituting the landmarks of your progress.

Conclusion

Personal and Project Development

The learning activities you select, from the point of view of your own self-development, will depend on the managerial self you wish to realize, and the stage you have reached in your managerial life cycle. It is likely, at the outset, that you will want to consolidate on strengths (your dominant self), and subsequently alleviate relative weaknesses (a lower order self). Ultimately, and in the best of all possible cases, you are able to become the full possible spectrum.

Individual and Manager Development

Development is not inevitable. But if you know the sort of direction it takes, you are more likely to develop yourself (see the select bibliography for prominent examples). Although there are at least seven different kinds of life path, all have to follow the natural laws of development. As you develop along any one path you explore, consolidate, renew and deepen your involvement with people and things. You thereby learn in quantum leaps.

There are four major development stages in adult life, succeeding three in childhood and youth. If you are to successfully undergo your own career transitions you need to anticipate them and to be willing to separate, on each occasion, your old self from your new one. It is never too late to develop yourself. Even if you have missed out on some developmental phases along the way, you can still grow mentally and emotionally, if not physically. It is just that it will require a little more effort than it might have done before.

Select Bibliography

Action manager: J. Harvey Jones, *Making it Happen* (Collins, London, 1987).
People manager: M. K. Ash, *On People Management* (Pan, London, 1984).
Change manager: J. Carlson, *Moments of Truth* (Ballinger, Boston, 1986).
Enterprising manager: L. Iacocca, *Iacocca* (Bantam, New York, 1984).
Analytical manager: H. Green, *Managing* (Grafton, London, 1984).
Developmental manager: J. Sculley, *Odyssey* (Fontana, London, 1988).
Innovative manager: M. Gorbachev, *Perestroika* (Fontana, London, 1988).

7

Charting the Seven Life Paths

Introduction

As I indicated in the previous chapter, there are seven very different paths to manager self-development. Three of these, which are relatively well worn, will be considered in the first part of this chapter. These are, respectively, the action manager's path of *action*, the people manager's *communal* path, and the analytical manager's *career* path.

The four less well-charted paths of development, the change agent's path of *change*, the enterprising manager's path of *enterprise*, the developmental manager's *evolutionary* path and the innovative manager's *creative* path, will be considered in the second part of this chapter.

Not only are there seven such learning or development paths but, in order to successfully evolve, managers need to pass through a series of stages along the way. Three such stages in childhood and youth, *physical*, *social* and *intellectual* development, are followed by four in adulthood; *exploration* and personal risk-taking, *consolidation* and role substantiation, *renewal* and conscious self-development, and *maturation* and role transcendence.

The following illustrations of this process of manager self-development are based on the life paths of individuals I have come across in my own teaching and consultancy experience, although their stories have all been 'fictionalized'.

CHARTING THE SEVEN LIFE PATHS 113

FROM ACTION TO CAREER PATHS

The Path of Action: Jim Corby – Adventurer

Jim joined a New York based sporting goods retailer, as personnel manager, in a burst of spontaneous enthusiasm. He was game for anything, especially when physical activity was involved. In fact what really attracted him to the group was their intention to market a line of running shoe. Jim specifically suggested that they approach the local shoe company to manufacture for them a running shoe that was particularly hard-wearing. He also offered to market a new product himself in a promotional run from Boston to New York in the following spring.

But few would have guessed, when Jim Corby was a young boy, that he would end up in his late teens, in that kind of position. . .

Childhood and Adolescence

Physical development

Jim was an asthmatic when he was young. Every few weeks he would be off school for several days. Life seemed to revolve around his state of health. Getting out of bed in the morning was all too often very difficult, and even eating could be a chore.

At the age of ten Jim's best friend was a gymnast who took his good health completely for granted. His cousin, who went to the same school as he did in the West country, loved netball and was forever playing outside. Jim just couldn't take it any more. One Sunday he came home from watching his friend compete in a gymnastics tournament and told his family that he was going to be a gymnast too! His family were both delighted and flabbergasted. How would Jim ever manage? He was such a thin and sickly child. They ended up discouraging him, which made him all the more determined.

The first few lessons he took were agony. His body hurt all over, and he was on the verge of giving up a thousand times. But somehow he persevered, and one day, thanks to his coach's incredible patience, he began to show signs of real progress. He was just about gaining control over his body. In fact, by the age of 12 his asthma was beginning to disappear. It would take another 30 years, though, to disappear completely.

Social development

At secondary school Jim joined the gymnastics team, as one of its most promising juniors. He also joined the athletics club as a middle-distance runner. Stretching himself in gymnastics, by that stage, had become an on-going challenge rather than a punishing experience. He also began to build up a circle of friends, something that was quite new to him. By the age of 16 he and his closest friends would spend at least one weekend a month going to see gymnastics tournaments in different parts of the country. They also spent two spring vacations rowing on the continent, competing for their school.

Intellectual development

Jim had never been much of an academic. He preferred to spend time on the sports field, especially once he became good at gym and at running, rather than in the classroom. However, he did find that after his two visits to the Rhône valley in the spring holidays his French began to improve. He discovered that he had a bit of a talent for languages.

The other subject that began to interest him was biology. The net result was that when he took his first summer job with a shoe manufacturer Jim not only got to know much more about human physiology, with a special emphasis on feet, but he also got to use his language skills. He voted himself into the position of export salesman for the South of France, and secured a sponsorship for his trip over there. Needless to say he managed to sell over $4000 worth of shoes in a fortnight, and improved his French no end in the process.

Much to his surprise, Jim finished school with good grades in biology and French. He also managed to win the inter-schools cross country event in his final year, while falling in love with his classmate Eva, who had intentions of studying medicine. Meanwhile, Jim decided that he was going to go into teacher training.

Youth: the Age of Exploration

Jim went to a College of Education and trained to be a teacher, majoring in biology and physical education. He decided to keep up his languages (by now he was also studying Portuguese, because his latest girlfriend was originally from Brazil) as a hobby rather than for his profession.

At College he quickly came to realize that the courses themselves were generally a bore. Although Jim enjoyed keeping physically active and meeting lots of fellow sportsmen and women, he sensed his overall motivation gradually declining. Believe it or not, he found himself yearning for his schooldays – and then he had a brainwave.

In his second year Jim got together with two of his classmates and decided to plan a trip to the Amazon for their coming summer vacations. Not only did he drool at the thought of venturing into the world's most celebrated jungle, but he would also have a chance to practice his new Portuguese language skills. Finally, as a biology student who was also becoming interested in zoology, the animal and insect life in prospect was unsurpassable. Needless to say, having contacted the Brazilian commercial attaché and the Royal Geographical Society, Jim's next port of call was the local shoe company for sponsorship. He called on his old acquaintance, Bill Potter, in the marketing department, and managed very successfully to whet Bill's appetite, using all the influencing skills he had picked up while selling sports shoes in France.

Jim and his two best friends did get to the Amazon that summer. There they not only learnt how to be self-sufficient but, despite a great fear of snakes, Jim discovered how to administer snake serum to his girlfriend. Fortunately, the three of them were also joined by a Brazilian student after a month, so that they were able to progress more easily. Finally, not only did Jim's Portuguese prove to be very useful, but he felt he learnt more zoology than he would have done in three years at college.

Jim actually went back to the Amazon once more for his final-year project, to investigate the influence of climate on physical fitness. These two trips, together with the gym and athletics, kept Jim going at college. He also managed to spend three spring vacations in Rio, where his girlfriend's parents now lived, so that by the time he graduated he was fluent in both French and Portuguese.

In the five years after graduation Jim worked in no less than four different teaching posts, including one in Brazilia and another in Paris. At the age of 26 he married a Californian girl whom he had actually met while teaching in Paris: she was a doctor, just like his girlfriend at school.

Young Adulthood: Consolidation

Within six years Jim and his wife had three children. For the first four of these years Jim really enjoyed domestic bliss. He was obviously ready to settle down, having taken up a teaching post in Montana. But then boredom began to creep in, with a vengeance.

Strangely enough, although he had plenty of opportunity to go running across the beautiful Montana plains, that kind of activity no longer satisfied him. For the first time in Jim's life his work seemed more important to him than his recreation, and he wasn't getting ahead as a physical education teacher at the school. He was itching to use his brains more, whether in biology or with languages. So he decided to join NYU's Science Foundation Course. Jim remembered that while he had been involved with the shoe company his marketing contact, Bill, had attended an NYU course, and had loved it. In fact he used to bring his tutorial assignments into work, and would ask Jim to answer some of the biology questions for him. Naturally, Bill Potter was the first person Jim contacted when he decided to go for the course.

After a further six years Jim finally graduated with an NYU science degree. In the meantime he had received two promotions at the school and was now head of the physical education department. But instead of feeling elated, at graduation, he felt a sense of malaise. He still didn't really feel that he had found himself.

Midlife: the Age of Renewal

By his late thirties Jim was going through some kind of life crisis. Gymnastics seemed to be a thing of the past, and he hadn't yet done anything significant with either his science degree or with his languages. Also he'd had enough of teaching, or so it seemed at the time. It had been an intellectual challenge to complete his degree but it did not seem to mean much more to him. The family were growing up and his wife was happily involved teaching English as a foreign language to Mexican immigrants. The question was, what should he do?

Friends suggested that Jim should open up his own sports shop, having been such a successful salesman in his youth, but he didn't have that kind of guts He wasn't an entrepreneur. He thought of teaching science, but that seemed a backward step. Moreover, he and his wife were now having some marital problems and he needed to pay attention to that area: in fact, they started going to marriage guidance.

Gradually Jim felt he was coming home. He remembered his marvellous gym teacher, in those early and painful days, who had given him so much encouragement. He also recalled how, during his schooldays, he had benefitted so much from Bill Potter's counselling. He came to realize, slowly but surely, that psychological exploration through the jungle of his own innermost emotions was as important to him now as his journeys to the impenetrable depths of the Amazon had been then. Perhaps the neuropsychology module at NYU had opened up a new interest in him: certainly the course tutor had contributed amazing insight.

So Jim decided to undertake a two-year, practically based counselling course, while taking on the new post of human resources manager at a local sports goods retailer, in fact the branch of a large American retailing group.

Maturity: the Age of Maturation

In two years Jim had graduated from being a student counsellor into being professionally qualified. Once again, just as in his youth, he was venturing into the unknown. But at the same time, probably as a form of security, he continued his teaching of physical exercise. Now, in his forties, Jim's asthma had disappeared completely, for the first time, and this seemed to act as some kind of signal. Although he had enjoyed his personnel job, Jim felt that it was time to move on. Something inside him had been touched, to the extent that he became increasingly dissatisfied with personnel work in isolation. It was too far removed from Jim the gymnast, from Jim the man of action. Then he had a phone call, literally from out of the blue.

Jim's old girlfriend Eva, from his schooldays, was now the company doctor working for the sport's shop's parent company. One of the company's subsidiaries was in fact involved in the pharmaceutics business, specifically researching and developing drugs for asthmatics. The post of deputy head at the research laboratory was vacant and Eva wondered whether Jim might be interested in applying for it. He knew immediately that his bell had tolled!

Today Jim is the laboratory director. He has introduced a radically new approach to the treatment of asthma, one that combines physical activities with medication. In fact Jim is now beginning to apply this combined physical and medical approach to their pharmaceutical business as a whole.

Gina's is another story: she is Italian, not American, and sought friendship rather than adventure.

The Communal Path: Gina Agnani – Animator

You would never have thought, given her background, that Gina Agnani would end up with the management role in which she now finds herself. Starting working life as a lowly administrator she is now not only a high-powered manager but, in fact, the life and soul of her organization. . .

Childhood and Adolescence

Physical development

Gina had one of those jolly round faces that folded naturally into a big smile. She was slightly on the plump side, and had spent most of her teenage years on one diet or another. It was as if eating was some kind of comfort or compensation for the emotional deprivation she had experienced as a young child.

Social development

The early years of Gina's childhood in Milan were a constant uphill struggle to please others. Somehow she was always the one to miss out. All she really wanted was to belong, to feel accepted as part of her family and social group. You see, her parents had been divorced when she was only three and, from that point on, home life never seemed to offer quite what she wanted.

Somehow other people seemed to call the tune. Her brother was a great sportsman, and was very much one of the boys. Gina's sister was the intelligent and knowledgeable one who impressed everybody. Gina was virtually a social outcast: everyone seemed to look down on her, so at primary school she would try especially hard to act in ways that made her acceptable to her classmates. She didn't dare to be different from anyone else in case she would be shunned. She talked like them, walked like them and thought like them, for fear of being excluded.

By the time Gina entered secondary school things were only just beginning to improve. She started to get at least a small share of the attention that she had worked so hard to obtain. Gina's brother and sister took more notice of her. They used to 'cry on her shoulder' when either of them had an emotional problem. At that stage Gina's sister was going through her teenage rebellion.

By the time Gina was 16 she was feeling secure enough to hold parties, and to even invite people whom she hardly knew – and they seemed to enjoy themselves! She began to realize that she had a talent for making people feel at home. She had obviously learnt how to make others feel wanted, from her own bitter experience.

Intellectual development

Gina had never been academically gifted, and was always too scared to speak out in class for fear of being ridiculed. She was hopeless at maths and the sciences, and her only saving graces were Italian and domestic science. She enjoyed reading novels, especially those that described the lives of hapless children, who rose up from mediocrity.

Gina left school at 17 with no formal qualifications, and went to secretarial college. There was pressure from home for her to go out and earn some money, and she was obviously not going to achieve much academically. After finishing the secretarial course she began work as a junior typist. Due to her diligence Gina managed to upgrade her typing and shorthand skills considerably. Once again, she found herself to be the 'social glue' within her typing pool – the one who could keep everyone happy. Her bosses, especially her immediate superior, Marco, recognized this quality and offered her a promotion. But Gina didn't feel up to it yet; besides, she was reluctant to give up the friendship of her peers.

Youth: the Age of Exploration

At the same time she had recently got married and was to have their first baby. Gina had met her husband-to-be while still at high school. They had decided that they would get married once both of them were earning a reasonable living. She had their first child at the age of 20, and the second one two years later.

Motherhood opened up a whole new world to Gina. As would be expected from someone with her background, she put all of herself into creating a secure home for her children. She started a mother and toddler group, bringing together all the young mums, and once again listening to all their problems. And with the help of her childhood friend, Maria, who was also a very good listener, she realized that she had made a mistake by not accepting the promotion at work. There was more to life than being a mum, and that led Gina to put a lot of energy into developing her little toddler group into a proper nursery school. At that stage she realized that her record-keeping skills, first uncovered when she was 16, were very useful.

When Gina was in her mid-twenties disaster struck. Ricardo, her husband, was declared redundant from his job as a draftsman. To make matters worse, they lived in a high-unemployment area in northern Italy. Gina had to go straight back to work while he helped out with the kids as best as he could. Her old firm, which she naturally returned to, once again offered her promotion – this time she knew she had to take it.

Her first week in the new job was a living hell. How could she order her friends about? She was no longer one of them: instead, she was their boss. She had to stand out from the crowd and even, on one occasion, side with her boss against them. She had nightmares about being cast out in the cold, and even called up her favourite schoolteacher from bygone days for support and advice. Needless to say, her teacher was round like a shot; she hadn't forgotten her young enthusiast. But the trauma lasted for a good three months before Gina began to come to terms with her new role.

Gradually she began to enjoy it more. She now saw herself as being responsible for providing others with job satisfaction within a happy work environment. Gina even began to read management books, such as Mary Kay's *On People Management.* In the eyes of her husband, Ricardo, Gina was becoming a different person, and he wasn't sure what he felt about it. Of course Gina felt very threatened by Ricardo's discomfort. One thing that she knew was that nothing would stand in the way of her providing a secure home for her kids.

Nevertheless, and almost without realizing it, Gina was changing from a follower into, well, almost a ringleader. She gradually began to see responsibility as a challenge rather than as a chore. After a year she actually began to feel comfortable in her role. It also helped that Ricardo was now back at work, and no longer felt threatened by Gina's personal growth.

Young Adulthood: the Age of Consolidation

For the first time in her life Gina was aware of the fact that she was actually able to use her head! Her job title now was office administrator, and she was sent on a book-keeping and stock control course. Never had she concentrated so hard on work. A year later she attended a follow-up course on data processing, and soon after that one on personnel management.

Strangely enough, Gina was pretty good at all those things, and she began to wonder why she had been labelled as such a dunce at school. Although it was always a struggle to keep up with the lecturers unless, like Frederico – the accounts lecturer – they were able to make learning fun, she did absorb it all eventually. She was once again aware of the way she was able to make everyone around her feel at ease. Frederico, for one, really did take to her.

No sooner, then, had Gina begun to impress her boss by the way she was now managing her people and her department than Ricardo got a transfer, by way of a promotion, from Milan to Rome. Gina was heartbroken at the thought of having to move home and job. She thought she was going to become an outcast again – and what about the disruption to the kids? At first she resisted fiercely, but there was no arguing with Ricardo when he had made his mind up.

When Gina moved from Milan to Rome she had to make a decision. She didn't have to work, at least not for financial reasons. Gina loved her family and the prospect of being at home again warmed her heart. She wouldn't have to stretch herself the way she had been doing at work. Moreover, Gina had felt guilty being away from her two girls.

For the first time in her life, or so it seemed, at the age of 34, Gina had to use her head to make a decision, rather than being swayed by mainly emotionally based arguments. She listed all the pro's and con's of staying at home versus going back to work. She consulted not only with Ricardo but also with her friend Maria, and gave herself six months to decide.

In the middle of all this, Gina's old accounts lecturer Frederico contacted her. Coincidentally, he had also moved from Milan to a nearby town, only seven miles from where Gina was now living. He was now general manager of the local leisure centre, which was owned by Gina's former company, and was looking for a right-hand person, someone who could act as a 'master of ceremonies'. He thought she was perfectly suited for the job.

Once again Gina was terrified: she'd never done anything like this before. And yet, remembering the parties she had organized for her fellow mums and toddlers, it wasn't completely foreign territory. An important factor in this job was that Gina was able to work on a flexible basis. So she eventually accepted.

She found herself being not only the 'master of ceremonies', but also taking over the general administration. In many ways she ran the centre, while Frederico spent his time at meetings with the parent company, the local authority and the local suppliers. Gina became involved with the public at large, which was an excellent way of getting herself known and accepted in this new environment.

Midlife: the Age of Renewal

Gina spent five years at the Romana Leisure Centre and enjoyed every minute of it. She converted it from a marginal social facility into a profitable and trendy place – people began to come from miles around. It had a special atmosphere: there was a warmth and friendliness that neighbouring public-sector leisure centres lacked.

But in her sixth year there Gina felt it was time for a change. She was now turning 40, the kids had left home, and although she loved her work, Gina knew there was something missing. Increasingly, home life – cooking, knitting and sewing for her family and friends – was taking over, emotionally.

Gina's eldest daughter had in fact taken a course in fashion and textiles at college, and was now designing and selling her own fabrics. One of her outlets was the local crafts centre. The staff there were always asking Gina to lend a hand in her spare time, because of her administrative skills. Then one day Gina's daughter said to her, 'Why don't you get more involved in the centre mum? You're good at organizing people and things, and you love the sorts of things they sell. You could get your company to give you the financial backing you would need'.

A year later Gina gave her notice in at the leisure centre. Frederico was heartbroken, but he could see that she now belonged somewhere else. Besides, over the past few years, husband Ricardo had become increasingly interested in design, and was itching to get out of the constrained environment of a conventional drawing office. Gina felt an ever growing pull from her family, from the world of crafts and, interestingly enough, from her old mentor Maria, who was now chief buyer at a local department store. So when she was approached by the woman who ran the crafts centre to take it over, and after influencing her old employer to take a large equity stake in the business, the Agnani family agreed to take the plunge. They sold their house and moved into the home adjacent to the centre.

In just two years from the time Gina took over, the turnover tripled. As her customers told her, the place had become transformed from a crafts shop into a social centre. It also did the image of her old employer no end of good.

Maturity: the Age of Maturation

The Agnani family then suffered another major setback – Ricardo was declared redundant again. He was now over 50, and the job outlook was grim indeed. The whole family dreaded the thought of having to move again. By now Gina had become totally integrated into the local community, and was putting as much in as she got out of it. It was her other daughter, Sophia, now a nurse, who then had a brainwave – she suggested that her dad join the crafts centre. Ricardo had, in fact, been a skilled craftsman all his life, but had never had the inclination to go out on his own.

Nevertheless, it took a year of not-so-gentle persuasion and fruitless job-hunting before Ricardo gave in, and his first customer was his daughter Sophia, who had just moved into a new house. Over that year, though, he had unwittingly begun to involve himself more and more with the centre, by doing odd jobs there for Gina. Eventually he joined her, as a kind of general factotum, and he also began to sell some of his own furniture there. He gradually took over the general maintenance and stock control while Gina concentrated on buying and selling.

At first Gina found the responsibility of buying utterly daunting. While the accounting side came easily to her she was, to begin with, hopeless at negotiating. Funnily enough, it was her designer daughter Carla who proved to be most helpful, in enabling Gina to overcome her fears of rejection. By now Carla had become quite an entrepreneur in her own right.

Finally, then, as a woman in her late fifties, Gina had become a businesslady of sorts. In fact, having been involved with the business for five years, the Agnani family bought out half the parent company's share in the enterprise. It wasn't the money, though, that really motivated Gina, but the involvement with a community of craftsmen and women.

Heinz's case was different again: he was much more the sort of person to follow a conventional career path.

The Career Path: Heinz Erlich – Executive

Heinz advanced along a conventional career path within his Zurich-based financial services company, until he became a company director. In later years, he also became a prominent figure in his local community. It was as if positions of management and leadership came naturally to him, wherever he was. . .

Childhood and Adolescence

Physical development

From his earliest years Heinz was a successful sportsman, although, at least at primary school, he had not been 'one of the boys'. It was only in later years, after one particularly formative experience, that he began to assume a more commanding presence on the sports field. A year after this experience his air of authority had become so pronounced that Heinz's coach, Rudie, who had already taken a particular interest in the boy, appointed him captain of the school football team.

By the age of 16, then, Heinz had become not only football captain but also Head of House. His performance as a high-jumper had improved markedly over the past year, and he was now a member of the school's athletics team. As his fellow pupils gained more respect for him so his physical and social stature rose.

Social development

Heinz was born in Berne in the 1920s. His father was a colonel in the armed forces and his mother was an active member of the local Lutheran church. She had been taught ever since Heinz was a babe in arms that there was a right and a wrong way of doing things. Heinz's father was autocratic by nature, and he immediately instilled a dutiful sense of obedience in his son. The only contrary influence in Heinz's early life was his grandad, who had remained a rebel all his life.

Heinz was sure that his parents, as well as the teachers at primary school, knew best. He never questioned their authority. By the time he entered secondary school he had become extremely diligent at his work, although he was not especially bright. He was well liked by the teachers for his dedication, and he fitted into the classroom atmosphere very well. He was not one to show off or to argue back.

When he was 15, though, something happened that Heinz would remember for the rest of his life. As he walked back from school he witnessed an awful accident. A schoolboy was knocked over by a car right in front of him. Something made Heinz react immediately. Applying all the knowledge of first aid that he had learnt in Sunday school he attended to the boy until the ambulance arrived. It was as if he had reached into another part of himself. When he returned home he told his parents what he had done, with a great sense of pride. Heinz was particularly keen to gain his father's approval. 'My son', his father said to him, ,'you have done me proud'. This was the boost he obviously needed.

Intellectual development

Heinz's academic performance had never been more than average. Although he was competent in the sciences, and just about managed to get by in the arts subjects, the star performers in the class left him well behind. However, when he joined the school's cadet force, Heinz's classmates looked to this newly emergent leader for guidance. He obviously had an ability to command.

Heinz therefore decided to switch to maths and economics for his matriculation, now that he saw his future in management rather than in science or engineering. He managed to scrape through these two subjects and, helped substantially by his character references, became an articled clerk with a very reputable firm of accountants. Although Heinz could probably have gone on to higher education he felt that the academic work would have been too much of a struggle.

Youth: the Age of Exploration

Heinz had been forewarned, by his economics teacher at school, that articles would be hard work. Although the routine suited his personality he was, at the same time, determined to introduce some additional responsibilities into his work and life. For a start, therefore, he continued to play football, and became captain of his local team when he was transferred to Zurich. As such he organized two team visits to Austria each year, as well as tours around Holland.

Within his accountancy firm Heinz impressed his superiors from the start. His general diligence with his correspondence studies and his interest in the practicalities of management also impressed them considerably. As a result, when he told his principal Johan Schmidt that he wanted to audit a very wide range of companies, in many different parts of the country, Johan responded very positively.

Indeed, when he was in his second year of articles, Heinz was assigned to the firm's South West African office for two years. He loved the weather there, the sporting life and also the hard-working people. Moreover, during his second year in Africa he was given partial responsibility for running the small local office. Erich Pohl, his immediate boss, was an incredibly able man: Heinz learnt more from him about man management than from anybody else he had so far come across.

After his second year in Windhoek, Heinz requested another transfer abroad, and was sent this time to Singapore. Because of the correspondence nature of the accountancy course he was able to complete his articles there and, thereafter, was appointed head of the local office. His organizational abilities had become clearly apparent to the firm and, at 24, he was one of their youngest managers.

However, Heinz could not see himself spending the rest of his life in a professional practice. He felt a need to be of service to industry at large. So, after returning to Switzerland for a year, he applied for a job with a financial services company, which had particularly close links with industry, and was appointed company secretary.

Young Adulthood: the Age of Consolidation

Heinz got married, at the age of 27, to his old sweetheart from school, and over the next five years they had three children. He consolidated his position with the company, based, at first, at the head office in Zurich. But Heinz knew that the time would soon come when he would want to move out of his staff position into the front line. After putting several feelers out, and waiting patiently for the right opportunity to come along, he found himself, at the age of 32, running one of the company's main divisions.

Based now in Basle, Heinz decided that he wanted to do a course in management studies at the local technical college, and he duly graduated three years later. Having rounded out his knowledge he was now preparing himself for a further promotion within the company. He applied for several higher positions, including one in Kuwait, which he was duly offered.

During three years in Kuwait he acquired many of the 'political skills' which would serve him well in the future. He also found himself much more involved in the personnel function, as a general manager, than he had previously been. At the age of 37 Heinz was plucked out of the Middle East and sent to run a brand new subsidiary in Norway. This enabled him to improve his cross-cultural management skills. The Norwegian operation was essentially a marketing subsidiary, so Heinz could draw on the knowledge he had gained during his management studies and apply it in practical situations. He had now become a fully fledged general manager.

Midlife: the Age of Renewal

Now, at 39, Heinz was at an awkward stage of his career. He was really ready for a major promotion and yet there were no immediate opportunities in sight. He began to get nervous. For a year or so he really was not on top of his job. At the same time his wife Anna had gone back to work, teaching German as a foreign language, and was reluctant to move the family once again. It was as if there was no way forward and no way back.

Then fate intervened – Heinz's immediate boss at head office resigned. The company needed a new Head of European Marketing, and Heinz was appointed to the job. For the next three years he took hold of the marketing operation and turned it inside out. He used his international experience to good effect, focusing on the need to market differently in different cultures – after all, Bernale was a multinational company.

By his late forties Heinz felt himself to be ready to move onto the company board. He waited and nothing came. Then, at 51, his opportunity did at last arrive: Heinz was appointed board member with special responsibility for marketing, and for the Middle East. Over the next ten years his responsibilities broadened even further. In his mid-fifties he had aspirations of becoming chairman, but by his late fifties he realized that time was passing him by.

Maturity: the Age of Maturation

At this stage Heinz felt a pull from his Lutheran roots. He not only felt the need to return to the church fold from whence he came, but also to contribute directly to the local economy. At first he thought he might want to return to the operational side of Bernale's business, in Berne. But he soon realized that this would be retrogressive.

So, aged 60, Heinz resigned from the board of Bernale to take up the post of Chairman of the Regional Development Council. Now based in Berne again, and as a leading member of the Lutheran church, Heinz has returned home physically, economically and spiritually. He is seen to be a leader not only in the business world but also in the local and national community.

Heinz and Anna's two grandchildren attend the same high school that their grandparents did as youngsters: needless to say, Heinz is a school governor. What, then, has changed? Of course the high-tech industries that are now in fashion did not exist when Heinz was a boy, but the principles of management and leadership have remained the same. For Heinz, in his sixties, there is more continuity than change. He and Anna are carrying on where his father and mother left off. He also regularly keeps in touch with Bernale, who are keen to finance the start-up of new enterprises in the locality.

FROM THE PATH OF CHANGE TO INNOVATION

The four relatively uncharted development paths are those of the manager of change, the enterprising manager, the developmental manager and the innovative manager, respectively. In fact, as you will soon see, each, to be true to themselves, needs to pursue a rather unconventional 'career', involving some intriguing shifts from one kind of organization to another, albeit retaining links between each.

The Path of Change: Hedda Carlson – Agent of Change

Hedda was a free spirit. She got involved with her particular work because she wanted to do something different from the usual routine. However, after an initial burst of interest, the attraction would inevitably wear off. She had this continual need to be moving on, and for the world to be moving, and changing, with her. . .

Childhood and Adolescence

Physical development

Hedda was definitely a 'brainy box', as her classmates from nursery school on called her, rather than a sporty type. In fact, ever since primary school, she felt she had possessed 'two left feet'. Because the secondary school she attended put a lot of pressure on sporting achievement she felt something of an outsider, which accentuated her feeling of being different.

Social development

Maths and computing aside, Hedda was extremely bored at school in Copenhagen. So, from the age of 15 onwards, she and her friends spent the summer holidays hitch-hiking around Europe, and picking up farm jobs to earn their keep. There was so much to see and so many people to meet. She found travel very exciting.

In her final year she also became interested in politics, and joined the school's debating society. Hedda became preoccupied with the role of women in a technological society and developed a 'Science in Society' group to debate the issues involved. She couldn't bear to see all those women caught up in dead-end data processing jobs, punching an endless sequence of holes into endless cards.

Intellectual development

At home and at school, for as far back as she can remember, Hedda wanted to know about everything. She was one of those often infuriating children who always want to know why. In fact, her parents didn't know how to handle her. Father was an enthusiastic trade unionist who was away much of the time and, when he was at home, needed peace and quiet. Mother was very devoted to her brood of three children, and had pretty conventional views on life. She wanted her two girls to be happy, but certainly did not envisage them becoming career women. After all, she had devoted her life to being a good homemaker.

Hedda's teachers at primary school were a little more 'modern' in their outlook, but even they found it difficult to answer those interminable questions. So by the time Hedda entered high school she was horribly confused. The only person who seemed to respond fully to her inquiring mind was Soren Ullman, her maths teacher. Soren happened to be interested in the technological revolution that was going on around him, and would get involved in long discussions with Hedda about 'man and machine'.

Not surprisingly, maths and computing were the two subjects in which Hedda excelled. Unfortunately, though, Soren had been promoted to head of middle school by the time Hedda did her first major exams, and therefore no longer taught her maths. He only came her way, once again, when she became involved in the young enterprise programme that he looked after. It was then that Soren had the brainwave to suggest that Hedda write a computer program for her group, just when her interest in the enterprise had begun to wane.

Youth: the Age of Exploration

Hedda applied and got into Cambridge University in England but decided to go to her local Danish university instead, just to be anti-establishment. She enrolled for a B.Sc. in computer science, and almost failed her first year's exams because she was too involved in student politics to take her studies seriously. Hedda also found herself a string of boyfriends!

So in her second year she took off a year to do voluntary service overseas as a maths teacher in Papua New Guinea. Hedda lived in a mud hut without any running water. In fact she had to cycle about five miles every morning to collect a fresh supply – that did her physical well-being no end of good! The school itself was one mile's walk away, up a steep hill. The saving grace, of course, was that the pupils were incredibly keen. And Hedda was seen to be the fount of all wisdom, which certainly stretched her mentally. She had to try and answer all their questions, in geography and English language as well as in mathematics. Hedda also picked up quite a bit of the local language before the year was out.

When she returned to Copenhagen it was naturally something of a disappointment. Although she'd had enough of teaching maths to 12-year-olds she was itching for another mental challenge. Therefore she started a new society at the university, concerning itself with the role of information technology in the developing world. She and three friends then organized a conference to which participants were invited from all over the world. Using a similar kind of database program to the one she had devised for young enterprise, Hedda set up an on-going IT network.

In the third year Hedda eventually buckled down to her studies and completed the degree. Subsequently, exhausted, she took six months off to travel before picking up a freelance contract as 'technology' editor for a new magazine. That job lasted, three days a week, for four years while, at the same time, Hedda picked up a string of programming assignments for software houses.

Young Adulthood: the Age of Exploration

When she was 25 Hedda moved in with her boyfriend, Erik, and they had their first child. While she was a very enthusiastic mother who immediately became involved with the local playgroup, she found life much too restrictive. At the same time she found herself becoming increasingly involved with childrearing from a psychological perspective.

By the age of 32, now with two more children, Hedda had not only acquired a degree in experimental psychology, but had developed a dozen different educational software programs for well-known software publishers. At that stage she and Erik not only decided to get married but also to establish an educational software company of their own. He had the commercial know-how and she was the mathematical genius. In fact Erik had spent 12 years in COMPTACT, on the sales side, and was itching to move on; so he managed to influence the local COMPTACT subsidiary to set them up in business, duly providing them with a service contract and taking a 40 per cent equity stake.

It was not so much the urge to make a lot of money that spurred the two of them on, but more the desire to work together, to have fun and to produce something of social value. Hedda remembered vividly, harking back to her young enterprise days, how strongly she felt about creating products and services that were worthwhile. Finally, interestingly enough and perhaps leaving her adolescent rebellion behind her, Hedda was beginning to feel that it was time to bring dad into the picture. In actual fact his organizational experience proved invaluable in the first few years of their software venture. By the time, then, that she was in her early forties, she was the joint managing director of a successful little business.

Midlife: the Age of Renewal

Through her political interests Hedda was encouraged to make a further change in her lifestyle. She had become increasingly dissatisfied with technology, in isolation from the profound sense of social purpose that was represented in her trade union heritage. This was brought out into the open for her by her father, who had become a real mentor to Hedda very late in life. He, in his turn, had left his company to become a lay clergyman.

Hedda felt that she had to return to Papua New Guinea to regain contact with life at its most basic. Fortunately her children were off her hands by now, and Erik was a very understanding husband. So she became a volunteer for the second time in her life, this time as a technology transfer agent rather than as a schoolteacher. For the next six years, therefore, she spent three months of the year in Papua, advising the government on the use of communications technology in education, and setting up three experimental programmes around the country. Fortunately for Hedda, COMPTACT supported her financially, as part of its community participation programme in this developing country.

Maturity: the Age of Maturation

Hedda is now well into her fifties and has become actively involved in local politics in Copenhagen, where she now lives. She is a liberal representative on the borough council, with a special responsibility for education. On top of all that, Erik and herself have created an integrated software package for use by the more innovative schools, duly marketed in conjunction with the latest range of PC's.

Hedda had been very struck by the way the Papua New Guineans lived in such close physical proximity. She felt that in Europe we had lost that kind of community spirit. So on returning to Denmark, politics aside, Hedda convinced Erik and COMPTACT to help her branch out into a community software company. Their company specializes in the production of educational software for the home, producing programs that necessarily involve parents, children and even grandchildren and grandparents learning from one another. Hedda had come up with a contemporary version of an extended learning community. It was as if she had altogether transformed her own childhood experiences in later life. The next step for her, if she still had the stamina in her sixties, was to convince the mighty COMPTACT to go down the same road, at least in her native Denmark!

Tanja's life path was a very different one: in fact, she followed the typical path of an entrepreneur, at least for the first half of her life.

The Path of Enterprise: Tanja Weil – Entrepreneur

The Axis group has never quite been the same since it welcomed Tanja Weil into its midst, for Tanja is a manager with a difference, certainly very different from what they are accustomed to in the UK. In fact it is difficult to gauge whether she has the temperament of an entrepreneur, a musician or an actress, not to mention her affinity with Solidarity in Poland. . .

Childhood and Adolescence

Physical development

Tanja was a very beautiful girl. Not only did she win an infant's beauty competition in Warsaw when she was only two, but by the unusually early age of 10 she had begun to flaunt her good looks, and by 15 had a long list of boyfriends. Needless to say she was more popular amongst the boys than the girls. By the age of 17 Tanja had already received two firm proposals of marriage.

Social development

Tanja was the only child of Eastern European parents. She was born in Poland but came to the UK when she was only four. Her parents had been well to do in their own country, but in England they always had to struggle to make ends meet: Tanja's mother had to work as a domestic, and her father as a factory hand.

Tanja was a very emotional child. When she was at primary school there was always some drama or another in the classroom, and Tanja was usually the one at the receiving end of it. In fact she gradually secured a reputation for herself as 'terrible Tanja'. She would always be looking for an opportunity to create trouble. At home her parents found her difficult to cope with, to say the least. She'd either come home triumphant because she'd succeeded in pulling the wool over a teacher's eyes, or she would be howling because someone had ganged up on her.

Intellectual development

In those early days, then, Tanja invariably felt herself to be a victim of circumstances. Only occasionally, when she had triumphed over authority, did she feel herself to be in control. Yet as she entered secondary school the balance began to shift; for Tanja was discovered by the drama teacher, Mr Hall. She definitely did have acting ability, most particularly when she was in the starring role!

Through her drama Tanja began to get to know some of the great literature of our time. She acted in two of Shakespeare's plays – *Romeo and Juliet* being her favourite – and grew particularly fond of Tennessee Williams. So, at the age of 15, for the first time in her life, Tanja found herself reading 'good' books. However, time for studying was limited. Because her parents never had two pennies to rub together Tanja had to work every weekend and school holiday at the local delicatessen. Max Wilenski, the owner of the shop, liked her to be there because she used to entertain his clientele with her impersonations of people in the neighbourhood. Tanja was very good at mimicking and mocking people. At the same time she picked up invaluable knowledge of merchandizing, and some skill in buying and selling – which Max allowed her to do, more and more, in his absence.

Youth: the Age of Exploration

Just prior to her seventeenth birthday Tanja first became involved in her very own business venture. Max, who supplied fruit and vegetables to the school, talked her into it. He thought she'd be able to teach the other kids at school a thing or two about 'the real business world', and raise funds for the Polish community in the UK.

At the first meeting, with the interested kids duly assembled, Tanja immediately stood up and declared that she wanted to set up a dozen different market stalls in the school grounds every Saturday. She would take charge of all the buying, and would look after the financial side of things. All she needed was other kids to produce some of the merchandise, and to man the stalls.

Pupils from Tanja's class were flabbergasted. They'd never seen her play such a constructive part in school, never mind take the lead. In fact, if it hadn't been for her drama teacher, who added his weight of authority to her spontaneous initiative, they would have refused to listen.

Over the course of the next six months, however, with Tanja taking the entrepreneurial lead, her new friend Tom keeping things properly organized, and drama teacher Greg keeping up the group spirit, the young 'Market Makers', as they called themselves, became an ardent financial and social success. Tanja found herself making trips to Spain and Portugal to pick up merchandise at rock-bottom prices. While in Spain she made a point of learning Flamenco dancing: she and Greg organized a highly successful Flamenco evening to round off a year of splendid 'market making'.

The school's corporate sponsors were so impressed wth Tanja that they paid for her to go to Hong Kong during the spring vacation. Needless to say, Tanja had put together a business plan for them before securing the sponsorship. While she was over there she bought a consignment of $5000 worth of radios, which were subsequently sold off for $15,000.

By the time the 'market making' was over Tanja, much to Greg Hall's dismay, was ready to leave school. She felt it had nothing more to offer her, and she was in a hurry to make her fortune. So Tanja went straight to Max and suggested he open another delicatessen –

his third – and let her run it. Max, who was also a refugee from Eastern Europe, had no children of his own. He had therefore been a father figure to Tanja for many years. Therefore he decided to set Tanja up in business. Of course, because she was barely 18, he took a special interest in her new delicatessen himself. He looked after the accounts personally, and helped her recruit staff. Tanja, as she had done before, took charge of the buying and selling.

While running her store, though, Tanja didn't lose touch with her acting side; indeed at the tender age of 20 she directed an Edward Albee play for her local amateur dramatics group. As she acted and directed she dreamt of becoming a woman of substance, imagining herself with a Dior outfit and a diamond necklace, strutting through the Ritz. Unlike many of her old classmates who had wanted to marry a millionaire she was intent on becoming one. She was going to make damn sure the world would take notice of Tanja Weil.

As a result she buckled down to her labours, often spending up to 16 hours a day working, inbetween being on the stage. After three years, though, she felt she had learnt as much about building up a delicatessen business as she cared to. She sold the shop, making £10,000 clear profit for both Max and herself. She chose to invest the money in a video shop which her current boyfriend, Kim, had started. Kim thought that his shop could do with Tanja's special brand of salesmanship, so he offered her a half share in the business.

Kim was right. Tanja proved to be a real star and in no time they had made enough money to invest in another video shop for her to run. However, after one more sensational year, disaster struck: the shop burnt down and Tanja was under-insured. She lost the business and her boyfriend all in one go. Her natural inclination was to go back home, to Max.

But she resisted – her ego was at stake. Instead she took a job at a local record store, one of a chain, and in no time was promoted to manageress. She lasted 15 months before, at the age of 24, she took off. Tanja couldn't stand working for someone else.

Young Adulthood: the Age of Consolidation

For the first time in her life, then, Tanja took time out to think, to take stock of her life and her prospects. She knew, by now, that merchandizing came naturally to her, and that she had got to know the food, record and video retailing businesses. She had connections in Spain and in Hong Kong, and had also, by now, spotted a gap in the market in London. There were no trendy places in north London where you could eat good, reasonably priced food and, while waiting, do a bit of browsing for your favourite records.

Tanja therefore put a proposition to her substitute father, Max, with whom she had continued to remain closely in touch. In the meantime he had sold out his businesses to a large retail concern, and was in virtual retirement. Naturally he jumped at the opportunity of going into business with his favourite young lady, and used his connections with the company who had bought him out. The shareholding was split three ways, between Tanja, the retailers and himself. After two tough years the shop/restaurant they set up eventually took off. Over the ten years that followed Tanja combined getting married and having two children with opening up six more such places, including one in Barcelona and another in Hong Kong. By the time she had opened up in Hong Kong her husband Raymond, who was a solicitor, had joined the business full-time. Also, during all this time, Max hovered in the background, helping financially whenever he was needed. In the meantime the Axis retailing group not only secured a more than adequate return on their investment, but watched their new venture grow with interest.

Having proved to herself and to the business establishment that she could succeed, Tanja was now willing to take things a bit more easily. Also Raymond had brought much more stability to her life and she was, of course, a very loving mother. It was now a question, at least to some extent, of brains on, hands off. Tanja managed to combine business and family life, in her thirties, by becoming more organized. Whenever she pictured such organization she had an image of Tom, from the 'market makers' days, in her mind.

By the time Tanja had turned forty, Max, Raymond and herself – as a business partnership – had built up 35 shop/restaurants in the UK, France and Spain, together with two in Hong Kong. Their combined turnover was £200 million, with a return on sales of just under 15 per cent. Moreover, 20 of the stores had been sold off to the Axis group. In that international context Tanja also had the chance to indulge in continuous bouts of concert- and theatre-going, in London, Barcelona and Paris. At times she would wonder, increasingly in more recent years, whether the theatre meant more to her than business, or vice versa. By this stage Tanja was a multi-millionaire.

Midlife: the Age of Renewal

Tanja had come from a family of actors and musicians as well as business people. Her one grandfather had been an impresario in Poland, and her grandmother, on the other side of the family, had been a well known opera singer in Hungary. The artistic side of her, while evident in her childhood, had been submerged by other things, including the need to survive. Now it had obviously risen to the surface again.

When Tanja turned 42 Max died, suddenly, on her birthday. She was so affected by it that she gave up working for a full year. She couldn't quite make out what was happening to her – it was as if her whole world had come to an end. She just stopped functioning as a wife, as a mother and as a businesswoman. The only person who could get through to her was her son Eric, who was now 15, and had become a gifted violinist. She would spend hours, lying in bed, listening to him playing violin sonatas. She would also take Eric into her confidence, repeating to him her feelings of shock and anger over Max's death, again and again.

Raymond and Jim Stokes, the Axis director in charge of Weil Entertainments, had to take over the running of the business completely. Strangely enough, it was only after Tanja had hit rock bottom that she began to come up again. Yet she was no longer her old self. She continued to take an interest, even more of an interest than she had previously, in the selection of records for the stores, and in the training and development of her staff. But the love of the marketplace, of the wheeling and dealing, had gone. In fact it was very fortunate, at this stage, that her daughter Deirdre, who was very much a chip off the old motherly block, had joined the family business.

Meanwhile Tanja started going to evening classes in music appreciation and, under the influence of a very educated lady whom she befriended there, she began to read non-fiction for the first time in her life. She was most taken by Gail Sheahy's books on *Passages* and *Pathfinders*. It was only then that Tanja fully realized the significance of her own most recent passage. She was moving from a relatively 'outer-directed' to a more 'inner-directed' phase of her life. Perhaps Greg Hall, from the old schooldays, had seen more in her than just a show-off actress and entrepreneur.

At the age of 46 Tanja then decided that she wanted to open

CHARTING THE SEVEN LIFE PATHS

another kind of shop, more up-market than the existing ones, catering for book and music lovers. She came increasingly under the influence of an eminent designer–retailer, and even approached him as a prospective business partner. The desire for money and power were no longer the major influences on Tanja's life. Funnily enough, such things had now become more important to Raymond, as well as to daughter Deirdre, than to her.

She was still unsure of what to do with the millions that Max had left her. Raymond was keen to develop the business in West Germany, but Tanja's heart was no longer in that kind of straightforward business expansion. Gradually, as her first new music shop took off, Tanja began to develop other thoughts.

Maturity: the Age of Maturation

Tanja decided that she would invest her business skills and the money Max had left her in a new concept of franchising. Called 'Musicshop', the concept involved a combination of good music, good books and a live, artistic environment. Tanja also felt that this new concept would fit in well with the up-market stance Jim Stokes was increasingly adopting at Axis. Conscious of the fact that people's leisure time was very much on the increase, she would provide a context in which the playing and the receiving of music could go together.

Tanja was also aware, in the mid-1980s, that the European movement would proceed apace, and that it would be important to provide a setting in which the different European cultures could appreciate one another. So her new franchise had books and records, from different countries, on the first floor, and language classes for businessmen and women on the second. When the intention to create a single market was declared, in 1987, her new concept took off like a bomb.

Wasn't it ironic, Tanja thought to herself, that she had left school at 17, and here she was setting up a new school for European business entrepreneurs. In 1990 Jim Stokes, Raymond and herself opened their first store in Warsaw, and had plans to move into Hungary, Czechoslovakia and Bulgaria. In fact Tanja was given the position of head of new ventures for the Axis group in Eastern Europe. It was with a song in her heart that she returned, at least for part of the time, to her native Poland.

Chantalle's development path was a very different one: she also became involved in a small business, but for very different reasons.

A Path of Self-development: Chantalle Dupont – Enabler

Chantalle Dupont was first coaxed into getting involved in business by her economics teacher, Etienne Olivier, who felt that, for all her obvious intelligence, she was hiding from 'the real world'. While she enjoyed studying economics, the business world seemed much too rough and tough for her liking. Surprisingly then, some 40 years later, Chantalle is playing a major part not only in running her own enterprise but also in revitalizing the economy of an entire region in southern France. . .

Childhood and Adolescence

Physical development

Although the boys and girls at school seemed loud and boisterous to her, Chantalle joined in the games and in fact proved to be a natural athlete – she probably inherited her physical prowess from her father. Therefore she travelled around the country with the school athletics team. However, she never got involved with the kind of rowdy antics that you would expect from a group of spirited 16 year olds, miles away from school and home. Instead she observed, from a psycho-logical distance. It was as if she would engage with life on the athletics track, and then detach herself when she was off it. However, Chantalle didn't entirely withdraw. She watched and she listened, while competing successfully.

Social development

Chantalle was a Franco-Algerian whose parents settled in Marseille when she was just a year old. The Second World War had just broken out and her French father, Pierre, was conscripted as a fighter pilot – she did not see him for the next five years. Her mother, Sahana, was a writer of not inconsiderable ability. She wrote poetry and short stories in her native Algerian tongue. During the war she was drafted into the local steelworks to do clerical work.

Chantalle's early memories, therefore, were of steel, grit and grime. Life was hard, and even after her father returned from the war there was little communication between Sahana and Pierre. Father was tough and 'macho', working as a foreman at the steelworks, and mother was delicate and feminine. As an only child Chantalle seemed destined to be the go-between. She loved her dad instinctively and admired her mum more objectively. She too dreamt of being a writer when she grew up: she would write about the men in the steelworks.

Chantalle was a very sensitive little child, but she hid her sensitivity from those around her. The only person with whom she would share her innermost feelings was her granny from Algiers, who stayed with the Duponts from the time her father had gone off to war. Granny never tired of telling little Chantalle stories about life in the little desert village in which Sahana had been brought up. The one she remembered most vividly described how her mother had to go out and beg for food during a time of famine. She kept such stories very much to herself, and would often be seen in the school playground on her own.

Intellectual development

Chantalle observed not only people but also nature. She loved the coastal valleys and would go for long walks with her mother, taking in the beautiful shapes and colours.. She had a love–hate relationship with her father's steelworks, hating the grime and the ugliness while being enthralled by the whole production process. It seemed as if crude ore was being transformed into refined steel by some kind of magic. The only situations which would conjure up similar feelings in her were those contained in the North African myths that she heard from her grandmother.

So at primary school Chantalle loved to draw and also to listen to stories. However, her favourite subject at secondary school was, interestingly enough, not art but French literature. She was crazy about Victor Hugo and read *Les Misérables* five times, at the age of 15. She was also interested in history, especially economic history, and at the local *lycée* she read whatever studies of the Industrial Revolution she could lay her hands on.

When she visited the steelworks she felt that she was re-living the

Industrial Revolution. Her father had now joined the ranks of middle management: she felt that he treated his workers quite abominably, and that the working conditions were absolutely appalling. By the age of 16 Chantalle had come to believe that there was little hope for a world that was filled with materialism and violence. While her father's bosses were driving their posh Renaults, her people in Algeria was starving.

Yet she realized how important material things were to people's quality of life. It was as if she had the task of reconciling her parents' attitudes – mum the artist, and dad the materialist. In the same way, when she contemplated her future she had to struggle with her own ambivalence.

Youth: the Age of Exploration

Chantalle's father was very ambitious for her, being his only child. Unlike many of his colleagues he did not feel that a woman's place is only in the home. He could see that future prospects in Marseille were not very good, so he wanted her to get a place at a leading Ecole Polytechnique near Paris. Her mother, on the other hand, didn't fancy the idea of such an elitist education far away from her daughter's roots.

Because Pierre was the strong character amongst the three of them, Chantalle listened to him, especially after the company's personnel director offered to help her. And so it was that Chantalle went to a Grand Ecole, to study philosophy, politics and economics. She also persisted with her athletics, and ended up running for her region. Interestingly enough, on the athletics track, she displayed quite a strong competitive streak, despite her mild and sensitive manner.

During the course of her studies Chantalle began to take a particular interest in the economics of underdevelopment and, on one of her summer vacations, took a trip to East Africa with a Norwegian friend whom she had met in Paris. In fact the personnel manager at the steelworks helped her out; his company was involved in a feasibility study in Tanzania, and he got her a summer job there as an economic researcher. As a result when she left university she decided to take up a post offered her as Assistant Development Officer, based in Entebbe. Over the next two years she became a great admirer of

Tanzania's then President, whom she actually met on one memorable occasion.

Young Adulthood: Consolidation

Working in the backwoods of Tanzania was less physically demanding than Chantalle had anticipated, but it was certainly more mentally taxing than she might have imagined. Wrestling with the problems of a developing country and economy proved no easy task. Political dogma, she quickly discovered, gets you nowhere. What was required above all, she found, was an in-depth understanding of the local people's needs, capabilities and potential. 'Listen to the people at the grass roots', Tanzania's President had said, 'Be open to their wants and needs, but then draw up your own interpretation of what has to be done'. In other words, it was ultimately up to her to make a judgement. It was her responsibility.

No sooner had she come to this conclusion, however, than her post was 'Africanized'. At first she thought of writing and appealing to the President but, on second thoughts, she concluded that her time had come – she needed to move on, and Tanzania had to develop its own people to do her job.

What she did do, before she left, was to write a letter to the President, thanking him for the opportunity that his country had provided her. She got a lovely response from him, in which he invited her to call on him in the future, at any time. Little did Chantalle realize how significant this reply would turn out to be.

When Chantalle returned to France she was 25 years of age. She was itching to get involved in more local economic development work, whereby she could use the knowledge and experience she had picked up in Tanzania. Therefore she applied for, and got, a post in an economic development unit in the Marseille region, with special responsibility for alleviating unemployment amongst young Algerians. Chantalle's job was to liaise between the youngsters, the local authority and the employers. Her responsibility was not only to match people and jobs, but also to bring harmony to an area in which there had been recent racial conflict. Chantalle found herself drawing not only on her own mixed heritage, but also on the knowledge of indigenous economics and business that she had picked up at the Grand Ecole and in Tanzania.

In the early years, then, she found the job to be a great challenge, and especially enjoyed working for Mahmood, an Algerian social worker with a great deal of experience of community work: over seven years they made significant, if intermittent progress. But gradually she became increasingly disillusioned. There were too many socially and politically minded people involved, and too few who understood the realities of economic development. She also began to feel a bit of a fraud in that, although she had experienced economic development from the outside, she had never worked in an actual business.

It so happened that, on her 35th birthday, Chantalle's father was declared redundant from his steelworks and used his redundancy money to buy into an employment agency, together with his old personnel director. The steelworks also offered assistance in kind, although not in cash, including some office premises. Chantalle suggested that she come in with them, and Pierre was naturally delighted at the prospect.

Midlife: the Age of Renewal

Now in her 36th year, Chantalle was beginning to feel that she would never get married: nobody seemed to offer her the kind of relationship that she was seeking. But, as so often happens, her husband-to-be arrived on the scene when she least expected it. At one stage, in Tanzania, she was on the verge of marrying a much older man, when the Murrays, who had become almost like foster parents to her, intervened. Ironically it was their son, Derek Murray, with whom she now fell in love with in Marseille, and married.

He was a sculptor and they first met at the house of a mutual friend – a Tanzanian in fact – studying in Paris. Both being impulsive by nature, they got married a month later. A year later they had their first and only child, but thanks to her grandmother's devotion Chantalle was able to return to work almost immediately. Derek also helped, being based at home.

Chantalle took to the work in her father's employment agency in a way she would never have expected. Somehow it was as if she had come home. At first she could not understand quite what was going on: indeed, it would be only four years later that the penny would really drop. In the meantime Chantalle undertook most of the interviewing in the agency, initially under the guidance of Xavier – the former personnel director – and she also handled relationships with the smaller business clients. Her father handled the administration and finance and Xavier recruited the larger corporate clients, also maintaining relationships with them, and with the management of the steelworks, who continued to take an interest in the new business.

The bureau undertook two major kinds of assignment: placing redundant steelworkers, including organizing for their retraining; and locating women, mainly secretarial, in part-time jobs. For the first kind of assignment Chantalle had to work very closely with Pierre and Xavier, as well as with the steelworks and the local Job Centre. She also decided to attend a counselling course at the local college.

In three years the agency had established itself as a successful business. During that time she noticed herself becoming tougher, and more businesslike, while Pierre softened up considerably. It was only then that Chantalle realized that part of her mission, in the business, was to balance out the lives of the hardened steelworkers who came her way.

However, soon after Chantalle had turned 40, she began to realize that something was amiss. For the following four years she did nothing about it, thinking that she would get over this temporary crisis. At work things were getting more difficult. Chantalle knew, in her heart of hearts, that only so many jobs could be found for all those redundant workers. Somehow a different approach was needed.

Maturity: the Age of Maturation

At this point Chantalle's husband suggested that they take a sort of sabbatical. He proposed that they go to Algeria, back to the land of Chantalle's birth. But Chantalle had other ideas. She felt that if she was looking for a new lease of life, she had to return to her oldest and dearest mentor in Tanzania. He had only recently retired from active politics, and she thought he may have some time to spare for her. So she wrote to him and, sure enough, he invited both of them to stay for a few days. As soon as they touched down on African soil Chantalle felt different. It was as if a mist had been removed from in front of her eyes. Gradually, after they had spent three weeks with the Murrays, she began to see things in a different light. But the real breakthrough came when Chantalle spent the weekend with the ex-President and his wife.

As the ex-President and elder statesman listened to her problem he said quietly to her, 'The trouble with you people living in Europe is that you have lost touch with your roots. You can only find your future by going back into your distant past, drawing on your old myths and legends for inspiration, and then relating them to a modern context'. Then Chantalle vividly recalled how she used to feel when grandmother related those folk stories to her. She also recalled, in an instant association, the steelmaking process as a magical transformation. Then the answer came to her. It was the self-image of the Franco-Algerian people as a whole that had to be changed if she was to make real progress. The vacuum lay not within business but around it. The first thing that she now had to do was to spend a few months in Algeria.

So Chantalle took off a further three months and spent the time with her aunt in Algiers. Her mother also joined them for one month, and they revisited their cultural heritage together. Chantalle reflected on the nature of poverty, both material and spiritual, and even began to write stories, for the first time since she had left primary school. It then occurred to her how rich an oral tradition the Algerians were able to draw upon. It also struck her that whereas Lyon was the very heart of France, and Lille was its body, Paris was its mind, and Marseille its soul. When she returned home to Marseille, after spending a week with her husband and child, she set to work, drawing up a master plan to put to the Regional Development Agency. It was to incorporate nothing less than the economic and cultural renaissance of the Marseille region. Chantalle spent many hours with Xavier and Mahmood, both natives of Marseille, uncovering many of the region's longstanding French and Algerian traditions. All in all it took four years of persistent discussion and persuasion before the Development Agency was finally convinced.

Six years later, the employment agency has now become a 'Life Centre', in fact the best known such centre in the country. Chantalle and her staff of 30 people – her father Pierre is now semi-retired – are working hand in hand with the local schools, the Training Services, the major employers in the area including the old steelworks, the Development Agency and the Regional Arts Council. The idea is to help individuals, at different stages of their lives, to discover and to chart their life paths.

So the Franco-Algerians, with their strong and combined traditions, have taken a lead within France in developing new kinds of life scripts for people, young and old, to follow. The regional economic and cultural development programmes have also been transformed in that light. Literature, history and business have joined forces. Chantalle has already written three books, based on her thoughts and achievements, and Derek has supplied the artwork. Her next project, during her fifties and sixties, is to position her Life Centre more centrally, within the steelworks, which has lost its heart and soul. In so doing she will bring together classical and romantic worlds, as she has done North and South. Not surprisingly, a copy of her first book sits proudly on a Tanzanian mantlepiece, with an inscription inside 'To my dearest mentor, with love from Chantalle'.

Finally, Shigeru's path was even more bizarre than Chantalle's: after all, he was, and is, an innovator.

The Creative Path: Shigeru Mahesh – Innovator

Shigeru was an innovator on the outskirts of San Francisco, unique unto himself, virtually from the time he was born! He started to produce extraordinary compositions on the guitar from the age of two, and when a 'Young Achievement' programme was set up, Sam Cohn, from the school's music department, immediately asked Shigeru if they could sell the 200 compositions that he had already recorded and produced at school, all around the country. From that point, interspersed with many breakdowns and breakthroughs along the way, Shigeru's creative path was set. . .

Childhood and Adolescence

Physical development

In early childhood Shigeru let out his frustrations physically. He loved to climb trees, and spring from branch to branch like a jungle boy. Sitting on top of a tree and gazing at the barren world in the San Francisco slum area before him, he would imagine a totally transformed *sound*scape, where all was beautiful.

Social development

Shigeru was an unlikely mix of Japanese and Pakistani stock. His father, a small-time restaurateur, whose family had originally come over from Osaka, was a Buddhist. His mother, a seamstress in a local factory, was a Muslim. The physical environment in which Shigeru was brought up was relatively impoverished, and the social one equally so.

The way people like Shigeru's parents were imprisoned within their own respective cultural blinkers, despite their marriage to one another, maddened him from a very young age. His spontaneous compositions were remarkable. They conveyed not only a passion but also a sense of form which was well beyond his years. By the age of 12, when he was able to articulate these things verbally, he expressed, through his songs, precocious dismay at people's inability to work things out for themselves in life. For his parents were constantly at loggerheads with one another, whether over race or religion, and yet they were expressing sentiments which were obviously not individually their own.

So life for Shigeru, until high school, was a continuing struggle to break out of the mundane, the uncreative mass of conformity.

Intellectual development

At secondary school Shigeru turned his attention seriously to music, which was the only subject that attracted him. The rest was a lot of tired old stuff churned out by other people: at least in the music class, thanks to his dedicated teacher Sam, he could compose his own work. In fact by the age of 15 he had become convinced that the music he wrote was more real than the actual sounds he heard around him. His most distinctive compositions were bizarre mixtures of religious music, combining tribal Pakistan with tribal Japan, sometimes interspersed with negro spiritual.

Shigeru's parents had virtually disowned him by the time he was 12. In fact he spent more time at Sam's place than in his own home. He made little contact with any of the other teachers, with the possible exception of the physics teacher, Shamus, with whom he used to discuss the nature of sound, and of musical harmonics. Interestingly enough, because of this personal connection, physics – other than music – was the only subject that Shigeru could handle.

So Shigeru, Sam and Shamus would often take mental and emotional journeys together into a fantasy land of their own combined creation. Shigeru had been an avid reader of Roald Dahl as a child. For musical nourishment, aside from traditional Japanese music, and

Jamaican reggae, he would listen for hours to Duke Ellington and Stravinsky.

Youth: the Age of Exploration

By the age of 17 Shigeru had had enough of his impoverished surroundings. He left school and home and became a deckhand on an ocean liner. For two years he travelled south and east, leading a life that was both arduous and exotic. In between work aboard ship he took every opportunity to go ashore. His eyes and ears were feasted on the infinite variety of people and sounds that he discovered. In fact, when he reached Malaysia he was so fascinated by the sights and sounds that he got himself a job in a little village, serving in a restaurant, before rejoining his ship on its return journey. During that brief period of time Shigeru not only picked up some of the local language but he also began to blend some of the Malaysian folk tunes with his own Indo-Japanese compositions. With the money he had earned as a deckhand he also purchased several indigenous musical instruments.

Aboard ship again, and somewhat to his own surprise, he befriended the ship's entertainer Christos, who was not much of a pianist, but who had incredible flair as a singer and as a master of ceremonies. Inevitably, when he discovered Shigeru's talents, he invited him to join the act.

Young Adulthood: the Age of Consolidation

In no time the two of them teamed up, Shigeru playing and composing and Christos singing. Gradually the ship's captain began to notice how many people were now coming along to the evening's entertainment. He was especially struck by the versatility of the new team of entertainers. As a result, and at the end of the voyage, he suggested that the two of them join up with a sister ship that carried four times as many passengers. They were an instant success, and spent a further two years cruising around the world. Needless to say, Shigeru continued to use every opportunity to absorb musical influences.

By the time he had turned 24, and Christos had reached 30, the two of them decided that it was time to branch out. For all this time Shigeru had continued to correspond with Sam, his old music teacher and, in the meantime, Sam's daugther Kelly had become an administrator at the Bay Area Arts Centre in San Francisco. So he and his would-be agent, Christos, went along to see her, to investigate whether she would sign Shigeru up. When he presented her with his new compositions she was instantly impressed, and invited her boss to hear her protégé. Shigeru and Christos were instantly signed up for a series of three performances.

Over the next ten years the two of them gave performances around the world and gained a considerable reputation. But that lifestyle could not last forever. Shigeru was not just a composer and a performer: he was a man with a mission, and that mission was becoming increasingly clear. Music had to be something more than entertainment. At that point, sadly, he and Christos parted company; also, Shigeru and Kelly got married.

Shigeru was now 35, and restless – he had to do more with his life. He wanted to get his kind of music established on the world's music stage. The obvious thing was for Kelly and himself to form a music publishing company.

Over the course of the next seven years Shigeru continued to compose – usually for piano, double bass, drums and guitar – for both public performance and publication as sheet music. Over time they got together a regular group of three performers, aside from Shigeru himself, and they toured both Europe and the US. Much of his music was now on record, and Shigeru had become a major recording artist.

Midlife: the Age of Renewal

As he turned 42 Shigeru, while doing fairly well financially, was becoming restless again. He still was not realizing his vision which, in essence, was to bring peace and harmony to a strife-torn world through music. The closest he had probably got was 20 years back, when the Bay Area Symphony Orchestra had performed to a combined Afro-American, Hispanic and Caucasian audience.

In the 1970s, and under adverse circumstances, Shigeru experienced a breakthrough. In 25 years he had seen his parents only twice: they continued to be as bigoted as they had ever been. But in 1975 his sister was killed in a street brawl between rival gangs. After the initial shock and dismay, and completely unpredictably, his mother became transformed, deploring the state of prejudice that had resulted in the futile killing of her only daughter. That seemed to be some kind of signal for Shigeru. He and Kelly returned home determined to do something.

In joining the civil rights movement they began to organize concerts of his music to invited audiences from all religious groups. After the concerts they would hold discussions to try and uncover the reasons for prejudice, as well as ways of overcoming it. For three years Shigeru combined these events with more conventional concert performances around the globe. Particularly rewarding was a trip to Islamabad, when he was able to return to his origins for a renewed source of inspiration.

Maturity: the Age of Maturation

Approaching 50, Shigeru felt – for virtually the first time in his life – that he was coming to terms with himself. Shigeru and Kelly decided to buy a house in the Bay area and to set up a new music school in their neighbourhood. By this time his recording company had been taken over by a Japanese corporation, and Shigeru managed to influence his Japanese countrymen to help him out with both finance and equipment. Naturally he agreed to call his school the Pacific 'Soundscape'.

The idea was to combine music with the study of different cultures, all under one roof. During the day tuition, in both popular and classical music, would be offered for children, and in the evenings businessmen would attend classes not only on languages but also on cross-cultural management. In all cases, though, music was presented as the background and context for the study of a nation's culture.

After four years Shigeru felt sufficiently confident in the future of their enterprise to withdraw from the administrative side of things and to return, entirely, to composing music. By this stage he felt that his compositions were drawing on all four quarters of the globe. Somehow, from his acutely impoverished background, he had succeeded in becoming a citizen of the world. The company had by now taken him under their wing as an 'adopted son'. As a company rooted in a universal means of communication they were, in collaborating with Shigeru and Kelly, crossing cultural barriers between East and West, if not also North and South.

Conclusion

As you can see, to gauge from the seven self-development paths, the learning organization that accommodates them has to reach substantially above and beyond the normal bounds of business activity. In the first place, it is clearly apparent that the boundary between small- and large-scale business needs to become increasingly blurred. Secondly, the gap between commercial, social and cultural activity has to be consistently narrowed.

To the extent that organizations enable individuals within them to grow and develop, so they have to learn to accommodate ever greater diversity. This theme of unity within variety is one which will constantly recur in this book, whether it pertains to variety of a psychological, technological, economic or cultural nature. We now turn from the manager's self-development to his or her acquisition, and application, of knowledge and skill.

PART III

Transforming Your Business Knowledge

8

Transforming the Business Functions: Markets, Money, Motivation

Introduction

Information Processing

At this point in our journey into 'the learning organization' we enter the 'knowledge field'. To the extent that knowledge-based organizations become a reality, so the management, or processing, of information will take precedence over the more tangible management of physical, human and financial resources. Such information processing has both horizontal and vertical dimensions.

Horizontally, there are seven different roles to be personally played, in the acquisition and application of management knowledge. Vertically, there are seven impersonally represented functions of learning (upward movement) and of innovation (downward movement). The fully functioning knowledge-based organization requires all of these horizontal roles and vertical functions.

In this introduction I shall describe these knowledge-based roles and functions, in general terms. But first I want to review the horizontal knowledge roles and vertical functions, overall.

Horizontal Roles

The horizontal roles extend from the knowledge originator – the most unusual – to the knowledge implementor – the most commonplace.

Knowledge originator

Knowledge originators, such as Isaac Newton in science, Pablo Picasso in art and Peter Drucker in management, open up entire new fields of knowledge where, seemingly, none had existed before. Whereas such inventive minds are actively sought out in research-based environments they are much less well known within the management mainstream. However, such managerial origination is becoming increasingly important, if we are to keep pace with the rate of technological innovation. After all, prior to the 1950s the discipline of marketing was non-existent; and prior to the 1980s the field of 'corporate culture' had not yet been identified. Successive 'manager-ial revolutions' will be dependent upon the true originators in the management field.

Knowledge developer

Knowledge developers, as acknowledged in conventionally based research functions, uncover potential for the application of newly discovered knowledge across a wide diversity of fields. Moreover, they play a significant part in developing such knowledge, or technology, to the point at which it is more accessible to the user than in its original and pristine form. The two established fields for such activity are technically based research and development, and psycho-logically based organization development. An emerging field for such developmental activity is that of management information systems.

Knowledge refiner

Such people refine the knowledge that originators and developers have created, duly converting it into systems, routines and proced-ures. In marketing, for example, such an analyst would conceptualize and specify the system required for the introduction of a new product. In accounting, such a person would work out a new system for dealing with just-in-time inventory control, but one that was based on existing accounting principles and practices. Finally, such analysis can be conducted on a large or a small scale, for a whole business or for a small part of one.

Knowledge promoter

Knowledge promoters invest in new technologies, expert systems, training packages or databases with a view to making a profitable return on their investment. Alternatively, they champion such a 'system', within the company or without, selling the benefits that will allegedly accrue to the customer. Whereas such promoters may 'customize' the knowledge, adding marketing features to suit the user, they will not do any original, developmental or analytical work on it. Their role is of an energizing rather than of a creative or conceptual nature.

Knowledge adaptor

Adaptors solve problems in the application of knowledge to specific situations at specific times and places. In so doing they are likely to have to adapt a system, a product or a service, to a particular and often changing set of requirements. The knowledge they apply is specific and professionally based – often reflected in training packages or user manuals – rather than general and conceptually grounded.

They display quick-wittedness and flexibility of mind rather than depth of insight and genuine originality. Such 'troubleshooters' are conventionally to be found in manufacturing and in management services, but, as the rate of change affecting all business functions accelerates, so their services are increasingly in demand.

Knowledge animateur

Knowledge 'animateurs' have the ability and inclination to turn sophisticated technologies or depersonalized sources of information into animated, 'user-friendly' applications. Knowledge, for them, has to be made directly amenable to everyday people – whether as staff or customers – before it becomes useful. Their own attitude to knowledge is that of the craftsman rather than that of the artist or scientist. On the shopfloor, or in the salesforce, such animateurs play a useful role in 'demystifying' technical or sales jargon. They have no interest in knowledge for its own sake, and therefore take the time and trouble to ensure that users not only find it practicable but are also comfortable with, and even enjoy it.

Knowledge implementer

Knowledge implementers, in the context of the learning organization, have the ultimate responsibility for ensuring that the knowledge source physically reaches its ultimate and required destination. They are not concerned with its origination, development, refinement, promotion, adaptation or animation: rather, they are responsible for physical production or distribution in, or to, the right place, at the right time. Increasingly, such physically based implementation is being undertaken by machines rather than people.

Vertical Functions

Management knowledge is fully utilized when seven information processing functions are both acquired and applied. Whereas the acquisition of knowledge – learning – is essentially an introverted function, its application – innovation – is primarily an extraverted one.

Knowledge acquisition: learning

A hunger for knowledge is an initial precondition for learning. A subsequent willingness to make social links with fellow learners, and to enthusiastically follow the example of coaches and mentors, is all important. Moreover, these physical and social preconditions need to be followed by a mental openness, or spirit of curiosity, involving a continual questioning of people, of things, and of events that surround you. And such an intellectually based curiosity needs to be supplemented by an emotionally based inclination to expose yourself to personally unchartered managerial territories, thereby acquiring new experience.

Only then will the methodical study of a 'business' subject reap genuine learning dividends. Moreover, these dividends will be multiplied to the extent that you are subsequently able to relate the body of knowledge you have acquired to both yourself and to the wider context in which you operate. Finally, such learning is perpetuated when you cultivate the ability to imagine yourself learning and developing.

Knowledge application: innovation

Knowledge acquisition, for managers, is of no consequence without its subsequent application. The first step is to envision what you ultimately want to create. Thereafter, you need to recognize the significance and scope of the knowledge to hand, not in specific detail, but in relation to the particular context. The next step is to determine in precise detail how best to apply the theory to enable you to deal effectively with practice. Then you commit yourself to action, using the concepts you have acquired to achieve your desired end.

The commitment you make will initially be of a generalized nature. Subsequently you will need to experiment with alternative and specific techniques, duly enlisting the help of communications technology. Ultimately of course, no matter how sophisticated the techniques, the approach you take will fail unless you enthusiastically involve other people with you. And in the final analysis you, more often than not today with the aid of some form of automation, will apply the internalized knowledge (see figure 8.1).

I now want to briefly apply the horizontal and vertical analysis to each of the specialist 'business' functions, starting with marketing.

Marketing Management

The Horizontal Roles

Conventional and academically based approaches to marketing management have been analytically based. For over 20 years, Philip Kotler in the US has championed such an approach:

Marketing is the analysing, organising, planning and controlling of the firm's customer impinging resources, policies and activities with a view to satisfying the needs of chosen customer groups at a profit.[1]

In more recent years this view has been challenged by Hugh Murray[2] in the UK. For Murray, what is most important is that the marketing approach be adapted according to the requirements of different marketplaces. As a result, there are a number of different marketing roles, ranging from that of an innovator – creating whole new markets – to that of a basic trader – dealing in commodity markets.

Figure 8.1   Knowledge acquisition and application.

Market innovator

The market innovator can create markets, as yet unforeseen, for combinations of products and services in the process of being developed, or which they recommend for development. Working in close contact with research and development such marketing people, albeit few and far between, can transform entire markets to conform to an image that they have of how things should be – as often done in the fashion business.

Market developer

The developer will see product and market potential in the most unlikely of places. Such developers will take particular account of underlying customer or client needs as opposed to manifest wants. Similarly, such a person will take account of the underlying characteristics of an institutional, communal or national source of custom. Having done this the market developer will then provide a context for the fulfilment of these needs through the organization's products and services.

Marketing manager

Conventional marketing managers take responsibility for the planning, organizing and controlling of the proverbial four P's – product, place, price and promotion – of marketing. In so doing they lay emphasis upon the analytical aspects of management, including marketing research and segmentation (planning), marketing logistics and distribution (place), costing, budgeting and pricing (price) and cost-effective selling, advertising and public relations (promotion). Their overall aim is to establish an effective match between product and market.

Sales manager

Typical sales managers are more entrepreneurial in their approach than their marketing counterpart. Their primary focus is on energizing the sales force to sell products and services that satisfy customer, or client, wants. To that extent they are always looking for ways and means of packaging or customizing the offer or support to suit the individual or institutional purchaser. The atmosphere surrounding their managerial work is emotional and behavioural rather than thoughtful or analytical.

Product or brand manager

Product or brand managers need to be highly flexible, adapting their product or service to different geographical, demographic, cultural or social trends and contexts. Moreover, unlike the more established marketing or sales managers, they will often switch from one product or brand to another, at regular intervals. Finally, because of their connection with the offer or support involved, they may well play a consultancy role with a client, based upon expert knowledge.

Customer services manager

With the renewed focus on 'customer care' within major public and private enterprises, the need arises for customer service managers who 'care' for the people with whom they are dealing. This people orientation places the emphasis on service, on relationships and on catering for the immediate wants of customers and clients rather than on their underlying needs.

Market trader

The market trader, whether in Bangladesh or in London's East End, is engaged in buying and selling what he or she regards as 'commodities', be they soya beans, cups and saucers or computer games. The object is to 'pile 'em high and sell 'em cheap'. What counts, at the end of the day, is the amount of cash coming into the till. The determinants of marketing success or failure are the trader's acting skills, stamina, and ability to 'get inside the customer's skin'.

The Vertical Functions

Acquiring marketing knowledge: learning

The learning process begins, in a marketing context, when you open your five senses to what is going on around you, physically reacting to what you touch, smell, taste, hear and see.[3] It is further reinforced by your enthusiastic response to people, and their immediate wants or needs.[4] Your learning will then be enhanced if you are able to mentally adapt to different sets of customer requirements, over space and time.[5]

However, all the learning you have so far undergone will be restricted if you are not able to forge bonds with prospective customers, with whom you can test out possible deals.[6] By this time your market knowledge will be well enough grounded so that the methodical analysis[7] you subsequently undertake will have a solid base to it. This overall analysis will lead you into a deeper insight of market dynamics only if you have gained an understanding of the underlying harmonies linking your own needs with those of others.[8] Finally, to the extent that you are able to imagine these needs being actualized[9] you will be able to function fully as a learner–marketeer.

Applying marketing knowledge: innovation

To the extent that you are able to envision new needs being actualized, so you are in a position to create wholly new markets, at least in your mind's eye; an interconnected range of original products and services would be the prospective outcome. Subsequent to such origination there is a need to develop exclusive, interconnected ranges, evolved for and through different cultural and social environments. Thereafter, and as the market opportunities expand, you should be marketing specialized products and services for standardized market segments, as opposed to the limited edition, exclusive ranges.

As competition intensifies, standardized markets need to be supplanted by customized products or services, duly promoted as tailor-made for particular customers within each market segment. As the focus becomes more and more specific, the marketeer becomes a consultant, solving problems for his or her client. Getting subsequently even closer to the customer he or she becomes involved with a form of craftsmanship. Finally, as the product or service is transformed from the most profound source of information – creative spirit – into the most extensive form of product – mass-produced commodity – raw trading instinct replaces customer care as the basis for marketing and selling (see figure 8.2).

Helen Pfister: Marketing Manager

Helen had worked for three years as public relations officer for a medium-sized publishing company in Boston, USA, before she was promoted to the

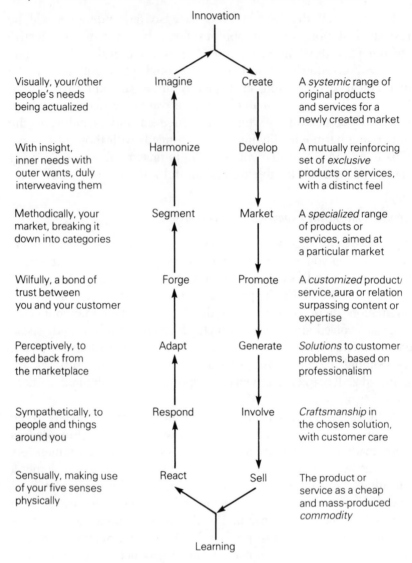

Figure 8.2   Marketing learning and innovation.

role of marketing manager. The company was poised to expand, internationally, so she faced quite a challenge; particularly because she had received no formal training in marketing, although she had read the odd book, and was very bright.

Acquiring Marketing Knowledge

Reacting

Helen started out by visiting the major bookstores on the East Coast, gradually getting a feel for the market. She chatted to sales assistants, observed customers' buying habits, and took in the different atmospheres of the stores. Helen then called in the 75 sales representatives to a meeting, and asked them to air their feelings: listening to their comments, and picking up their 'vibes', she found that she was not afraid to feed back her own intuitive *reactions* when called upon. She repeated this process nationwide, visiting 35 stores and meeting over 250 representatives in all.

Responding

Being naturally active, Helen found this first stage of her induction easy to take on board. The next phase, which she regarded as very important, came less naturally, as Helen was not particularly sociable. She arranged 20 separate 'getting to know you' meetings, with her representatives across the US and Western Europe, meeting no more than a dozen people at a time. She now wanted to be able to *respond* much more directly to their problems, and to get to know the people individually. At this point, Tom Peters, with his views on 'getting close to the customer', had become very influential – a kind of distant mentor.

Adapting

Having got to know her salesforce, and major bookstore staff, pretty well, Helen began to realize that her task was not going to be easy. It was not that difficult to 'get close', but each person was different: some extremely money-minded, others more people-oriented, yet another group very 'bookish'. Somehow or other, she would have to *adapt* her style and tactics accordingly.

Forging

Helen asked head office to assemble for her all the available statistical information about the buying habits of the different customer groups, in the US, the Pacific Rim and Europe. Armed with this knowledge, and six months into the job, she now felt confident to go back to the major retail outlets, and the direct mail trade, to forge a personal relationship with each key player. She was also now encouraged to attend a three-day workshop on 'Negotiation Skills' at Boston University; after which she found herself growing out of her old PR shoes, and into new, rather more brash ones, which felt none too comfortable.

Segmenting

Helen was not averse to asserting herself, but was not what you might call a 'conceptualizer', and she was increasingly finding this to be a disadvantage. Not only did she find it difficult to assimilate Kotler's *Analytical Marketing*, but she was still unable to *segment* her market in a useful way. Therefore she took herself off on a fully fledged two-week marketing course, at Brandeis University – she found the programme so stressful that she spent next weekend off in bed, with a blinding headache. But she was now able to undertake a proper segmentation exercise on her market, which made her feel much more confident.

Harmonizing

At this point, one year into the job, Helen was just beginning to feel comfortable with it, having got to know her market both analytically and practically: she was beginning to understand overall market trends, and her particular niche – and she had been able to resolve the conflict between her career and family roles. She could also now see ways and means in which her inner need to become a more influential manager could be *harmonized* with the company's need to expand that market.

Imagining

For the first time, then, she could *imagine* herself occupying an important influential and significant position within the company, whereby her thoughts, feelings and actions would make a visible impact.

Applying Market Knowledge

Creating

Helen began to see herself transforming the whole marketing approach of the company. She could now see that a whole new market was emerging for works of both fiction and non-fiction that transcended national boundaries. She could clearly *envisage* an integrated range of biographies on the one hand, and of business, economics and ecological texts on the other – books that were intrinsically cross-cultural. Such a publishing programme would require the transformation of the inherently parochial approach to publishing and marketing in the US.

Developing

First, Helen had to *develop* a less parochial attitude amongst her marketing staff and key representatives in the US, and prospectively in Europe and the Pacific Rim. To that end, she brought in an independent consultant, to help her evolve the company's corporate culture; and at the same time she held intensive discussions with editorial staff, to help them recognize and promote the kinds of authors they needed, and to stimulate an interdisciplinary approach.

Marketing

The first three titles in the new TRANSCEND series – transcending not only disciplines but also the fiction/non-fiction divide – were published simultaneously; a biography of Vaclav Havel, a new work by the British ecologist James Lovelock, and an anthology of short stories by the Japanese Catholic writer Shusaku Endo. The books were *marketed* jointly; but, in effect, Helen had to promote this concept to her own salesforce before she attempted to reach the retailers, or the public at large.

Promoting

Once she had transformed the outlook of her own people, Helen was in a position to *promote* her concept to the retail trade, in her three geographical markets. Her advertising colleagues in Boston put together a package including an up-market video, incorporating all three authors in both their audiovisual and printed materials. And Helen's overall financial projections, based on two alternative pricing structures and new distribution arrangements, served to demonstrate the economic viability of the new series.

Generating

In fact, the company decided to experiment with the two different distribution arrangements, settling after six months on mail order in Eastern Europe, Japan and Singapore, and direct retail sales in the US and the rest of Europe. Each arrangement *generated* its own particular problems and opportunities. During the trial period, Helen also made a point of encouraging all her representatives to generate ideas on sales gimmicks, which were then brought together at a collective brainstorming session.

Involving

Subsequent to this collective effort, a general consensus emerged on the best overall approach to the marketing of this new series. Then, to keep people continually *involved*, Helen appointed an animator, or chief sales enthusiast, in each of the 36 different sales regions around the globe.

Selling

The target that Helen set the international sales force was to *sell* a million copies of each book, with sales distributed evenly between the US, Europe and the East. Three months thereafter, she was delighted to find that they were already one third of the way towards reaching their target, although US sales were well ahead of performance in the other two territories. She began to wonder how she should react, but decided to visit the various countries – to gain a first-hand impression – before deciding on any course of action.

Conclusion

As we can see then, the learning process is one of building up, or evolution, whereas the innovation process is one of breaking down, or involution. Both form a necessary part of the managerial whole, from a knowledge-based perspective. We now turn from external to internal relations, from marketing to human resource management.

Human Resource Management

Horizontal Roles

Conventionally based 'personnel management' is rooted in the welfare role played by personnel officers at the turn of the century. Almost a hundred years later 'human resource management' has supposedly come of age, duly concerned with the planning, recruitment, training and appraisal of personnel. However, such human resource managers play very much a support role to the line managers.

In their more proactive capacity personnel managers may follow the lead established by Warren Bennis in the 1960s:

Bureaucracy was a monumental discovery for harnessing muscle power via guilt and instinctual renunciation. In today's world it is a prosthetic device, no longer useful. For we now require organic-adaptive systems, as structures of freedom, to permit the expression of play and imagination, and to exploit the new pleasure of work.[10]

These 'structures of freedom' are more akin to the knowledge-based organization than the conventional bureaucracy. At the same time both have their place, as we shall discover when I unravel the horizontal roles, which extend from what I call the personnel 'empowerer' to the proverbial 'headhunter'.

Personnel empowerer

The fundamentally creative personnel role is played by those few psychologists who can empower people to actualize their individual potential within an organizational setting. Abraham Maslow, the American humanistic psychologist, has been one outstanding case in point.

For such empowerers as Maslow personnel work is transformed from 'managing human resources' into actualizing human beings at work. The product they offer is both original and systemic, rather than specific, infusing all the other business functions with its humanistic orientation.

Personnel facilitator

Developmentally inclined personnel managers, that is facilitators, see themselves as enhancing the potential of individualized human beings rather than that of depersonalized human resources. Working systemically, like the empowerer, they develop potential through interfusion, rather than creating it through fusion. They see personnel work, then, as means to enhance the productive potential of individual people as well as interdependent groups, and not as a direct means of serving the bottom line. In that capacity they work closely together with the organizational and the corporate developers.

Human resources manager

The human resources manager is the commonly depicted personnel manager who plans, organizes and controls the flow of such 'human resources' within the whole of an organization. His or her function – together with those of the operations, marketing and finance managers – is to serve whatever happens to be the declared purpose of a particular enterprise, duly channelling the flow of human resources efficiently and effectively. Critical vantage points, within such a flow, are recruitment, training, administration and job evaluation. In that capacity the human resource manager offers a particular set of services rather than a systemic web of integrated activities.

Social entrepreneur

Social entrepreneurs, in a personnel context, are interested in manipulating the organization within which they work to the advantage of both themselves and the personnel within it. Unlike human resource managers, who take a detached interest in people, social entrepreneurs see their personnel-related activities as a direct extension of themselves. As such they personalize and customize human resource 'packages', making them saleable to the organization, and hence profitable to both the personnel concerned and to themselves. They may also seek to sell such packages on the open market.

Management trainer

Trainers, in today's sophisticated and turbulent organizational world, are increasingly educated, research-oriented and professionally based. As such they adapt existing training packages, including computer-based ones, to particular organizational purposes. Unlike the more rigid trainers of old they need to be eminently flexible to take account of multiple individual user needs. As a result they operate more as consultants, providing access to individualized learning, than as conventional instructors. Finally, such trainers form themselves into networks of fellow professionals, within and across organizations.

Personnel officer

Personnel officers, to the extent that they can be qualitatively distinguished from trainers or managers, are craftspeople rather than professionals. In taking care of the day to day welfare needs of personnel, they are involved with people *as* people, rather than as resources or recipients of welfare. They are typically concerned with what Herzberg called 'hygiene' – as opposed to 'motivational' – needs, such as working conditions and social facilities. Finally, they genuinely and warmly care for the people whom they serve.

Headhunter

Headhunters, as the name suggests, are proverbial fast operators who seldom lift themselves above the immediacy of the placement fray. Their aptitude lies in speed of response and in their knowledge of the particular attributes of the people being traded, be they financial controllers, commercial artists or software engineers. Acquiring people, for them, is akin to hunting, and the people being hunted are like physical commodities, with varying prices on their heads. Finally, the job market is seen to be a jungle, in which the most sharp-witted and fleet-footed of the headhunters survive and the weakest go under.

Vertical Functions: Human Resource Learning and Innovation

Learning – the upward movement

Learning, in the context of human resource management, begins when you deploy your five senses to react to people.[11] Having opened up your senses to others you reinforce your learning when you open up your heart, responding to people warmly and spontaneously.[12] Such physical and social behaviour is mentally enriched when you are able to consciously adapt your style of communication to particular people in particular circumstances.[13] Furthermore, to the extent that you are able to probe into the forces of power and influence,[14] so your ability to manage people accelerates.

Enhanced learning, of a human resource variety, takes place when you become able to methodically analyse the job, training and welfare requirements[15] of employees. It is your capacity to recognize the underlying needs of people,[16] though, that enables you to stand out from the personnel crowd. Finally, to the extent that you are able to imagine your people being transformed into peak performers,[17] so you will have learnt how to be creative with people.

Innovation – the downward movement

The great social innovators, such as Robert Owen of Lanark Mills, transformed a mass of workers – to some extent at least – into groups of self-actualizing individuals. Thereafter, new business and organizational opportunities can be developed out of the enhanced capacities of these people. These businesses will have to be subsequently administered, making best use of recruitment, training and appraisal methodologies.

To secure the social innovation, though, the human resource function needs to manoeuvre itself into a position of influence within the organization as a whole. Subsequently it will be in a position to generate a wide range of training techniques, flexibly geared towards the self-development of the individual. At the same time, in order to provide the social stability that serves to balance change, people would need to become involved in the organization through social and welfare-based activities. Finally, and inevitably, in order to bring new blood into the organization some degree of trading in the job market would be required (see figure 8.3).

Sergei Ligaev: Human Resource Manager

Sergei was one of the first so-called 'human resource managers' to be appointed in the Soviet Union, in the wake of *perestroika* and *glasnost*. He had previously been factory manager at a local car plant in Kiev, which had now linked up in a joint venture with Volvo. At first, the Swedes wanted to send Sergei to INSEAD, to do an MBA, but they then thought better of it – it seemed more important, at this point, that he should learn and develop from his own grass roots.

Acquiring Knowledge of Human Resource Management

Reacting

In this new plant employing 3000 people, Sergei first followed his natural instincts as an ex-production manager, wandering around the shop floor, talking, observing and generally appraising the atmosphere. In the process, duly *reacting* with his senses, Sergei was able to form his initial impressions of the workforce: they seemed to be an unruly bunch, poorly motivated, and working more out of necessity than anything else.

Responding

Therefore, the next step Sergei took was to visit workers at home, to be able to *respond* better to them as people. He sat around the fireside with their families, listening to stories about the old factory and the new, and about the heroes and villains. He also discovered that the test track was the only part of the works in which a real family spirit existed – here the men actually enjoyed their work. That aside, the heart and soul of the workforce community was not to be found in the 'Kievlenin Works' but at the dance club, where traditional folklore and dance thrived.

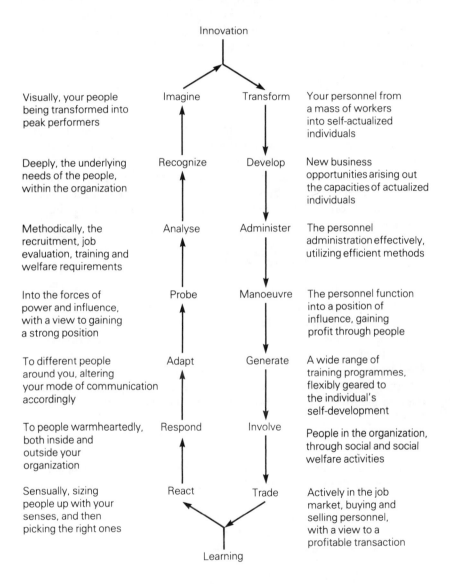

Figure 8.3   Human resource learning and innovation.

174 TRANSFORMING YOUR BUSINESS KNOWLEDGE

Adapting

Sergei now wanted to find out more about the different social and working groups. First, he discovered that there was an enormous gulf between workers and management, despite their common socialist principles. There was an equally important disparity in expectations and behaviour between the 'shopfloor' and 'white collar' staff. He found that he had to *adapt*, speaking almost in different languages to the two groups, which went very much against the grain, as he had always regarded himself as a man of all the people.

Probing

Not only did Sergei have to adapt to individual differences, but it became immediately apparent that he would make little progress unless he came to understand the workplace power politics. So he *probed*, both formally and informally, with a view to developing his own sphere of influence. It took him the best part of six months to make any headway – and the task ahead of him still seemed formidable – but he persevered, encouraged by the new management.

Analysing

Armed, eventually, with this combination of physical, social and personal knowledge, Sergei began to formulate ideas for recruitment, job evaluation, training and development. But he felt very uncertain, even after almost a year, and therefore asked to be sent on a human resource management course being run, in English, at Stockholm University. He was particularly keen to meet practitioners from other countries. It proved to be quite a sobering experience, as he both met a wide variety of people, and applied his mind to the whole gamut of problems facing him back home.

Recognizing

Upon returning home, Sergei felt that his knowledge of the personnel role had been much improved, but that he still had difficulty in placing it in perspective. After all, this was Soviet Russia, not the US or Scandinavia. Therefore, he turned to the works of Tolstoy and Turgeniev: Could he *recognize* Tolstoy's Russian peasants in the Kiev factory, or had the people been irrevocably changed by the Revolution?

Imagining

Sergei immersed himself in Russian culture, from the films of Eisenstein, through the paintings of Kandinski, to the symphonies of Shostakovich. Painstakingly, and with a little help from Leo Tolstoy on the one hand and Peter Drucker on the other, and after hundreds of hours of conversations with workers and their families, he began to *imagine* the kind of organization he might wish to create.

Applying Knowledge of Human Resource Management

Transforming

Sergei envisioned his auto works being *transformed* into a place where people wore smiles on their faces, achieved vast increases in productivity and attended evening classes after a hard day's work. There they would study the works of Dostoevsky, Tolstoy, Yevteshenko and Karl Marx, as well as Adam Smith, on the one hand; while they also investigated the ideas of Frederick Taylor and Elton Mayo, of Maslow and Herzberg, and of Henry Ford and Shoshana Zuboff. In fact, it took just a year to turn this vision into action.

Developing

In the process, and as the workers' and managers' hearts and minds were opened up, a whole series of new business opportunities were recognized, two of which were *developed* over the course of the next year. With Volvo's support, the factory diversified into machine tools and simple electronic switchgear. At the same time, a 'learning organization' was inaugurated, and the wide range of classes was attended by no less than 85 per cent of the plant's personnel.

Administering

As all these activities took off, Sergei found himself having to *administer* a much expanded human resource function, incorporating recruitment and training, job evaluation and payments administration, as well as a far-reaching programme in organization development. Sergei received amazingly effective support from the Swedes – past masters in personnel administration – throughout.

Manoeuvring

However positive all this may sound, Sergei still found himself hard-pressed to make his influence continually felt. The trials and tribulations of national economic and social transformation filtered down to the local level, affecting the Kiev region and the factory alike. Sergei therefore had to keep lobbying at a political level, both inside and outside the company, to *manoeuvre* himself and his department into a position of continuing influence.

Generating

Faced with the daunting prospect of simultaneous economic, social and technological change, Sergei had to *generate* a continuing series of experiments, both socially and technically. Amongst innumerable training programmes, he initiated Coverdale training, management by objectives, and the 'managerial grid'. He also worked closely with the Swedes to introduce new, computerized technologies.

Involving

Throughout the three years during which he retained his post, Sergei continually *involved* people at all levels, both within the organization and without. He arranged plant visits for wives and families, as well as visits from folk dancers, poets and writers. He even adopted the UK's Arts Council idea of an 'artist in residence'. Finally, he supplanted the conventional anniversary celebrations of the Russian Revolution with a Kiev-based production festival, not only to celebrate the achievements of his most productive work group but also those of the star performers in the local economy as a whole.

Trading

In the final analysis, and in the spirit of genuine *perestroika*, Sergei was constantly on the lookout, worldwide, for the best possible human resource consultants, those who were able to appreciate the Soviet Union's unique situation. Over time, he became enormously astute at trading off their expertise and involvement against the enjoyment and experience he could offer them of living and working in the Soviet Union during this unique period of development.

Conclusion

As we can see, there is much more to human resource management than meets the conventional eye. To become a successful personnel manager (learning) involves you in stretching yourself all the way from instinctive reactions to people to imagining such people being transformed. To perpetuate that success (innovation) involves stretching yourself from such elevated, transformational activity to everyday trading in the personnel market. We now turn from people to money, from human resource to financial management.

Financial Management

Horizontal Roles

Conventionally based accounting and financial management reaches back to double-entry book-keeping in seventeenth-century Italy:

Book-keeping is the systematic recording of business transactions in a manner which enables the financial relationship of the business, with other persons, to be clearly disclosed, and the cumulative effect of the transactions on the financial position of the business itself, to be ascertained. Business transactions comprise the exchange of value, either in the form of money or of goods and services, which are measured and expressed in terms of money.[18]

Subsequent developments of the financial function, often mathematically based, have further extended its rationality. Discounted cash flow, capital budgeting, portfolio analysis and financial model building have added degrees of analytical sophistication to an already conceptually refined discipline. However, in the past few years, a combination of competitive instinct and intellectual wizardry, heightened by the internationalization of markets, has produced a financial revolution.

In the words of Walter Wriston, former head of Citicorp:

The information standard has replaced the gold standard as the basis for international finance. Communications now enable and ensure that money moves anywhere around the globe, in answer to the latest information or misinformation. There now exists a new order, a global marketplace for ideas, money, goods and services that know no boundaries.[19]

Financial managers, therefore, have become information processors, intent on learning and innovating at a speed that exceeds the rate of change in the global marketplace. As such they range all the way from creative financial impresarios to proverbial market traders.

Financial impresario

The fundamentally creative financial role is played by those few people who are able to imagine original large-scale projects, of social and economic benefit. Architects with financial acumen, operating on a grand scale, or music impresarios with lofty imaginations, often occupy such positions. For them money, or finance, is a means to a cultural or social end, as was the case for Bob Geldof with 'Live Aid'. The product they offer, like that of the developer, is systemic rather than specific. For such an impresario, however, such a product is entirely original.

Financial developer

The 'developmentally inclined' property magnate, venture capitalist or banker to the Third World, sees finance as a means of enhancing the productive potential of individual people and things, or of whole communities and environments. Such people apply their financial acumen to the integrated development of physical, economic or human potential. For them capital, as part of a much greater whole, is a means to a recognized social end.

Financial controller

The financial controller, conventionally trained as a chartered accountant, is the commonly depicted financial manager who plans, allocates and controls the flow of money within a part or the whole of an organization. His or her function is to serve whatever happens to be the declared purpose of a particular line of business, channelling the financial flows efficiently.

Financial entrepreneur

Entrepreneurs – as the proverbial wheeler–dealers – are interested in manipulating the sources and uses of funds to their own personal and business advantage. Unlike financial controllers, who take a detached interest in the company accounts, entrepreneurs see the cash flows as a direct extension of themselves and their business relationships. As such they personalize and customize financial 'packages'.

Financial planner

In today's sophisticated and turbulent financial world, financial planners are increasingly educated, research-oriented and professionally based. As such they not only adapt existing financial instruments to particular organizational purposes, but also create new instruments, such as 'junk bonds' and 'swaps'. Unlike the more rigid planners of old they need to be eminently flexible to take account of multiple exigencies, operating, therefore, more as consultants than as bureaucrats.

Financial book-keeper/accountant

The straightforward book-keeper or accountant, who is more of a craftsman than a manager or a professional, takes care of the day-to-day administration of the books. Such people are concerned with ways and means of making the accounting activities neat and tidy, and the outcomes of such activities of benefit to individuals for whom these craftspeople genuinely care.

Financial trader

Market traders, or their equivalent, are the proverbial fast operators who seldom lift themselves above the immediacy of the financial fray. Their aptitude lies in their speed of response and in their knowledge of the particular items being traded, be they tobacco or pork bellies. Finance, for them, is intertwined with a particular commodity, rather than being something abstracted from physical reality.

Vertical Roles: Financial Learning and Innovation

Learning – the upward movement

Learning, in the financial arena, begins with trading – in stocks, options, or even stamps or coins. It is that reactive instinct,[20] rooted in the physical senses, that sets the learning process. Only thereafter should the learner–financier be exposed to the most tangible accounting skill, involving the recording of transactions through basic book-keeping.[21] Subsequently the more intellectually founded financial disciplines such as cash flow forecasting and discounted cash flows[22] have their place. Once this combination of instinctive and intellectually based knowledge has been acquired, then the budding financial manager should have the opportunity to mould together a set of financial accounts.[23]

Having got his or her hands dirty, as it were, the learner should then be involved in analysis and interpretation of financial statements.[24] This is the precondition for the next stage of a more fundamental appreciation of the underlying needs and trends that the figures reveal.[25]

Ultimately, the learner–financier should begin to be able to imagine the transformation of an organization's financial future.[26]

Innovation – the downward movement

The financial impresario is able to transform the financial structure of an organization, thereby creating a new business entity. Having done this he or she should be able to develop new business in accordance with the transformed capacities and subsequently identify trends. The resulting business, as a whole, would then need to be controlled tightly, with budgets set, actual versus desirable performance compared, and corrective actions specified.

Subsequently, and continually, situations would need to be exploited to the business' advantage, manoeuvring the company cash flows astutely. Thereafter, in experimental vein, alternative sources and uses of money would need to be generated, making extensive usage of financial modelling and flexible financial instruments.

It is also important to involve people through stock options and also through employee reports that enable staff to participate in the company's financial affairs. Finally, and inevitably, active and on-going trading in the market is required to keep the money turning over fast (see figure 8.4).

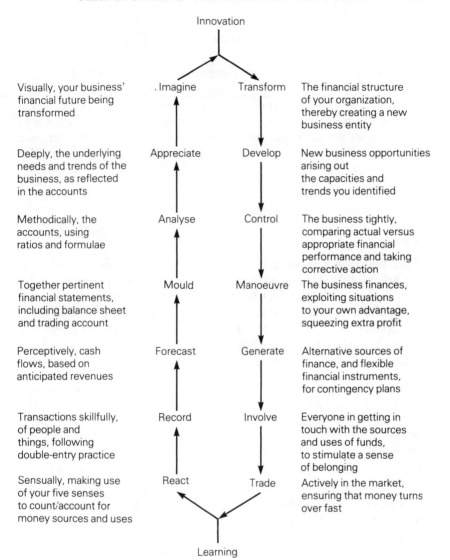

Figure 8.4 Financial learning and innovation.

Jock Henderson: Management Controller

Jock was recently installed as management controller for the largest subsidiary of a diversified financial services group, based in Edinburgh. As a canny Scot, trained as a chartered accountant, Jock was eager to take up the post. At the same time, as he had been running his own small business in Singapore for the past eight years, he knew that it would take him some time to get used to this new position, back in his home country – and working for someone else.

Acquiring Knowledge of Financial Management

Reacting

When Jock took over, the Edinburgh subsidiary was in a pretty poor state. His brief was therefore to work with the new managing director to put the company back on its feet. Jock felt that it would take him a good six months to appraise the situation as it was. In fact, having spent the first week poring over balance sheets and profit-and-loss accounts, he decided to go out into the field, accompanying the insurance salesmen on their rounds. After a month of this, he felt that he was almost, but not quite, able to identify the problem. His gut *reactions* were still tentatively based. While he cut 20 per cent off the expense budgets, as a gesture of stringency, he wasn't quite sure why he was doing it.

Responding

Jock decided to get 'closer to his customers'; that is, the sales force on the one hand and the office administration on the other. In effect, he took control of the day-to-day book-keeping, so that by duly recording all transactions himself, he could get a real feel for what was coming and going. In the process, he also engaged himself in endless discussions with clerical and sales staff. The finance office couldn't understand why their boss was taking so much time and trouble to *respond* to people – this wasn't how they expected a finance man to act!

Forecasting

After three months of this mundane activity, Jock felt that he had a real feeling for the whole operation, so much as that he could *forecast* anticipated revenues and expenditures, for the year, on the basis of current trends: he anticipated a loss of £100,000 in the forthcoming financial year.

Moulding

Jock then proceeded to *mould* together a set of financial statements based on a break-even situation. He enlisted the help of the company's IT specialist, Jeannie Clark, who was familiar with all the financial packages on the market. Surprisingly in his eight-year lay-off from mainstream accounting, Jock had forgotten how to prepare these statements himself. He was amazed to find that the new packages enabled him to put a set of accounts together without more than a smattering of specialist financial knowledge.

Analysing

With Jeannie's continuing assistance, he was now able to *analyse* the company's financial situation quite precisely, clearly separating out fixed from variable costs, and 'people' costs from the costs of physical things.

Interpreting

However, he soon realized that these analyses were too sterile and difficult to *interpret* without a better understanding of trends in the industry at large. Therefore, over the next couple of months, he attended three different seminars on the financial services industry. He also made it his business to meet the most erudite academics and consultants in the field, and to study the most up-to-date market research reports. Needless to say, he also had many long discussions with senior management in the subsidiary, and within closely connected institutions in the group. Eight months after he had joined the company, Jock finally felt that he was really beginning to appreciate what was going on – the figures were merely the symptoms of a deeper underlying problem.

Imagining

In his mind's eye, Jock began to *imagine* a (profitably) transformed set of accounts, based on a very different operation. It was not a picture of a slimmed-down administration: on the contrary, he foresaw a group of professional salesmen carrying a much widened portfolio of financial services. In financial terms, therefore, risks would be spread over a much wider range of activities. At the same time, Margaret Thatcher's vision of a shareholders' democracy would be reflected in the company's *avant garde* style and ethos.

Applying Financial Knowledge

Transforming

In effect, Jock envisaged a complete *transformation* of the business. They were now to be in the business of 'Composite Financial Services', with one aspect complementing, or reinforcing, another. He even designed a new logo, and a colour scheme for the modernized offices – all carefully costed into his budget. At the same time, recalling some of the knowledge he had gained as a trainee accountant, Jock restructured the company's short-term investments, both to secure a better return and to improve the company's image with its bankers.

Developing

Jock and his managing director were now able to identify, and *develop*, a wide range of new business opportunities, that had significant financial implications. In the short term, of course, the drain on cash was greater than the inflow of revenue, but this situation reversed itself within only six months.

Controlling

Naturally, it fell to Jock to *control* the flow of finances very tightly. Unlike the development time span, which stretched between six months and two years, financial control was conducted on a monthly basis. In fact, the new computer software that they had recently installed enabled them to monitor the precise cash flows in and out of the business at weekly intervals.

Manoeuvring

Control was a passive, depersonalized activity, but Jock was sometimes called upon to deliberately *manoeuvre* the flow of finances to accommodate the interests of the group as a whole, from the vantage point of quoted share price and tax liability. Like most other quoted companies of the day, the earnings per share had to be carefully watched, albeit legitimately, to minimize the risk of an attempted takeover.

Generating

Whereas such manoeuvring called upon Jock's somewhat devious 'creative accounting' abilities, his ability to tap alternative sources of funds was very much more in the intellectual mainstream! During the first two years of the appointment, he lived up to his reputation by *generating* all kinds of schemes for raising finance at comparatively low cost. This very much helped the company to enter into profitable new ventures without incurring too heavy a financial drain.

Involving

Jock proved to be very successful in his ability to get on with people. It was difficult at first, as established staff were suspicious of an obviously meddlesome newcomer, but he won them over (sometimes by going to such extremes as wearing his kilt – and even playing the bagpipes – in the office!). Later on, he took great care to *involve* the 100-strong sales force and administration staff in an understanding of where the cash came from and went to. Finally, after two years, he received the MD's approval to introduce a profit-sharing scheme.

Trading

One of the reasons why Jock was able to introduce this scheme, after two years, is that the company had now grown to be very profitable. This was partly due to the new business strategy, and partly due to Jock's acumen in *trading* on the stock market. He had secured the MD's permission to invest 10 per cent of the subsidiary's profits, every year, and had managed to secure a fourfold return on each occasion. No-one was surprised, therefore, when it was announced that Jock was to take over as financial controller for the group as a whole, after two and a half years.

Conclusion

Interestingly, then, finance can also be viewed as a process of learning and innovation. We now turn from these specialist disciplines to the generalist disiplines.

Notes

1 P. Kotler, *Marketing Management* (Prentice Hall, Englewood Cliffs, NJ, 1968).
2 H. Murray, Markets and marketing (unpublished paper, 1986).
3 T. Peters and N. Austin, *A Passion for Excellence* (Collins, London, 1985).
4 H. Turner, *The Gentle Art of Sales* (Fontana, London, 1985).
5 J. O'Shaugnessy, *Competitive Marketing* (Allen & Unwin, London, 1983).
6 H. Goldman, *How to Win Customers* (Pan, London, 1978).
7 Kotler, *Marketing Management*.

8 E. de Bono, *Opportunities* (Penguin, London, 1983).

9 T. Levitt, *The Marketing Imagination* (McGraw-Hill, New York, 1978).

10 W. Bennis, *Changing Organisations* (McGraw-Hill, New York, 1968).

11 M. McCormack, *What They Don't Teach You at Harvard Business School* (Fontana, London, 1987).

12 M. Kay Ash, *On People Management* (Pan, London, 1984).

13 R. Revans, *Action Learning* (Blond Briggs, London, 1980).

14 A. Jay, *Management and Machiavelli* (Penguin, London, 1974).

15 P. Torrington, *Personnel Management* (Irwin, London, 1978).

16 F. Herzberg, *Work and the Nature of Man* (McGraw-Hill, New York, 1964).

17 A. Maslow, *Motivation and Personality* (Harper & Row, London, 1964).

18 W. Biggs et al., *Modern Accounting* (Spicer & Pegler, 1954).

19 A. Hamilton, *The Financial Revolution* (Unwin Hyman, London, 1986).

20 R. Heller, *The Naked Investor* (Hodder & Stoughton, London, 1968).

21 S. Sims, *The Affairs of Polonius* (Kogan Page, London, 1967).

22 Hamilton, *The Financial Revolution*.

23 J. Gillies, *Moneylove* (Warner, Los Angeles, 1978).

24 T. Farmer, *Making Sense of Company Reports* (Pitman, London, 1976).

25 F. Wilken, *The Liberation of Capital* (Heinemann, London, 1983).

26 N. Hill, *Think and Grow Rich* (Wilshire, New York, 1958).

9

Rediscovering the Core of Business: Strategy, Structure, Systems

Introduction

We now consider operations, organizational and strategic management from a learning/innovation perspective. Whereas organizational behaviour and corporate strategy are conventionally recognized as generalist in nature, operations or technology management – incorporating information technology – is increasingly becoming so. In fact the most substantive thinking on organizational learning is now coming from that operational quarter.

Operations and Information Management

Horizontal Roles

Conventional and analytically based approaches to production or operations management have been both rationally and mathematically based. Ray Wild, one of the best known of the traditional authorities on the subject in the UK, describes an operating system as 'a configuration of resources combined for the provision of goods or services'.[1] Within such a system, he says, physical inputs, outputs and conversion processes will normally predominate.

In more recent years, particularly with the advent of information technology, a fundamentally different approach to operations management has emerged. Three professors at HBS, where this learning-oriented approach has gained pre-eminence, have put their case succinctly:

Our task today is to incorporate particular new technologies and heightened product variety into high volume manufacturing systems and to do so without the luxury of long lead times. What is therefore needed is a view of production as an enterprise of unlimited potential, an enterprise in which current arrangements are but the starting point for continuous organisational learning.[2]

It is this perspective, adopted by Professors Abernathy, Clark and Kantrow, that we shall be espousing here. Starting with the different roles in the learning spectrum we range from the technological innovator, at one end, to the production operator at the other.

Technological innovator

The technological innovator, outside of conventionally based research and development, can invent systems and processes, as yet unforeseen, usually by extending the current horizons of information technology. Working in close contact with research and development such inventive people, albeit few and far between, can transform entire operations to conform to an image that they have of how things should be. Henry Ford, with his introduction of the assembly line, was a classic case in point. The image that he was obsessed by, and felt compelled to transform, was that of farm hands being physically consumed by the brute force of manual labour.

Information architect

The information architect will see potential for networking across the most disparate of places, and develop such potential into an integrated systems architecture. Through their sensitivity for harmony such architects will take account of underlying operational needs, as opposed to manifest wants, and for interdependent requirements, as opposed to independent ones. The information architect, drawing off the innovator's original inspiration, will then provide a context for the fulfilment of these operational needs through the design of interacting human and machine intelligences.

Operations manager

Operations managers take responsibility for planning, organizing and controlling the production and distribution of goods and services. In so doing they lay emphasis upon the analytical aspects of management, including the scheduling of operations, the control of inventories, the coordination of transportation and the monitoring of costs. Their overall aim is to establish a cost-effective operation, and to shield the operation from turbulence in the environment. In that capacity they are aided by the systems analysts who structure the flow of information to correspond with these operational demands.

Operational strategist

Operational strategists are more entrepreneurial in their approach than their analytical counterparts. Their primary focus is on energizing the technological innovators, the information architects and the systems analysts to come up with designs and processes that will give the company a competitive edge in the marketplace. To that extent they are always looking for ways and means of customizing the operation, including manufacturing and distribution, to suit an individual or institutional purchaser. Moreover, in today's increasingly competitive environments, they are ever more engaged in forging strategic alliances, to share operational costs and market risks.

Technological forecaster

Technological forecasters feed the innovators and information architects with information that leads them to adapt their product or service to different geographical, demographic, cultural or social contexts. In other words, they play a consultancy role, based upon their expert knowledge of a particular product or service, and of the changing environment in which it is set. They enable the organization to learn faster than the rate of change. Finally, because of their love of variety and mental stimulus, such technological forecasters regularly shift their focus from one product or process base to another.

Quality supervisor

With the renewed focus on 'total quality management' in major companies today, the need arises for quality managers who 'care' for the product and people with whom they are involved. This quality orientation places the emphasis on craftsmanship and on service. Like their counterparts, the customer services managers, they therefore 'feel' more than they think or do.

Production operator

The 'shopfloor' operator – whether in Ohio, Oldham or Osaka – is physically engaged in producing or distributing 'commodities', be they MacDonald's hamburgers, Wedgwood tea sets or silicon chips. The object is to 'get them out the door' – fast and furious. What counts, at the end of the day, is throughput. The determinants of operational success or failure are the operators' stamina, pacing and dexterity. In fact such physical activity, today, is being increasingly automated.

Vertical Functions: Operational Learning and Innovation

Operational learning – the upward function

Operational learning begins on 'the shop floor' or in whatever its equivalent happens to be in a non-manufacturing environment, be it in a dealing room or in a district sales office. Reacting, through your five senses, to the rhythm and pace, the glare and odour, the force and weight of the physical activities and environment,[3] is the individual and managerial starting point for operational learning. It is for this reason that the traditionally oriented businessman gets his son to start his management career in the proverbial 'packing room'.

Starting at the bottom, physically, is often associated with such a bottom-up approach, socially. In other words, by working alongside the packers, within the firm, or with everyday customers, the traditional learner–manager is obliged to respond to people's mundane needs. For the Japanese,[4] who generally favour this bottom-up approach to management development, quality circles – for example – are formed around the basic operations, both physical and social, of the company. This physical and social appreciation precedes intellectual acumen in the learning hierarchy.

The capacity to adapt, mentally to feed back from the environment, is embodied in the flexible manufacturing systems being built into modern production facilities.[5] Adpative information systems are enhancing individual and managerial flexibility.

Moreover, in recent years, innumerable strategic alliances have been forged to enhance not only flexibility but also technology-led competitiveness,[6] whereby consortium participants learn from one another – faster than the competition.

Such learning is further accelerated when analytical ability is acquired to map out the complete 'management information system'[7] underlying the company's physical operation. Then, over this information system, a new breed of operational manager builds an 'information architecture' that connects the individual, the operation and the learning process:

Information technology makes its contribution to the product, but it also reflects back on the system of activities to which it is related. Information technology not only produces action but also produces a voice that symbolically renders events, objects and processes audible, knowledgeable and shareable in a new way.[8]

Finally, the capacity to imagine the complete transformation of an enterprise from mass to information[9] is rare indeed, but is a necessary precondition for technological innovation in many operational environments today.

Marie Citroen: Information Manager

Marie had recently been promoted from systems analyst, in the large, up-market Grenoble dress factory in which she worked, to the new post of Operations Manager. Over the course of the past five years, the company had been transformed from a low-tech, family owned business into a high-tech public company, employing over 2000 people. Marie's post was a new one, combining production coordination with information management.

Acquiring Knowledge of Operations and Information Management

Reacting

As a cerebral sort of person, Marie initially made a point of trying to cast aside her preconceptions, and place herself physically in the factory environment. In effect, she became a seamstress for six weeks, getting to experience the work and the physical environment at first hand. At first she *reacted* adversely to the relentless pressure of work, and also to the bawdy language of shopfloor conversations – she had to learn to become less middle class, and to overcome some of her physical and social inhibitions.

Responding

Surprisingly, after a month of this painful 'unlearning', Marie began to enjoy herself, at least some of the time, *responding* to the women's earthy sense of humour and, for the first time in her life, cracking 'dirty jokes' amongst her friends. She particularly took to one group of workers, from a neighbouring rural area, who were extremely dedicated to their work. She took them more and more under her wing, to the extent of inviting them to a housewarming party when her six-week stint was over. And in the process, she learnt a great deal about the 'craft' of dressmaking, which still coexisted with the modern mass production set-up.

Adapting

Two months into the job, then, Marie began seriously to address the problem of production control, now committed to the idea of combining efficiency and effectiveness with a humane working environment. Armed with the latest texts on operations management, just in time systems, and Japanese-style quality circles, she set out to relate these up-to-date management techniques to her immediate experience of the ladies on the shop floor; using her considerable intellectual prowess to map out a scheme for a flexible manufacturing system that took account of both technical and human factors. She was also aware of the need to *adapt* production to an increasingly up-market, individualistic and designer-led clientele.

Forging

Alongside such manufacturing arrangements, an ever greater need arose for integration between the company's production and marketing departments, and also between the company and its suppliers. The daunting prospect of *forging* such alliances convinced her to attend a three-day course on 'Self Assertiveness', run by a local business school.

Analysing

With subsequently heightened self-confidence, and due familiarity with the practical situation, Marie and her IT group undertook a full-scale systems *analysis* of the socio-technical requirements of a flexibly based manufacturing system. Halfway through the exercise, and needing to top up her state-of-the-art knowledge, she persuaded the firm to sponsor her on an educational visit to Japan, where she met Yonedi Masuda, and the US, where she met Shoshana Zuboff – both of whom she found equally inspiring.

Building

Marie and her team spent the next six months *building* up a new information architecture. At the same time, Olivier Gerard, her very stoic deputy, kept the existing production operation on course. Marie was intent on building a genuine learning organization into her design, and therefore drew her favourite gang of workers into the overall development: one worker in particular was selected to attend evening classes on computer programming, and was subsequently appointed as project assistant.

Imagining

Towards the end of her six months of development work, Marie was able to *imagine* the total transformation of her production base from a materially based operation to one based on information. To that end, she envisaged involving the workforce in a massive educational exercise, both technologically and cognitively oriented. In fact she brought out Masuda and Zuboff as high-level consultants, and also involved some livewires from the local *polytechnique*.

Applying Knowledge of Information and Operations Management

Envisioning

One year into her new job, Marie was able to present a full-scale simulation of the new system in operation, to both management and workers. Using a combination of audiovisual techniques and an appropriate visualization exercise, she got them to *envision* their future. The finance director was sceptical (in view of the massive investment required), but the MD and the workforce were very enthusiastic – they had, of course, been involved all along.

Developing

One of the project keynotes was the *development* of a learning community, which Marie had already piloted through her gang of seamstresses, led by her protégé. That gang of four, together with a further three workers, came to play a very important part in creating the simulation and, in the process, learnt a great deal, not only about computer hardware and software, but also about influencing skills in management.

Structuring

Having got the go-ahead from the MD, and with the blessing of the workforce, Marie and her small group of systems analysts formed a larger project group, taking in representatives from around the company. Over the course of the next three months, they put together a detailed systems *structure* and financial specification, which in turn formed the basis of the factory reorganization plan, which was devised over the subsequent three months.

Competing

At this point, Marie turned her attention outward, sitting down with the marketing personnel and the MD to devise prospectively *competitive* strategies. Since the whole idea was to reposition the company, strategically, so that buyers not only in France but also worldwide would be newly attracted to their adaptable production schedule and individualized designs, market-based learning was just as important as internally focused organizational learning.

Generating

To that end, Marie invited some of the leading buyers, from all over Europe, America and Japan, to watch the simulated production system at work. The buyers were also able to simulate different alternatives for themselves, covering both scheduling and design. By the end of the day, the buyers were buzzing with ideas that they had *generated*, and that Marie might incorporate in the new system.

Involving

Six months later, when the new system was actually up and running, Marie invited the same buyers to visit the reorganized factory to see how their ideas had been put into effect – they were thrilled, and orders inevitably followed. In the process of installing the new hardware and software, not to mention the new plant itself, Marie had *involved* the workforce (particularly the gang of four) at every step of the way.

Producing

Two years to the day after Marie had been appointed, the new system was operational. Inevitable teething troubles were soon overcome. Marie was thrilled to see the first items coming off the new line: she couldn't help thinking back to her time as a seamstress on the old factory floor, in a mass production system that had now been supplanted by an automated and 'informated' *production* system.

Operational innovation – the downward function

The vision of an information-centred, knowledge-based, learning organization forms the starting point for operational innovation. The context in which it is set is that of a learning community of mutually evolving intelligences: 'The flow of value adding knowledge helps legitimate the organisation as a learning community.'[10] Moreover, this learning community extends beyond an organization's own boundaries to incorporate closely connected stakeholders.

Such a diversified community, stretching out from an inner, visionary core in concentric circles, will be integrated through a tightly structured management information system. Such information should enable it to compete via a technology and information-led strategy, enabling it to customize its offerings.

Similarly, 'economies of scope' are supplanting pure economies of scale: 'Programmable automation permits an automated machine to perform a range of tasks. This permits a single range of equipment to produce a variety of products, creating flexibility.'[11] Learning and variety is generated.

Quality control of such a diverse set of offerings is facilitated by the involvement of people at each stage of the operation, and between each of these stages. Here, again, the Japanese have scored with the communal work environment that they have created in their large companies. Finally, economies of scale and scope, through which products and services are produced on both a flexible basis and on a large scale, are combined (see figure 9.1).

Conclusion

The fields of operational and information management are becoming increasingly intertwined as the knowledge-based organization

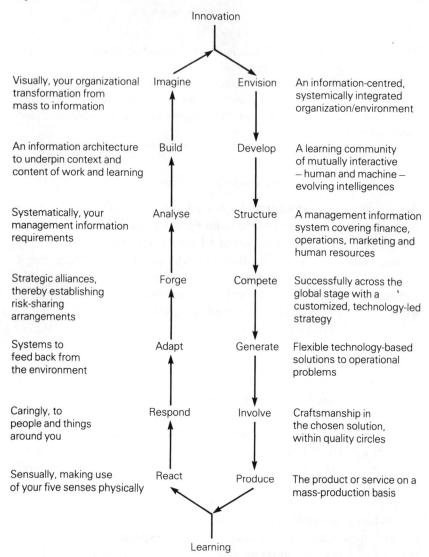

Figure 9.1   Operational learning and innovation.

becomes the norm rather than the exception in developed economies. Also, and as a direct result, the technology of learning and the learning community are becoming ever more closely integrated as informational and social architectures respectively. We now turn to the management of organizations to continue our journey.

Management of Organizations

The Horizontal Roles

Conventionally based organizational behaviour is rooted in the administrative sciences that reached their heyday in the early part of this century:

We can distinguish two main lines of development in traditional organisational theory. The first, deriving from the work of Taylor, focusses upon the basic physical activities involved in production and is typified by time and methods study. The second, of which the works of Gulick and Urwick provide good examples, is more concerned with the grand organisational problems of departmental division of work.[12]

Contemporary developments in management and organization theory draw more on the behavioural sciences than the administrative ones. In addition, unlike the traditional approach, which relies on social engineering, the contemporary approach draws more on what might be termed 'social ecology'. In the words of the Dutchman Bernard Lievegoed, one of the leading thinkers in this area:

The manager will have to acquire two sorts of knowledge – insight into the development of the human being during the course of life, so that he can include his development in all his plans; understanding of the development of social structures, of commercial organisations in particular and of society in general.[13]

Whereas, then – at the two ends of the learning and innovation spectrum – the organizational innovator will need to be familiar with these underlying philosophies of organization and management, the action manager will be inclined to 'shoot from the hip', regardless of any organizational or management theory.

Organizational innovator

The organizational, or social innovator is that rare breed of a person who creates original organizational forms, as unique blends of traditionally based cultures and modern-day technologies. Such innovators need to take due account of the prevailing myths and rituals within the organization and its cultural environment, and envision structures and processes that can both accommodate and transform them. Their point of focus, duly aligned with that of the business visionary and the technological innovator, is upon co-creation within and between institutions and cultures.

Organization developer

The organization developer's role is to recognize and to harness the potential of individuals, groups and departments, both within and across the boundaries of the core organization. Such an enabler of individual and organization development needs to work hand in hand with the 'information' and 'corporate' architects to ensure that evolving strategies, structures and processes are attuned with one another. He or she has a particular interest in co-operative arrangements between individuals, groups and organizations engaged in joint ventures.

Executive officer

The role of the executive – or analytical manager – is to plan, organize, direct and control the activities of a business function, a business division, or of the organization as a whole. Moreover, his or her activity needs to be coordinated with that of fellow executives. Such executives, therefore, are the most directly involved of all the roles in 'managing people' in the conventional sense; that is, in coordinating their activities. In fact, most management texts assume that such an analytically based role is the only valid one in organizational behaviour.

Intrapreneur

The 'intrapreneur', a role only created in the late 1970s, is an entrepreneur operating within an existing organization. Alternatively designated as a 'champion', a 'winner' or even a 'new venturer', such a wilful operator links up with the business strategist, the sales manager, and the wheeler–dealer financier, as a kindred competitive spirit. In an era of prolific buy-outs, mergers and acquisitions, such acquisitive and opportunistic characters are much in demand. In an organizational context, however, his or her role is to head up an intrapreneurial team rather than to operate as maverick individual.

Agent of change

The agent of change operates on the organizational periphery, rather than in the core, adapting to changes in the physical, economic, technological or social environment. Linking up with the futuristic planners, the product managers and the information technologists, they head up project groups concerned with implementing techno- logical and organizational change. Their managerial concerns are specific rather than general, tactical rather than strategic, and mentally rather than emotionally or behaviourally stretching.

Animateurs

Animateurs, conventionally operating in sales and customer service, on the shop floor or in social service, care for people as individuals and in small groups, rather than across the organizational board. Their world is concrete rather than abstract, filled with warm feelings rather than cool thoughts or racey actions. They are the glue that holds the organization together, working with the business animateurs and with customer services to keep people, within and without, happy.

Expeditor

Tom Peters, with his now oft-quoted expression 'managing by walking about', introduced the 'action man' into the organizational scene. Whereas market traders, sharply exhibiting all five senses, have long been a recognized part of the entrepreneurial business establishment, it is only recently that an organizational equivalent has entered the scene. As someone whose approach is that of 'ready, fire, aim', he or she blends very well with seasoned trader, or with the hardy expeditor.

The Vertical Roles: Organizational Learning and Innovation

Management and organizational learning – the upward movement

Learning begins, for you as a manager, when you make the kind of contact with people and things that Tom Peters advocates in his plea for us to go 'back to basics'. This kind of immediate contact with people, within the company and without, is epitomized by his now renowned MBWA – management by walking about.[14] For Peters, management must touch, feel and taste its customers, its suppliers, its people and its product. Only then will it be able to react fast enough to be able to 'thrive on chaos'.

Similarly, in calling for us to 'listen naively', to pay attention to people's needs, to be zestful and enthusiastic, Peters is inviting us to respond immediately and spontaneously to the people with whom we work.[15] Furthermore, through our bias for action and our urge for experimentation, we should be continually adapting to a changing environment. In that respect he is at one with Charles Handy, who argues that 'discontinuous change is the only way forward from a tramlined society.'[16]

To react, respond and adapt is not enough, though, if we are to return to Peters' business basics. All of that has to be married up with the desire to win that is ingrained within the 'intrapreneuring'[17] that is now seen to be such a necessary part of corporate life.

At this point we complete the journey back to basics, and managerial and organizational learning ensues at a level of further sophistication, less instinctual and more analytical. You are now called upon to study, methodically, the structures and processes of management and organization.[18] Having married up instinct and intelligence you then need to exercise insight, unravelling the phases in individual, organizational and commercial evolution.[19] Ultimately, and picturesquely, you need to be able to imagine the tapestry of myth and ritual, story and legend, in corporate culture.[20]

Lovemore Mbigi: Development Manager

Lovemore Mbigi had recently graduated from the University of Zimbabwe, as a sociologist, when he came across David Sutherland, who had set up a correspondence college aimed at black Zimbabweans who were hungry for education. Mbigi quickly saw that the correspondence college was not fulfilling its potential, primarily because Sutherland himself, not being a 'man of the people', failed to properly identify with his personnel. Lovemore joined the company and, after a year, had tripled its turnover by operating from a grass-roots level. He then decided to take up a post with Eastern Highlands Tea Estates, as a personnel manager.

Acquiring Knowledge of Organizational Behaviour

Reacting

The tea estate, in the remote Eastern Highlands, was in a parlous state. Ravaged by the recently ended war of independence, its European managers had barely succeeded in preventing total rack and ruin; and young Mbigi, with a reputation for being a radical, had been brought in as a last resort. He immediately began to rub shoulders with the 3000-strong workforce, travelling around the estate both by jeep and on foot. He had to *react* immediately to workers' demands, some of which were outrageous; and while on the one hand he clamped down on ridiculous demands, on the other he became very much a man of the people, visiting them in the unkempt fields by day, and in their shabby homes by night.

Responding

Having lived in this part of Zimbabwe himself, Mbigi was able to appreciate the local folklore and customs, and while visiting their homes he could take part of his workers' daily rituals and family events. At the same time, he *responded* and indeed acceded, to some of their requests by, for example, inaugurating a home improvement scheme, and encouraging the formation of women's groups and the setting up of play schemes for young children.

Adapting

At the same time, he realized that not all of the answers lay in a reaffirmation of communal traditions. It was important to *adapt* to technological change, and to adopt contemporary managerial practices, as and when appropriate. He had to balance the needs of Black and White, and also tradition and modernity. As a recent university graduate he realized the importance of marrying up the Zimbabwean spirit with Western technique, and so he attended short courses, run by the Zimbabwean Institute of Management, on topics such as 'management by objectives' and 'performance appraisal' techniques.

Desiring

Notwithstanding all this, Mbigi knew that without an understanding of business he was bound to fail. If he was to gain the respect of the established management he would need to demonstrate his commercial prowess. He therefore had a burning *desire* to prove himself, business-wise. As he was too young and inexperienced to do this directly, he decided to attend business school, part time, to do an MBA.

Analysing

Whereas in the longer term the MBA would stand him in good stead, in the short term his studies immediately helped him to *analyse* situations better, particularly with regard to economics and finance; although it took considerable practice before he became at all adept. Yet he realized that his understanding of business and organization, as a whole, was dependent – at least in part – on such analytical prowess.

Unravelling

It was clearly apparent that a static analysis would fall short: he had to place it in the context of the evolution of his country, and also of his particular farm. After six to nine months he began to appreciate, in a way that he had not done before, the significance of the tea estates' particular history. As he began to *unravel* the company's unique development, he began to see that free enterprise and bureaucratic order both had their place in the scheme of things, as did free expression and communal order.

Imagining

Just about a year into the post, and having stemmed the tide of discontent through his display of sincerity and astuteness, he began to picture the kind of tea estate he wished to create. He *imagined*, quite genuinely, a place run by the people for the people, through a combination of aggressive free enterprise and supportive communal activities. It was also to be a place where the material and spiritual worlds converged, in ways that seemed entirely natural to the native Zimbabwean.

Applying Knowledge of Organizational Behaviour

Transforming

Gradually, Mbigi began to *transform* the spirit of the organization, from the bottom up. He shared his vision, of prolific individual enterprise supported by a wide range of communal activities, with the 3000 tea workers. It was most vividly represented in a production festival, which combined a traditional rain-making ceremony with a modern celebration of individual and group productivity.

Enabling

Mbigi first built up a team of youthful black managers, who assumed the front-line roles: he recognized in each of them an entrepreneurial verve combined with an ability to get along with the workers. In turn, these team leaders then put together small groups of tea planters, each of which began to form a shared identity. At the same time, each individual was *enabled* to develop his own work style and group role.

Structuring

In conjunction with the top management team, Mbigi then devised an organization *structure* whereby each individual had his personal territory within the tea plantation, contained within a larger group territory. These group cells formed the basic building blocks for the organization as a whole.

Acquiring

Inevitably, Mbigi had to use his powers of persuasion to *acquire* the kind of power and influence he needed to win over the White establishment. He was helped not only by the MD's generally progressive attitude, but also by his own growing reputation as an agent of change; it was by no means easy – and he had to confront continuing opposition from entrenched interests. As far as the workforce as a whole was concerned, he used a wide variety of financial incentives to raise their overall productivity level.

Generating

He adopted many different approaches to *generating* a positive attitude amongst the management, including sending them on conventional management courses. In that context, he drew heavily on his behavioural science training, and experimentation continued for a good two years before he began to get things right.

Involving

Mbigi's overall approach was to *involve* each worker's body, mind, heart and spirit, by improving working and living conditions, providing schooling and, perhaps most importantly, encouraging singing and dancing, as well as traditional rituals, to raise their collective spirit.

Acting

Mbigi *acted* the role of manager tirelessly and relentlessly, living on the premises and being on call at all hours of the day and night. After three years, and having played a major role in increasing productivity by virtually 1000 per cent, he could no longer sustain the pace he had set himself, and moved over to a consultancy role within the company. He is now trying to spread his particular management gospel around the whole of Zimbabwe.

Organizational innovation – the downward journey

The transformation of the culture of an organization is a precondition for innovation: it applies as much to Siemens or to Sears Roebuck as it does to Soviet Russia. The transformed culture creates new spirit and raises individual and organizational potential. To the extent that such spirit and potential is recognized, and then developed, so a greater degree of technological and social complexity can be accommodated and harnessed. This spirit and potential is effectively channelled once appropriate organizational structures are set in place. However, such potential is only released when the social entrepreneurs championing the organizational innovation have acquired sufficient power and influence (see figure 9.2).

Once the organization has committed itself to the innovation, as a whole, then it is time to experiment, piecemeal, and to generate specific solutions to particular organizational problems that arise. Of course, such solutions will only fit the bill if people are enthusiastically involved in the process. Finally, the innovation will only become visible and tangible, and the spirit materialized, if the manager manages by wandering about, acting with and upon immediacy.

Conclusion

Managerial and organizatioal learning starts with the physical, social, mental and emotional basics – to which Tom Peters so fervently alludes – and ends with the analytical, insightful and imaginative sophistication with which Peters is less familiar. Conversely, social innovation begins with vision and ends with action. In other words, the basics of management need to be interspersed with the complexities of organization if wholesome learning and innovation is

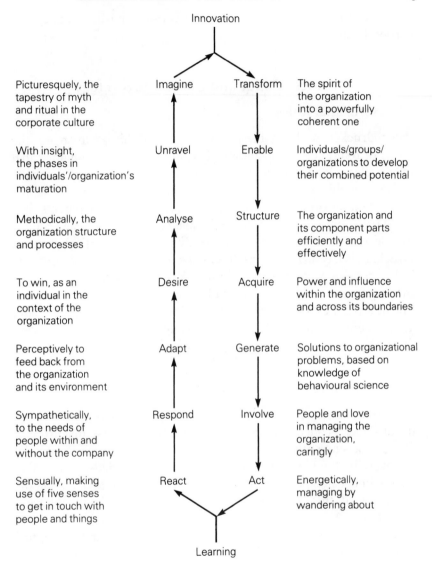

Figure 9.2   Organizational and managerial learning and innovation.

to ensue. Finally, we now move on to consider business policy and corporate strategy.

Business Policy and Corporate Strategy

The Horizontal Roles

Peter Drucker, probably the first management thinker to lay out the terms of reference for business policy, in the 1950s, maintained that only a clear definition of the mission and purpose of the business makes possible clear and realistic business objectives: 'It is the foundation for priorities, strategies, plans, and work assignments. It is the starting point for the design of managerial jobs, and above all, for the design of managerial structures.'[21] In that analytical context, Drucker closely aligned himself with his traditional, and administratively oriented, predecessors – Frederick Taylor, Gulick and Urwick. Some 30 years later, Drucker had changed his tune. In describing 'the new realities' in economics and business, as well as in politics and government, he describes the historically based shift of emphasis from analysis to what he terms perception.

From analysis to perception

The computer is, in one way, the ultimate present-day expression of the analytical, conceptual view of a mechanical universe that arose in the late seventeenth century. It rests, in the final analysis, on the discovery by the philosopher–mathematician Gottfried Liebnitz that all numbers can be expressed 'digitally', that is by 1 and 0, and on the extension of this analysis beyond numbers to logic in Bertrand Russell and Alfred Whitehead's *Principia Mathematica*.

But while it embodies the triumph of the analytical and conceptual model that goes back to Descartes, the computer also forces us to transcend that model. 'Information' itself is indeed analytical and conceptual. But information is the organizing principle behind every biological process. Life, modern biology teaches, is embodied in a 'genetic code' that is programmed information – and biological process is not analytical. Biological phenomena are 'wholes': they are different from the sum of their parts. Information is indeed conceptual, but meaning is not – it is perception.[22] In Drucker's words:

Increasingly, we will balance the conceptual and the perceptual. Contemporary philosophers deal with configurations – with signs and symbols, with patterns, with myth, with language. They deal with perception. Thus the shift from the mechanical to the biological universe will eventually require a new philosophical synthesis.[23]

Similarly, corporate strategy is in need of a new synthesis, combining mechanism and organism, analysis and perception, concept and myth, in the way that Drucker suggests – a horizontal movement from the visionary to the expediter, via the corporate architect and planner.

Corporate visionary

The much sought after visionary, such as a Henry Ford or a Mikhail Gorbachev, is able to envisage an entirely new industry or society, when differently constituted elements existed before. As a result he or she is not only able to tap the spirit of one or more cultures, but also create a product or service that actualizes some deeply hidden need within them. As a strategist, then, such a person envisions a technological, social or economic future and – through others – establishes ways and means of actualizing it.

Corporate architect

The corporate architect establishes a strategic context within which all the business functions, and the associated business entities, can become attuned and aligned with an evolving technology and marketplace. Such a context, through its proactive structures and processes, stimulates departments and functions to grow and develop in line with the enterprise and its environment. It is based on co-operation: the corporate architect therefore constructs a bridge between the inspired visionary and the analytically based strategist.

Corporate planner

The corporate planner, of the more formal variety, is responsible for analysing the strengths and the weaknesses, the opportunities and threats that the company faces, and for formulating a strategy to cater for them. Such a strategy should include policies, long-term plans, budgets and procedures, encompassing all the major business functions.

Competitive strategist

The competitive strategist operates more on 'gut feel' than the analytically based planner. While taking some time out to assess the strengths and weaknesses of his or her competition, such an entrepreneurial operator moves directly into corrective action rather than remaining on the reflective sidelines. Such a strategist then, is more of an opportunist than an analyst, keeping his or her market instincts, and personal connections, finely honed.

Business futurist

The futurist, 'technological' forecaster or scenario builder, is a free spirit living on the edges of corporate life. Such a person will be involved with the very long range aspects of planning, such as environmental or technology assessment, looking 10 or 20 years ahead. As ecologists, sociologists, economists or anthropologists, such planners will be a long way removed from the corridors of power.

Corporate animateur

The animateur is better known in public life than in private enterprise. The role that such community developers play is to involve people in the planning process, not only inviting their participation in devising the plans themselves but also stimulating them to become involved, for its own sake. In the private sector such people may become the 'showmen' to which Tom Peters alludes.

Business expeditor

The role of the expeditor is to make specific plans happen. Such a person is mainly concerned with the immediate, practical implications of the plan rather than with its long-term impact. His or her role is therefore practical and 'political'.

The Vertical Roles: Strategic Learning and Innovation

Strategic learning – the upward movement

Strategic learning begins when managers expose themselves to the business environment, again by wandering about, reacting – with their senses – to the everyday circumstances of customers or suppliers, competitors or collaborators, public officials or people in the community at large.[24] Subsequently learning is enhanced as and when the managers respond to the needs of such people in an immediate and informal manner, enthusiastically incorporating these expectations into an evolving strategy.[25]

Having raised the intensity of their physical and social response, learner–strategists should use the information fed back to them from the surrounding environment to mentally adapt[26] their strategic frame of reference. Then, drawing astutely on all these inputs, they need to openly confront[27] themselves 'warts and all', *vis-à-vis* the competition. Having opened up physically, socially, mentally and emotionally, learner–strategists need to methodically analyse[28] the formal structures and systems they require to plan effectively. In moving from analysis to what Drucker calls 'perception' they will subsequently need to unravel[29] the long-term potential of their business and environment before, ultimately, imagining[30] the part the strategy will play in releasing the spirit of whole nations.

David Hurst: Chief Executive

David Hurst was taken on by Midland Steel of Hamilton, Ontario, in the mid-1980s to turn round their ailing company. While he had a reputation for being something of a bottom-line merchant, he also carried with him a certain mystique. Despite his background as a civil engineer, in some ways he saw himself as a frustrated academic, with fanciful – even esoteric – ideas of his own.

Acquiring Knowledge of Corporate Strategy

Reacting

When Hurst first called on Midland's three plants, spread around the country, he *reacted* so strongly that it made him feel physically ill. The sheer waste of resources was unbelievable: in at least two of the operations, bits of steel were strewn all over the place, the stench from the furnaces pervaded everything, and the workforce looked dishevelled and downcast. In fact, after only three weeks, he felt like giving the whole thing up.

Responding

However, he couldn't help but *respond* to the scale of the human misery that he saw around him, not to mention the total lack of quality and workmanship. His response was not that of a great humanist, but merely one of discomfort when confronted with such degradation. Naturally he took every opportunity to talk to workers about their feelings, while at the same time familiarizing himself with the basic production facilities and methods. As a 'steel man' of some 20 years standing he knew, in his bones, the difference between good product and bad.

Adapting

Hurst gradually built up a dossier on each of the three plants and, despite his initial gut reaction, was increasingly struck by the differences between them. He found the Winnipeg operation to be in far better shape than the other two: the first impressions belied the truth – productivity ratios at Winnipeg met up to the industry average despite obviously low morale. In *adapting* his pespective, Hurst became able to appreciate the contribution of Jack Warren, the veteran plant supervisor at Winnipeg who, while he apparently muddled through, was actually very astute. Sadly, he got no proper backing from senior management.

Confronting

Six months into the post, and after having instigated some essential redundancies in two of the plants, Hurst *confronted* his Board with the facts and figures, as well as his overall impressions. He was not averse to using his power and influence; nor to resigning if he did not have his way. In this flexing and testing of his political muscle, how much clout was he going to have? Despite attempts to play his cards right, particularly before the opinionated company chairman, his candid assessment of the company's competitive strengths and weaknesses was sufficiently combative to invoke a strong reaction.

Analysing

Nevertheless, he effectively got the go-ahead, and set out to assess current systems and procedures, and how they would have to change. As he was primarily an engineer, he took himself on a one-week executive programme on strategic planning, held at York University in Toronto. His financial controller, who was generally a more adept analyst, went with him. Fortunately, Hurst was able to enlist the help of the York faculty, to *analyse* his company's competitive environment and come up with some possible alternative strategies.

Unravelling

In his heart of hearts, though, Hurst returned from the course feeling unhappy. He now had the strategic tools, but they did not seem to have been *unravelled* and applied in true context. In fact, his empathy with the steel business told him that the York faculty's new strategies were somehow inappropriate. Defying the conventional wisdom of the advocated niche marketing, Hurst just knew that a series of acquisitions and strategic alliances, that would make Midland a general, rather than specialist, steelmaker, would be the right way to go.

Imagining

After continuing deliberation, Hurst suddenly realized that the Jack Warren culture at Winnipeg provided the clue: Warren was a classic all-rounder, who combined a feel for the product with an extraordinarily up-to-date knowledge of process technology and market developments in the steel business. Hurst *imagined* a dozen Jack Warrens in the new company, bringing about the best of both worlds – a combination of long-standing steel traditions and the most forward-looking technologies.

Applying Knowledge of Corporate Strategy

Transforming

Hurst began to implant his strategic vision into the company, starting by raising Warren's own awareness of his strategic value to the company as a whole. Over the course of three intensive months, Hurst, Warren and the group finance director worked on a strategic plan that would totally *transform* Midland's operations and marketplace. Converting it into evocative pictures, they began to share their vision with the company as a whole, the objective at this stage being more to inspire people than to inform them – Midland was become the key player in the North American steel industry.

Enabling

This corporate vision could only be realized if the potential of all three plants was fully developed. Therefore task groups were set up in each to recognize prospects for synergy within and across the plants. Similarly, a group was established at Board level to look out for joint ventures of mutual benefit to all parties concerned. Finally, Hurst asked his human resources director to come up with an ambitious organization development programme, involving the whole company. Hurst wanted to create a series of *enabling* activities whereby the company would be developed commercially, technologically and culturally.

Structuring

The work of these task groups led to a conventional set of objectives, plans and procedures. At this point, Midland's finance director came into his own, with his planning *structures*, although he never eclipsed Hurst's broadly and visionary based thrust.

Acquiring

In the course of the next year, Midland *acquired* one major competitor, and forged joint ventures with three other companies, in both Canada and the US, in allied businesses. At this point, Hurst was concerned that the company should exert, and substantially increase, its power and influence in the marketplace.

Transacting

Hurst was also aware that the market for steel products was changing rapidly: in fact, it was breaking up into four or five markets. He therefore had to adapt his operations so that the company could handle various sorts of *transactions*: in commodity-type markets at one extreme, and with the demand for complete systems at the other, with a spectrum of other markets in between.

Involving

Not surprisingly, Hurst had to transform the company's culture not only to reinforce his synergistic intentions but also to accommodate these different marketplaces, each of which required an individual approach. Generally speaking, and often to his short-term cost, Hurst was committed to introducing Japanese-style consultation into the company, albeit with a Western twist. He was particularly influenced by Jan Carlson's approach to *involving* staff, in turning around Scandinavian Air Services: placing the customer at the top of the organizational hierarchy, with front-line service staff ranked next, and company executives way down at the bottom – Hurst found it very difficult to be that humble!

Acting

At the same time, and over the course of the next 18 months, Hurst was continually *acting* the role of manager by wandering about, not only to check whether the new vision was being realized, but also to keep morale high and give praise where praise was due – a supreme and exhausting effort.

Strategic innovation – the downard movement

Strategic innovation begins with an all embracing, all encompassing and all compelling vision of the business' future – one which serves to transform the spirit of the place. That transformed spirit creates potential. Such potential is developed through enabling contexts; that is, through either internal or external contexts that are, qualitatively speaking, growth oriented. That enhanced potential is subsequently channelled through appropriate structures and processes; that is, through effective business policies, objectives, plans and planning systems.

However, structures and systems remain inert until such a time as they are empowered by strategists who have acquired power and influence within the firm, and competitive advantage outside of it. In effect such strategic advantage is relative. It will depend on the particular marketplace in which the strategy is being transacted. Whatever the course planned, though, the strategic posture has to be integrated with the organizational culture, thereby involving people and even love. Finally, and inevitably, the plans have to be activated through the proverbial 'managing by wandering about' (see figure 9.3).

Conclusion

We now have had the chance to review all six of the 'business' disciplines in the context of reflective learning and active innovation, and to outline the transformed nature of each function – further elaboration is up to you. At this point then, we are ready to bring together learning and innovation, in the context of the learning organization.

From one perspective, which I have called 'horizontal', each knowledge area lends itself to a wide range of *learning roles*. As we saw

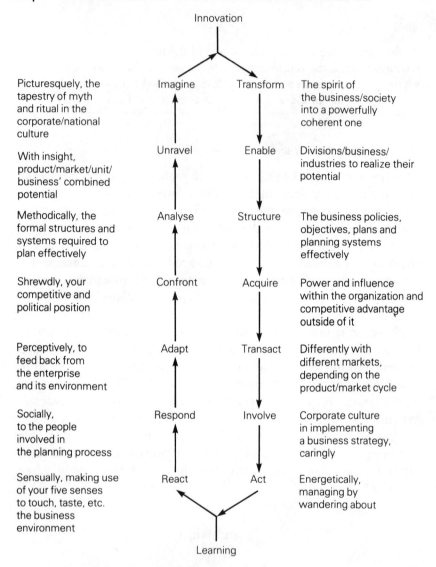

Figure 9.3   Business policy and corporate strategy.

in chapter 5, these roles are preconditioned by your individual learning style. From the other perspective, which I have called 'vertical', each business discipline lends itself to the same wide range of *functions*.

These functions are split into two. The function of learning is introverted and evolutionary, and therefore develops from the bottom up. From a manager's perspective, it involves a cumulative development of your thinking, feeling and behaving. The function of innovation is extraverted and *in*volutionary, and therefore transforms from the top down. From a management perspective, it involves a cumulative transformation of your thoughts, passions and actions. While inner-directed learning is a precondition for innovation, outer-directed innovation is the visible manifestation of what will otherwise remain invisible.

Although the combination of horizontal, upward and downward movements form an apparently neat and sequential structure, life and management never work with such overall consistency. In effect there will be more in the way of hopping and skipping and less in the way of coherent movement. Moreover, the extent to which you will be able to move horizontally and vertically will depend on your personal versatility (introvert) or your organizational and commercial versatility (extrovert).

Finally, there is obviously a direct connection between your preferred role and your functional acumen. In other words, and for example, a technological or social innovator is likely to be adept at envisioning operational or organizational transformations.

We now turn to skill development.

Notes

1 R. Wild, *Operations Management* (John Wiley, New York, 1979).
2 W. Abernathy, R. Clark and T. Kantrow, *The New Industrial Renaissance* (Harvard University Press, Harvard, 1983).
3 S. Zuboff, *In the Age of the Smart Machine* (Heinemann, London, 1988).
4 T. Taishikawa, *Total Quality Control* (Kobunsha, Tokyo, 1984).
5 R. Cohen and J. Zysman, *Manufacturing Matters* (Macmillan, London, 1987).
6 R. Moss Kanter, *When Elephants Learn to Dance* (Harper & Row, New York, 1989).
7 T. Murdick and W. Ross, *Management Information Systems* (John Wiley, New York, 1974).
8 Zuboff, *Age of the Smart Machine*.
9 Y. Masuda, *The Information Society* (Basil Blackwell, Oxford, 1990).
10 Zuboff, *Age of the Smart Machine*.
11 Cohen and Zysman, *Manufacturing Matters*.
12 R. March and H. Simon, *Organisations* (John Wiley, New York, 1958).
13 B. Lievegoed, *The Developing Organisation* (Basil Blackwell, Oxford, 1990).

14 T. Peters and R. Waterman, *In Search of Excellence* (Harper & Row, New York, 1982).
15 T. Peters and N. Austin, *A Passion for Excellence* (Collins, London, 1985).
16 C. Handy, *The Age of Unreason* (Hutchinson, London, 1989).
17 G. Pinchot, *Intrapreneuring* (Harper & Row, New York, 1984).
18 C. Handy, *Understanding Organisations* (Penguin, London, 1978).
19 R. Lessem, *Global Management Principles* (Prentice Hall, Englewood Cliffs, NJ, 1989).
20 H. Owen, *Spirit, Transformation and Development* (Abbott, Virginia, USA, 1987).
21 P. Drucker, *Management: Tasks, Responsibilities, Practices* (Heinemann, London, 1979).
22 P. Drucker, *The New Realities* (Heinemann, London, 1989).
23 Drucker, *New Realities*.
24 J. Harvey Jones, *Making it Happen* (Fontana, London, 1988).
25 T. Deal and A. Kennedy, *Corporate Cultures* (Penguin, London, 1982).
26 J. Quinn, *Managing Strategic Change* (Prentice Hall, Englewood Cliffs, NJ, 1981).
27 M. Porter, *Competitive Strategy* (Macmillan, London, 1982).
28 I. Ansoff, *Corporate Strategy* (McGraw-Hill, New York, 1964).
29 J. Gardner, *Self Renewal* (Harper, New York, 1978).
30 R. Lessem, *The Global Business* (Prentice Hall, Englewood Cliffs, NJ, 1987).

PART IV

Transforming Your Management
Skills

10

From Apprenticeship to Mastery

Introduction

Skill Development

The third set of managerial competencies are the action-oriented skills. There are seven broad groups of managerial skills, each with their own combinations of subskills. The traditionally recognized areas of skill are:

- the organizing skills of the analytical manager
- the directing skills of the action manager
- the social (or 'man' management) skills of the people manager

Newly emergent managerial skills include:

- the learning skills of the manager of change
- the influencing skills of the enterprising manager
- the facilitating skills of the developmental manager
- the creative skills of the innovative manager

In this chapter we shall identify how managerial skills are generally developed, in terms of the cast of skilled characters (the horizontal dimension) and then the process whereby managerial skill is both acquired and implemented (the vertical dimension). The established skills, and subskills, are considered in greater detail in Appendix A, while the emergent ones – including the leadership skills of the developmental and creative managers – are set out in Appendix B.

The Cast of Skilled Characters: the Horizontal Dimension

Like the different managerial selves there are varying approaches to skill acquisition and implementation. These approaches correspond, more or less, to management and learning style. In other words, whereas the developmental manager will aspire towards 'artistry', skillwise, the analytical manager will be more of a pragmatist. It is the innovative manager, meanwhile, who might aim to achieve absolute mastery.

Master

The master–learner is a more familiar figure in the martial arts, or in the classical music tradition, than in business or organizational life. However, noted businessmen and -women have become 'masters' in such arts as salesmanship, negotiation and even managing people. Such mastery involves not only a depth and breadth of experience, but also a combination of self-discipline and self-knowledge relating to the skill in question. Moreover, such masterly operators are invariably unique in their approach to delegating, influencing and team-building – or whatever the particular skill happens to be. Finally, they have the capacity to inspire others through their own skilled example.

Artist

Artist–learners do not possess the degree of originality of the master. They have not completely transcended their own personal limitations through their skill. However, to the extent that their skilled management has become a true art form they are able to interweave personal style and impersonal skill beautifully.

As a result their approach is a highly distinctive blend without being a totally original product. As negotiators, they see potential for mutual gain when everyone else remains bogged down in adversarial relationships. As problem-solvers they see wide-ranging opportunities where others see circumscribing constraints. Finally, they have the capacity to arouse the potential of others because of their combined insight and sensitivity.

Pragmatist

Pragmatic learners acquire skills, step by step, following the example of authoritative others, reading one or more of the extensive range of 'How to . . .' books now on the market, and attending a suitably methodical course of instruction. Such pragmatists cannot separate the acquisition of a skill from its implementation, the two being for them inextricably intertwined. They are not interested in acquiring any originality in their managerial skills but rather in doing something that works, efficiently and effectively. So, for example, their social skills will be considered and considerate rather than instinctive and spontaneous: their approach to creativity will be analytically rather than imaginatively based.

Opportunist

Opportunist learners acquire skills on the hop, as and when they are required. A course or a book on, say, influencing skills, will only be considered relevant in the heat of the moment. At the same time they will not hesitate to 'use people' to the extent that they might be able to learn from their skilled example. However, unlike the pragmatist who will respect a suitably accredited or authoritative individual, the opportunist will only respect he who delivers the goods.

Moreover, such opportunistic learners will readily 'buy in' skills, either in the form of talented people or, nowadays, in the form of expert systems. A skill is a 'commodity' to be bought and sold, just like any other.

Scientist

Managers who approach learning scientifically apply the kind of experimental approach to each task that has been documented by Kolb in the US and Revans in the UK. In other words a learning cycle includes active experimentation (test), concrete experience (audit), reflective observation (survey) and abstract conceptualization (hypothesis). The acquisition and implementation of a skill therefore requires the individual manager to complete the learning cycle, continually, whether in relation to performance appraisal, team-building, or salesmanship. Skill development therefore becomes a primarily intellectual process.

Craftsperson

Learner craftspeople pick up skills on the job, under the guidance of a master craftsman, with whom they can identify emotionally rather than intellectually. In other words they respect skilled operators – whether as a coach or problem-solver, a leader or a negotiator – because they can identify emotionally with them. Because master and learner share the same respect for the craft tradition, they feel they belong to one another. Outside of that social bond, or affinity, the learner craftsperson, as is usually the case with Japanese managers, is unable to acquire and implement skills. Culturally or corporately, alien people, no matter how strong their managerial skills, cannot directly influence such craftspeople.

Actor

Management, for Tom Peters, is showmanship. Actor–learners, in a managerial context, are people who develop skills by physically mimicking skilled people around them. As actors, in this imitative sense, they are close observers of the skilled coach, the expert salesman, or the astute problem-solver, but only from the outside. In other words, they mimic managerial behaviour to a greater extent than managerial thought or feeling. To that extent such 'actors' are the direct opposite of the learner as artist.

In conclusion, whether you aim to develop organizing or directing skills, or facilitating or influencing abilities, you may approach the task from the vantage point of a master or an actor, a pragmatist or an artist. A fully functioning organization, however, would wish to have a complete cast of skilled characters in its midst. We now turn to the process of acquiring and applying managerial skills.

Demetrius Vaclas: Regional Sales Manager

Upon his appointment as sales manager for Apple Computer's southern European region, covering Greece, Portugal, southern Italy and Spain, Demetrius Vaclas knew that while his aptitude as a salesman had got him the post he would now have to become more of a manager. He had been used to doing things himself, together with his close-knit sales team in Greece –

leading by example – but now he had to become more skilful in organizing people, specifically the heads of the 25 distributors in the southern region.

Acquiring Organizing Skills

Reacting

In many ways, Demetrius felt that he was starting from scratch. At first, and in a fairly disorganized fashion, he set out on a 'grand tour' of the 25 distributorships, getting the feel of the various operations, and *reacting* instinctively to the demands of their staff. At the end of this exercise, he had vivid memories of each operation, both in terms of their trade and such things as office decor, sights and smells, and even the local cuisine. But, to be honest, he still felt very much at sea, as did the local sales managers in each of the four countries; and his suggestions for remedial action seemed to be a very random set of gut reactions.

Responding

He knew that this was not good enough, and was tempted to attend a three-day course on 'The Well Organized Manager' – but his instinct told him that this was not yet the right time. Instead he took a closer look at two other colleagues, the Spanish sales manager and his immediate boss, the sales director for the whole of Europe, both of whom seemed to be incredibly well organized – so much so that he found it hard to resist becoming a 'copycat', or even giving up his own self-sufficiency. Despite feelings of inferiority, he began to take detailed tips from his director, Mats Jensen; befriending both him and Eduardo (a Spaniard from the Basque country) in order to find out what really made them tick, and thereby become even better organized! After six months, he was *responding* much more warmly to both men, even to the point of becoming more like each one, especially when it came to self-organization.

Adapting

Demetrius was now able to relate what he had observed to the regional sales set-ups that he had seen in operation. At first he found it difficult to resist mimicking his masters, but he came to appreciate that different situations demanded different organizational approaches. Demetrius found that his chances of even half succeeding depended on his ability to *adapt*.

Exposing

After nine months in the job, and having gained sufficient confidence, Demetrius began to deliberately *expose* himself to unfamiliar situations, calling upon hitherto untapped powers of organization. For example, cutting completely across his personal 'grain', he set up formal board-type meetings for his national sales managers, coolly taking the chair in a way that he would not previously have thought possible. It was as if he had to allow his old, informal and spontaneous self to die, so that a newly depersonalized Demetrius could be born.

Analysing

At this point, exactly one year into the job, Demetrius felt that the time was right to go on a five-day management course. He had to strain his mind to the utmost to take aboard the management concepts – of planning, organizing, directing and control. However, by and large, he was now able to relate theory to practice, to the extent that he could both *analyse himself*, as an organized manager, his overall job, as regional sales manager and – with a real sense of achievement – his whole sales region.

Harmonizing

For the first time, after some 18 months, Demetrius began to feel at home. He was beginning to harmonize his own managerial role, including the organizational abilities required of him, with himself as a person. No longer did he feel that organizing others was somehow 'anti-social'; nor did he fear that delegating to others would cause loss of control. His self-image was beginning to change fundamentally.

Imagining

One of the skills that Demetrius had acquired – from his Italian ski instructor – was that of 'visualization'. He was now able to apply this to his role as a superbly organized manager, creating a self-image in his mind's eye that he would never have recognized a year ago.

Applying Organizing Skills

Envisioning

For the first time, Demetrius was now able to *envision*, for himself, what being a really well organized manager was about, in personal terms. And so he set out to create, over the next year, nothing less than the best organized Apple sales region in the Western hemisphere – dispelling prevailing beliefs about southern European management skills on the way. What's more, he would do it with characteristic southern flair, drawing on his own venerable traditions from Ancient Greece, and from the Greek gods who sat on Mount Olympus, each of whom would now come to make his individual contribution to the whole.

Recognizing

At the same time, he *recognized* that it would not be a simple matter to realize his vision over the time scale that he had set himself. The four nationalities had highly individual characteristics, not easily blended into one homogeneous organization, and their current sales performance fell well below that of the western European region.

Defining

Demetrius built into his managerial role the expectation that he would have to reduce the gap between his people's romantic aspirations and their spasmodic performance; by resurrecting (and duly updating) the principles and practices of the organized, democratic governments of the ancient Greek city–states. He modelled, and thereby *defined*, his own role after that of Apollo – taking a leaf or two out of Charles Handy's contemporary interpretation in *The Gods of Management*.

Committing

In *committing* himself to this plan of action, Demetrius declared his hand at the 1990 International Sales Conference. While his immediate boss respected his intentions, the plan was met with incredulity by many of the other regional managers. That only made him even more determined, and he was able to secure a significant increase in his training budget, to help him along the way.

Exploring

Over the course of the next year, Demetrius *explored* a number of different means to his organizational end: an inspirational video (on a new Apple-bound city–state); some spellbinding new software from Apple's Cupertino operation, as part of a training package; and some training staff, imported from the UK, to run appropriate role play exercises. The role play had the greatest effect; except on the Greeks themselves, who naturally took to the video, and built up their own training modules.

Involving

Needless to say, Demetrius put himself out to *involve* as many of the sales personnel as possible in 'Operation Apollo'; through a judicious mixture of the openness which came naturally to him and the formality which he – as a well organized manager – had now learnt to accommodate alongside informality.

Implementing

Fourteen months after he had declared his initial intentions, Demetrius was ready to *implement* the organizational change throughout the southern region. He created 30 such Apollonian cells, around his distributors; each had their own vision statement, rules and procedures, training modules and induction programme for new sales staff. Six months later, sales had literally doubled throughout the region. The 1991 International Sales Conference was held in Athens, and Demetrius became the star of the show. He was asked to assume responsibility for the whole of Europe, and began to envisage the spread of 'Apollo' throughout the continent, particularly into the emergent territories of Eastern Europe.

Skill Acquisition and Application: the Vertical Dimension

The term 'skill acquisition' is something of a misnomer. A particular course, book or film may stimulate your awareness of 'the conduct of an effective meeting' or of 'team-building skills' but, in isolation, it can have only a minimal effect on your enduring managerial competencies. Skill acquisition, then, is more of a journey than a destination, a learning process rather than a subject of instant recall. Moreover, as can be seen in figure 10.1, skill application is a creative undertaking in its own right.

We now turn to skill acquisition and application in more detail.

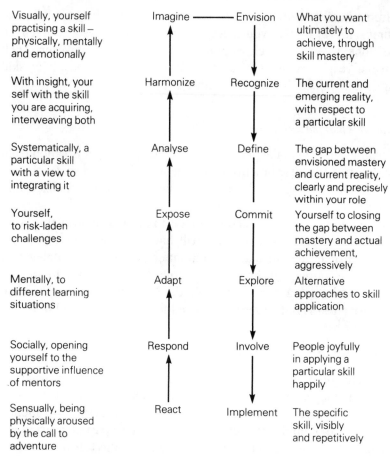

Figure 10.1   Skill development.

Skill Acquisition: Learning

React – the call to adventure

When learning ceases to be an adventure it loses its powerful, primordial appeal. The 'call to adventure' represents the first and physical step towards skill acquisition. Moreover, such a 'call' only arises when learner managers keep themselves on physical alert: sniffing around for what's going on, touching base with the troops, listening to the office grapevine, looking out for trouble, and seeing for themselves who is doing what.

Immediately before and after you go on a 'performance appraisal' course, for example, you need to physically expose yourself to situations in which such appraisal is conducted. However, such 'sensual' exposure is only a start. Without social sensitivity skill acquisition will be frustrated, almost at birth.

Respond – making social connections

Learning can never take place, at least for managers, in isolation from a supportive educator or a protective mentor. Without a social context into which learning can be placed it becomes depersonalized and sterile.

If you fail to respond to people, that is to those who inevitably cross your learning path, your journey will have been in vain – you will remain insular and insulated. Your attempt to acquire delegation skills, for example, will be divorced from the very people to and for whom such delegation is required. Nevertheless, such social responsiveness is not enough. You need to engage in a 'road of trials'.

Adapt – learning from experience

The 'road of trials' involves processes of trial and error, whereby learner–managers adapt to situations in which they find themselves, and then learn from their experiences. This period of mental alertness and of intellectual discovery is so much a part of growing up, managerially. It is the youthful phase built into the learning process before you consolidate in an adult manner. Any task you tackle, therefore, should lend itself to such exploration and adaptation before you commit yourself to a particular line of thought or action.

As a result, for example, you need to seek out and adapt to different social situations before working out your own approach to 'social skills'. Such experimentally based learning will involve a combination of travel, short courses, books and work-related experiences. However, such intellectually based exploration is not enough: you will also need to expose yourself to psychologically laden risk.

Expose yourself to emotional risk

Whatever ideas you pick up, intellectually, you need to have the courage to put both them and yourself to the test. In the process you may become a different person, disassembled and reassembled as a result of the emotional wrangles you have undergone. In fact, in order to significantly enhance your managerial skills in an area which has previously been weak, such a risk-taking process is unavoidable.

For example, in developing your information processing skills – should computer programming be alien to you – you will not only have to be mentally alert, but will also have to risk exposure and ridicule, for, inevitably, many of your fellow learners will speed ahead as you fall by the computer wayside. If you keep at it purposefully, and conquer your fears, then you face the next learning task of fitting the skill into your job, role or organization.

Analyse the skill, systematically

As your newly acquired skill becomes physically, socially and mentally integrated, within yourself, so the need arises to relate it to your job and to your organization. This ability to conceptualize, to analyse the parts and to relate the parts to the whole, as well as to relate theory to practice and practice to theory, serves to integrate your skill.

Analysis is enhanced when you investigate the different elements contained within a skill (subskills), and the way in which a particular subskill, such as 'listening', relates to a whole skill, such as 'facilitating'. Similarly, for example, listening ability in theory becomes integrated in practice when you are habitually called upon to exercise such skill, as part of your overall management role.

Develop insight – penetrating to the source

You may now have integrated a skill within yourself and your organization, without gaining any fundamental insight into its meaning and significance. For example, you may have developed problem-solving skills without much appreciation of their timing and context, particularly within different cultural settings. Such understanding requires depth of individual, organizational and societal insight.

The insight is developed through a capacity to listen, a power to observe, a willingness to be humbled, and an ability and inclination to link like with unlike, actual with potential, both in yourself and through others. It involves seeing meaning and context in all things.

However, even such powers of insight do not necessarily lead you into the realms of pure imagination, the ultimate in skill acquisition.

Imagine – enhancing your originality

True originality, in the process of learning a particular managerial skill, is only displayed when you develop the capacity to imagine yourself exercising that skill in your own unique way. By means of imagining you marry up your uniqueness as an individual manager with the particular skill at hand. Thus, for example, you could imagine yourself inspiring your people through a particular form of sporting imagery that is uniquely your own: metaphors of, say, sailing might be juxtaposed with a particular brand of management, drawn out of your creative imagination to convey a sense of momentum and direction.

In the final analysis, though, the acquisition of skill, *introverted* learning, is only a means to an end, the application of skill, *extraverted* innovation.

Skill Application: Innovation

The full application of managerial skill requires innovation, in its creative and active entirety, in the same way that the complete process of skill acquisition requires learning, in its most complete sense. Such innovation ranges from envisioning what you want to create, through the exercise of a particular skill, to the detailed implementation warranted. The questions you need to address at each point, in the course of applying the skill you have been acquiring, now follow.

Creating your vision

- What is your far-reaching mission in applying the skill?
- How is its application going to change the world around you?
- How will it change your life, work and vocation?
- What universal problem will the exercise of the skill solve?

Recognizing need

- What market or organizational potential will you be realizing?

- How is technology and society evolving so as to fit in with the application of your emergent skill?
- What underlying need will you serve?
- What linkages arise between one skill and another, in fulfilling that need?

Defining the skill

- What definable skill are you applying?
- What subskill components need to be applied?
- How does the application of the subskills fit with the skill as a whole, and the skill as a whole with other skills?
- How is integrity between you the manager, as applying subject, and the skill, as applied object, maintained?

Committing yourself

- What's in it for you personally, in applying the skill?
- What competitive advantage will you gain, internally and externally?
- Who will champion your skilled cause?
- How will you be selling your newly skilled self?

Exploring alternatives

- What are you aiming for, in applying your skill?
- What alternative approaches have you adopted?
- What feedback process have you introduced, for comparing actual with the desired results of exercizing your skill?
- How have you built exploration into the organizational fabric?

Involving people

- How do you effect shared values, whereby people will co-operate with you in your application of a particular skill?
- How do you ensure that whatever skill you apply is accessible to the people with whom you work?
- How do you keep things eminently practical?
- How do you keep people enthusiastic?

Finally, and ultimately, the originally envisaged skill needs to be embodied in a simple, tangible form, in order to inspire effort.

Implementing the skill

- How do you keep your people's energy level from waning, in relation to the skill being implemented?
- What will physically be produced at the end of the day?
- How do you impose a sense of urgency?
- How do you maintain a bias for action?

Now that you have dealt with the acquisition and application of skill as a whole it is time to revisit your managerial self.

PART V

Total Quality

II

Knowing Yourself as a Whole

Introduction

From Excellence to Arete

For managers, the 1980s have been marked by a passion for excellence that has known no bounds. A whole flotilla of American management books have followed in the wake of Tom Peters' search[1] and passion[2] for excellence. For Peters, above all else, excellent companies possessed 'fired-up champions' who had entrepreneurial autonomy, and strongly 'shared values', transmitted through a 'hands on' management style. In addition such companies kept close to the customer, achieved productivity through people, had a bias for action and – above all – kept things simple.

In fact, Europe has been so overwhelmed by this American wave that any managerial identity of its own has almost been washed underfoot. I say 'almost', because it was some ten years prior to the Tom Peters influx that the Pirsig wave swept across Europe. In this instance the wave, though supposedly American in origin, actually came from ancient Greece, notwithstanding some additional influence from the East.

As we recall from chapter 1, in Pirsig's terms, 'The Buddha, the Godhead, resides quite as comfortably in the circuits of a digital computer or the gears of a motorcycle transmission as he does at the top of a mountain'. Moreover, that 'Godhead' is contained in the ancient Greek term 'arete'.

Fifteen years after Pirsig, I took myself off to Crete to uncover, at first hand, his source of inspiration. I was also very aware that the British management philosopher, Professor Charles Handy, had written his own treatise on *The Gods of Management*, drawing purposefully and picturesquely on Greek mythology in his brilliant analysis of corporate cultures. I felt that somewhere in between Peters, Pirsig and Handy – mediated by the originating influence of ancient Greece – I would find Europe's managerial holy grail. The first book I happened to lay my hands on, in a local bookshop in Chania, northeastern Crete, was by the Greek scholar C. M. Bowra, through whom I discovered the term 'arete'.

'Whereas the gods', he said, 'are literally everlasting, a man who had done something really worth doing passes outside time into a timeless arete. The man so remembered was the true man, the essential self who *found his full range and passed outside the changing pattern of his development* into his ultimate reality'.[3]

As we can immediately see, the Greek notion of excellence is very different from its American successor. It is much more inner-directed than Peters' and more transcendental in nature. Let me now pursue the argument, comparing and contrasting European Greece with Tom Peters' America.

From Autonomy to Autarchy

Greece is a region of great variety. Mediterranean and sub-alpine conditions exist within a few miles of each other; fertile plains alternate with wild mountain country. Therefore Greek city–states were normally reasonably self-sufficient, and could enjoy a balanced corporate life. Such self-sufficiency – 'autarkia' or *autarchy*, was an essential part of Greek civilization.

This notion of autarchy is, in fact, not too far removed from Tom Peters' idea of autonomy. Arbitrary government, according to the classical historian Professor Kitto, 'offended the Greek in his very soul'. Were you to ask an ancient Greek what distinguished him from a 'barbarian' he would respond 'The barbarians are slaves; we Hellenes are free men'. In that respect the oriental custom of obedience was, then in Greek and now in American eyes, a similar affront to human dignity.

The Greeks' confidence in humanity, and its scope and possibilities, was such that – with the aid of the heroic outlook – they were able to shake off primitive superstitions and taboos. Indeed, they felt *man to be closest to divinity when he was most completely himself*. The ancient Greek imagination, inflamed by stories of vast undertakings and incomparable heroes, of Gods walking on the Earth as the friends of men, formed a *vision* of a heroic world which they cherished. Since, from an early age, these stories were the staple diet of Greek education they encouraged a conception of manhood in which *personal worth* held pride of place, reinforcing an ideal already favoured by other circumstances. The smallness and self-sufficiency of city–states promoted a degree of independence which was impossible in the centralized theocracies of Egypt and Asia.

The *individualism* which conditions imposed upon Greek life suited its inherited cult of *heroic manhood*, and endured in historical times as one of the most striking elements in its beliefs and behaviour. The essence of the heroic outlook is *the pursuit of honour through action*. The great man is he who, being endowed with superior qualities of body and mind, uses them to the utmost and wins the adulation of his fellows because he spares no effort and shirks no risk in his desire to *make the most* of his gifts and to *surpass* other men in his exercise of them.

At a first glance, then, ancient Greek and modern American may appear as strange bedfellows. However, in the Greek case, it was not an externalized passion for people, competitiveness or shared values that inspired the individual to attain excellence but an internalized standard – to make the most of his gifts, if not also those of the organization or community.

From Outer- to Inner-directedness

Heroic outlook

The cohesive force at the centre of this ancient Greek scheme of human balances was the concept of man's nature and place in the sum of things: the Greeks were aware of the humble nature of human origins, but saw in them a vast unrealized potential. The gods provoked man to rival them as far as he could, and made him aware of possibilities beyond his usual self.

At first the heroic ideal was confined to a chosen few: in Homer the great heroes dominate the scene, and the common soldiers are hardly mentioned. But in Athens, which is the only ancient Greek democracy on which we are well informed, equality of opportunity took the form of the expectation that the whole population was capable of behaving in a heroic manner.

This heroic outlook gave an unexpected prominence to *intelligence*. The Greeks liked and admired intelligence, whether practical or theoretical, and no doubt felt that they surpassed other people in their possession of it. But they did have qualms about its uninhibited exercise, and felt that it must be balanced by other qualities of *character* and *self-control*. The Homeric hero is not moved to acts of heroism by a sense of duty, as we understand it, but by a *duty to himself*. He strives after that which we translate as 'virtue', but which is the Greek 'arete' – excellence. Finally, the sense that a man owed a supreme sacrifice to his own people was deeply ingrained in the Greek character, as an adaptation of the heroic outlook to the *civic frame of reference*.

Because the Greeks felt they were different from other men, and that they had always to excel and surpass them, they broke away from the static patterns of society, and action in all its forms was sought and honoured as the natural end of man. So a bias for action was considered to be of value to the ancient Greeks, in life as a whole, just as it is to Tom Peters, in the business world. But whereas the Greeks valued, above all, intelligence, self-control and a duty to realize one's individual capabilities (self-development), our contemporary American seekers after excellence value sociability, self-assertiveness and a commitment to win against the competition (free enterprise). The respectively inner and outer directed, rationally and emotively based pursuits are at odds with one another. Similarly, the notions of heroism and individuality, as we shall now see, are fundamentally different.

'Manliness' and godliness

Ancient Greek religion is unusual: it has no eminent prophet or law-giver who expounded the nature of the gods, no sacred books, the authority of which is final on doctrine or morals, no central organization or hierarchy, no insistence on orthodoxy, and no concept of a dedicated religious life. In fact the gods and their human progeny, as Charles Handy has indicated, were very close to one another.

The Greek sense of the holy was based much less on a feeling of the goodness of the gods than on a devout *respect* for their incorruptible beauty and unfailing strength. If this was a price that the Greeks paid for seeing the gods in human shape, it had vast compensations: it presented an *ideal* which was indeed not possible to rival but which, by its fascinating challenge, made men feel that it was good to possess, even in the humblest degree, qualities shared with the gods.

One of the most notable of Greek contributions to ethical thought was precisely the idea that *the goodness of the action lies in the action itself*, and that a man may be judged by the degree of decision and choice which he gives to it – perhaps a development of the system of virtue or honour already described. A man felt that he owed certain obligations to himself and to his own idea of what he ought to be. If he carried these out, he was satisfied and asked for no further reward.

In search of self

Rational scientific concepts can help us sort out and grasp objects and things, but when it comes to ourselves and our lives we need the language of myths – emotion, drama and sensuality – in order to describe the battle of the gods being waged in our souls. We can thereby evoke a *universal significance* in the roles we play, as managers or as mankind. When, like the ancients, we search for the gods in the events of *our* lives – in our feelings, attitudes and motives – we find not only a hidden richness in our internal confusions but a *structure of meaning* underlying our raw experiences, turning our lives into an inner adventure of creative possibilities.

In our longing to understand ourselves and our world, the gods of the past can show us the way into our future. They can teach us a deep *acceptance* of others and of ourselves; and acceptance, as the myths tell us, is the first step on the way to change and transformation. Moreover, this universality can free us from the prevalent stereotypes. In fact, we have all the gods and goddesses within us, but in varying degrees of intensity, with different gods dominating our lives during different phases. The manager's function, should he follow through his European heritage in this respect, is to recognize and release the gods within himself and others, while paying due attention to cultural propriety!

The central tenet of Greek religion was summed up in the inscription on Apollo's temple at Delphi – 'Know thyself': as you are, and as you are becoming; in your feelings and in your destructive impulses, no less than in your glory and essential divinity. This passion for the truth served a very practical purpose, informing the art of living that led to the realization of man's divine potential:

In this context, the gods were transformed from forces that had to be propitiated in the course of an official religion to powerful symbols of the depth and complexity of man's experience. And the personification of the energies they represented made them powerful catalysts of self knowledge and understanding.[4]

In conclusion then, whereas for Tom Peters product champions and business heros are symbols of the power and simplicity of individual achievement, for the ancient Greeks their heroic figures symbolized existential depth and complexity. While the one scales the heights of 'doing' the other plumbed the depths of 'being'.

From Reality to the Imagination

Self-realization and shared values

On the surface both purveyors of excellence – modern American and ancient Greek – appreciate the importance of myth and symbol in management and organization: Tom Peters has argued that the best American companies are 'a tapestry of myth and ritual'. The American social psychologist, Philip Selznick, has said:

To create an institution you rely on many techniques for infusing day to day behaviour with long run meaning and purpose.

One of the most important of these techniques is the *elaboration of socially integrating myths*. They are efforts to state, in the language of uplift and idealism, what is distinctive about the aims and methods of the enterprise [emphasis added].[5]

In ancient Greece, myth provided the framework for drama, illustrating some important crisis or problem in a highly concrete and cogent way – that is why Greek tragedy can be called symbolic. The old stories are not only told again for their own sake, but also to exemplify some deep-seated problem, which is presented in this particular form. The heroes of the past keep their individuality, but also represent *aspects of human destiny*. Each man may see in them something which concerns himself, beyond which lies some universal issue which is thereby enhanced in significance. The essence of a symbol is that it expresses, in a concrete, particular form matters which are otherwise beyond our grasp.

The unfading youthfulness of Greek myths lies in their appeal to intelligence, the emotions and the imagination. They appeal to the *intelligence* because some solid consideration underlies their dramatic events, some positive assertion about existence which invites conclusions to be drawn from it. They appeal to the *emotions* because what happens in them evokes horror or fear, admiration or delight, and forces us to compare our own desires and aims with them. They appeal to the *imagination* because each of us needs some image against which to set ourselves, and see our own limitations. Only then can we transcend them, in the light which is shed on some familiar situation, or in an unforseen expansion of our faculties.

The Greek description of the power of myth is fairly close, in its meaning and scope, to that of Philip Selznick. Overall, however, the Greeks placed much more emphasis on the individual's development, whereas Tom Peters' focus is on communally shared values.

Tradition and modernity

In ancient Greece the poet was regarded as the instrument of some external incalculable power, which possessed him and spoke through him. He was a prophet, a seer: he saw what others did not see. Poetry was not confined to ceremonial occasions; it was part of everyday life, honoured and enjoyed by a large number of people, and it was needed for hymns to the gods. It was a repository of stories for a people deeply interested in the superb achievements of its ancestors. Poetry was needed at public festivals to celebrate the glory of a city when it rejoiced over a victory in war or at the games:

In poetical composition both inspiration and craftsmanship are equally necessary, and the Greeks were well aware of it, even if at some times they stressed the need of the one and at other times the need of the other. Their respect for technical skill made due allowance for inspiration by assuming that all crafts have their presiding deities, and that *it is from the combination of divine prompting and human labour* that the special appeal of poetry is born [emphasis added].[6]

This view of poetry as something divinely inspired might be seen as contradictory to another view: the Greeks also insisted that poetry was a *form of art*, a *practised skill*. The combination of skill and inspiration is 'sophia' – wisdom or skill. The term is applied not only to the fine arts but also to activities as varied as that of the helmsman, the builder, the general or the cook. Today we would undoubtedly want to add the practice of management to the list, and to speculate upon the blend of skill and inspiration, change and continuity required of it.

Tradition dominated Greek poetry without hampering its freedom. Precisely because it laid down the form of a certain kind of poem, it left the poet free to develop his skill in other directions, and the old stories could then become a vehicle for pressing, present-day issues. Because poetry was regarded as a rational activity, the Greeks put into it their own pondered and serious view of life. When the great playwright Aeschylus constructed a tragedy, he made his action illustrate the divine laws which operate through human life. His view of these laws was not just original; it was reached by a deep consideration of human affairs, and his presentation became vastly enriched by all the imaginative and emotional attention that he gave to it. In the words of the Greek philosopher Heraclitus, 'to think is the greatest virtue [arete] and wisdom consists of speaking what is true and acting in obedience to nature'.

Here is where European and American most fundamentally part company, for whereas the ancient Greeks placed primary emphasis on reason and intellect, Tom Peters decries such 'paralysis by analysis'. For the Greeks, such rationality went hand in hand with the valuing of difference.

The Theory of Cultural Propriety

Valuing difference

Charles Handy, as Professor of Management at the London Business School, was the first European to bring the Greek gods into the management arena. As an Irishman resident in England, Handy combines a passion for individual self-expression with a managerial pragmatism. And as a European, he has combined his appreciation for a diversity of *cults* with a sensitivity for a unifying theme, or pattern – that is, *culture*:

To the Greeks, religion was more a matter of custom than formal theology. Their gods stood for certain things and, to a degree, you chose your god because you shared the values and interests which they represented. You were a Zeus person or an Apollo person, the god of order and reason, a follower of Athena, the warrier goddess, or of Dionysus, to me the most individualist of gods.

I have used four gods to symbolise the *different ways of managing* that can be discerned in organizations, or, to put it another way, the different cultures that exist in organizations. Organizations, like tribes, have their own way of doing things, things that work for them and things that don't work. You have to read them right to be effective. Each culture, or each god, works on quite different assumptions about the basis of power and influence, about what motivates people, how they think and learn, how things can be changed [emphasis added].[7]

As a pragmatist, Handy has reduced the 14 gods (see below) that reigned on Mount Olympus to four, and has diluted the metaphysical thrust of the Greek cosmology for practical purposes. Even so, it is very clear that Charles Handy's European perspective is different from that of Tom Peters: whereas Handy values variety, and hence complexity, Peters reaches for simplicity.

Neither of these management gurus, then, do justice to the full European perspective. For all their Anglo-American differences, both Handy and Peters resist pursuing the truth – as an ancient Greek might have done – in the interests of Anglo-Saxon pragmatism.

Masculine and feminine

In dramatic contrast to the Western concept of one great god, and one great contending principle of evil, each Greek god contains a polarity, an inner tension, a light and a dark side. Hence man is as much 'in the image of the gods' when he is creative, joyful and triumphant, as when his dark underside is showing.

Similarly, the Greek gods and goddesses come in masculine and feminine (not the same as male and female) guises. Cults based on the mysterious life-giving powers of nature existed in Greece alongside the Olympian cults, and in sharp contrast with them. From a distance the Olympic Pantheon of the 14 gods, presided over by Zeus, looks impressively solid, but on closer inspection this solidity dissolves. While the goddesses, in general terms, were concerned with rebirth and regeneration, the gods were more preoccupied with the paying of honours due. Goddess and god, respectively, represent completely different concepts of religion: the 'goddess' and 'love'-oriented aspects derived directly from Minoan Crete, while the 'god' and 'power'-oriented aspects descend from Europe and the Mediterranean.

We are now ready to investigate the Olympian gods of Greece in their full character (arete), thus undoing both Peters' simplicity and Handy's practicality. I shall therefore be replacing Peters' uniform entrepreneurial personality, as well as Handy's four gods of management, with a multiplicity of managerial – albeit god-like – personalities.

The Gods of Management

In her book, *The Greek Gods*,[8] the modern Greek author and philosopher, Arianna Stassinopoulos, has identified 14 major gods and goddesses. These can be seen, in fact, as seven categories of gods, each with masculine and feminine counterparts. These, subsequently, can be related to the *processes* as well as *styles* of management and learning that constitute this book.

Creative: Hephaistos and Poseidon

Creative managers' orientations range from the innovative, techno-logical thrust of America's Henry Ford, who can be likened to the Greek god Hephaistos, to the ecologically based vision of Agha Hasan Abedi, the founder of the Bank of Credit and Commerce, who can be likened to Poseidon. Whereas Ford was an inventive engineer who created an automobile industry in the 1920s, Agha Hasan Abedi is a social innovator, originally from Pakistan, who created a new form of banking in the 1970s.

Hephaistos the innovator

Hephaistos is the embodiment of man's unquenched creativity, the creativity that is forged as a bridge between our primordial dependence on nature and the industrialized world. He is the symbol of endless resourcefulness and prodigious activity. Like the great architects and engineers of our modern era – be they Corbusier, Stephenson or Edison – he built magnificent palaces and made the first self-propelled machines.

In his workshop he is supreme, unrivalled, but – like the archetypal crazed inventor – he is a total loss outside of it. In other words, he is lost in a world of social intercourse where he cannot use an axe to forge or create. Indeed, his physical lameness is symptomatic of his

Table 11.1 Europe's cultural and managerial heritage

Culture	Role	God	Goddess	Hero	Heroine
Creative	Innovator Visionary	Hephaistos	Poseidon	Henry Ford	Hasan Abedi
Developmental	Enabler Designer	Hades	Dionysus	Akio Morita	Mary Quant
Authoritative	Executive Leader	Apollo	Aphrodite	Alfred Sloane	Carlos de Bennedetti
Enterprising	Entrepreneur Entrepreneuse	Zeus	Demeter	Alan Sugar	Mary Kay
Changeable	Change agent Networker	Hermes	Athena	Richard Branson	Steve Shirley
Communal	Animateur Gatherer	Hera	Hestia	Nelli Eichner	Mitsubishi
Energetic	Activator Adventurer	Ares	Artemis	Lee Iacocca	Anita Roddick

emotional disability. The master craftsman who achieves perfection in his artefacts and mechanical inventions undermines human relationships: Henry Ford, idiosyncratic founder of Ford Motors, was just such a person.

Visionary Poseidon

Poseidon ruled over the creatures of the sea, embodying the two age-old symbols of the unconscious, horses and water. What Poseidon's myth tells us is that the hero who will save us from dangers has to plunge into the sea and, having confronted its dangers, discover its mysteriously creative source and power of renewal.

Agha Hasan Abedi started his own new bank in the early 1970s, focusing his attentions on the developing world to an unprecedented extent. In so orienting his banking activities, set in the context of a search for global peace, Abedi tapped a previously hidden source of creativity and power.

Designers: Hades and Dionysus

Designer cultures range from continually evolving business corporations in Japan to highly individualistic design companies in Europe. Sony, with Akio Morita at its head, is an example of the former, and Mary Quant Designs, with Mary Quant as its founder, is an example of the latter. The first is represented by Hades and the second by Dionysus.

Hadesian renewal

Hades, the god of death, is today the hardest god to relate to. Hades teaches us acceptance of death as part of life. Even more importantly, and in Socrates' words, he urges us to 'practise death daily'. Practising death obliges us to continually evaluate what is lesser in our lives in terms of the greater. It reminds us that death must precede rebirth. Sony's philosophy of 'mu', or nothingness, whereby the company remains totally open to change and evolution, is reminiscent of this.

Hades presides over our individual and organizational descents, our emotional upheavals and our griefs, with the power to bring illumination and renewal. As the seed must flourish and then die to be born again, so a part of ourselves, our institutions or our whole societies, must die before we can give birth to the reality hidden in our depths.

In stirring our numbness to pain, Hades disturbs our safe, comfortable existence, breaks up the old patterns we cling to, and 'through the darkness leads us', individually or collectively, to a deeper-seeing, richer and more resonant being. Akio Morita, in breaking out of the traditional Japanese way of life to become an international businessman, underwent that very process of death and renewal.

Dionysian self-expression

Dionysus is the god of ecstasy, dance and song: he is the loosener, the liberator; he brings plasticity and flexibility into what was rigid and hard; he frees us from old bondages; he dissolves old claims – he lifts the age-old barriers which conceal the invisible and the infinite. Mary Quant, who created her business and innovative designs in the 1960s, is such a person. She responded to the signs of the expressive times, developing a 'liberated' look to complement women's social progression.

Dionysus is the enemy of rigidity and self-control. He embodies the madness of the supreme moment of creation, of the enchanted moment when man is flung out of his routine world, his ordered existence. Dionysus is the god of theatre: he, or she, is therefore most uncomfortable with the more formal styles of management and organization.

Formal: Apollo and Aphrodite

A typically hierarchical organization such as General Motors, with its well-known chief executive, Alfred Sloane, is an Apollonian culture; whereas a network-based organization, with overlapping interests and complementary forms, such as Carlos De Bennedetti's Olivetti, is represented by Aphrodite. Whereas General Motors is formally structured, Olivetti is aesthetically formed.

Apollo the executive

Apollo is the West's ideal of man. When Hamlet extols his vision of personhood he is extolling Apollo: 'What a piece of work is man! How noble in reason! how infinite in faculty! in form, in moving, how express and admirable! in action how like an angel! in apprehension how like a god!' Reason, form, action and apprehension are all Apollo's essential attributes, just like a conventional business executive.

The bringing of harmony into boundless confusion and the discovery of order in chaos, are both Apollonian gifts: 'Know thyself' and 'Nothing in excess' are the two great precepts that he has bequeathed humanity. The spirit of Apollo is embodied in 'the splendour of clarity and in the intelligent sway of order and moderation'.[9]

Love is the area in which the god of reason is least at home. The myths of his adventures with women are dominated by unsuccessful chases and fleeing maidens: the god who embodies light and truth wreaks havoc in the world of love and the feminine.

His will to exercise power, cut off from love and intuition, brings about a naive belief in the absolute manageability of human beings.

Aphrodite the leader

Aphrodite is the goddess of love and beauty. She is the longing she causes as well as the cause of longing: her essence is transformation through the power of beauty and love. We can either drown in it or be released through it into a life lived more intensely, more truthfully and more consciously.

Great scientists and artists alike, be they Einstein or Solzhenitsyn, have been aware of the power of love and beauty in their work. The contemporary philosopher Sir Karl Popper has put it this way: 'there is only one way for science – to meet a problem, to see its beauty and fall in love with it, to get married to it, and to live with it till death do us part.[10]

Love and form, individual and organizational harmony, and Aphroditean culture and the influence of aesthetics on organizational life are generally more accessible to the Italian manager than to his Anglo-American counterpart. Therefore De Bennedetti, with his uniquely Italian style and aesthetic sensitivity, demonstrates such Aphroditean leadership. Above and beyond his displays of primal entrepreneurship lies a sensitivity to physical and social form that distinguishes him from his powerful US counterparts in the electronics industry.

Powerful: Zeus and Demeter

The power cultures are either centred, like Alan Sugar's Amstrad, around an aggressive entrepreneur or, like Mary Kay Ash's 'Mary Kay Cosmetics', around an impassioned entrepreneuse. Whereas Alan Sugar can be likened to Zeus, Mary Kay can be likened to Demeter.

Zeus the entrepreneur

Zeus, the 'all seeing' and 'all high' lord of air and sky is the personification of power and influence. His very name comes from the Indo-European root '*dyu*', to shine. The character of Zeus as the *politician* amongst the gods is immediately established by the means he uses to gain supremacy. Against the brute force of the Titans, he deploys an uncanny instinct for strategy and for consolidating his power by key alliances with the older divinities. The recent collaboration between Alan Sugar in electronics and Rupert Murdoch in the media, over their satellite television project, is a typical case in point.

The god who embodies the forces of expansion and growth, however, seems incapable of inner growth and expansion. The force that expands and creates therefore also becomes the power that binds and restricts.

Demeter the entrepreneuse

Demeter is Earth mother, adoring mother, even clinging mother. A defensive clinging to the upper world, to the surface world, is Demeter's negative aspect. In her smothering, Demeter would rather destroy what she has given birth to, whether it is an institution, a project or an idea, than let it develop independently of herself. In her positive aspect, as the elemental mother, Demeter embodies the highest mysteries of a person's nature, and the alternating cycles of plenty and fallowness, including the change of seasons and the ebb and flow of our emotional lives. Hence Mary Kay Cosmetics has developed into not only a successful company, but also a supportive group of women, all over the US.

As long as Demeter resists her emotional depths, she grieves and rages and withers. When she can finally accept the deeper reality that lies beneath the surface, the potential as a 'seed in each moment of life', the Earth and her enterprise blooms and rejoices.

Adaptable: Hermes and Athena

Typically adaptable cultures range from the aggressively flexible Virgin Group, with Richard Branson as its Hermesian agent of change, to the inherently flexible F. I. Group in computer services in the UK, with Mrs Steve Shirley as its typically Athenian founder and networker.

Hermes the agent of change

Every god has a centre, a special imprint on an aspect of ourselves or our lives. Hermes' centre is everywhere, part of an ever-expanding spiral, and every colour in the expanding cosmic rainbow is his. He is equally at home on Olympus and in the subterranean depths, and is thus supremely adaptable. Hence Richard Branson can be found signing up recording stars, crossing the Atlantic in a hot air balloon, or developing the new 'Mates' condoms to combat AIDS. Introducing the unexpected into our lives is one of the means he uses to jerk us out of sleeping wakefulness, and to break through the rigidities and confinements of personal or institutional habits or conventions. Whenever things seem fixed, rigid or stuck Hermes introduces fluidity, new beginnings.

Magic and trickery, and mischief and lying, belong as naturally to Hermes' world as guiding people through periods of instability. He is always en route, never trapped. Like a great magician or comedian, a Houdini or a Jacques Tati: 'After we have laughed at his wit, been held in the grip of his drama, nourished ourselves in his wisdom, revelled in the colours and layers of his adventures, he still raises echo after echo in our mind and hearts'.[11]

Athena the networker

Athena fully aligns herself with the masculine order, but she breathes into it soul, mercy and wisdom. She is, above all, the goddess of civilization, an inventress and artisan. Artisans, craftsmen and tradesmen celebrate her as their teacher and patroness. Plato used Athena's role of weaver as a metaphor for the political process, where she is known for her powers of persuasiveness. The American psychologist James Hillman[12] amplifies the metaphor, likening Athena's art to the systematic plaiting of strands together, producing a whole fabric out of her art of combination. In this way Steve Shirley has created a network of 1000 women, the majority of whom 'telework' from, home, within a computer services business.

Athena's domain is this world, and the chink in the armour of the goddess of civilization is her reluctance to penetrate the mysteries of what lies below her: her pragmatic spirit directed towards tasks and agendas, becomes disconnected from soul and from earth. Athena's rejection of her powerful, instinctive feminity is part of the denial of the depths of her nature. When these are disowned, Athena becomes all head.

Communal: Hera and Hestia

Communal cultures are more characteristic of traditional societies than modern ones. However, a company with a strong, matriarchically based, family feeling, such as Nelli Eichner's Interlingua in the UK, or one with an anonymous, but communally based identity, such as Mitsubishi in Japan, would fit the Heran or Hestian bill, respectively.

Hera the animateur

As long as Hera projects on her husband all her unlived creativity, as long as she expects to find fulfilment in her role as wife alone, she creates her own betrayal. The other side of such destructive possessiveness is a deep instinct to protect and nurture. Hera's protective strength manifests itself not only in her relationship with her husband but also in her relationship with the community. Hera is a queen, and the wider realm of things is as much her province as her family. Her attempt to make communities both of Olympus and the Earth is an expression of the passionate concern for the communal life, for the whole.

Societies cannot survive without Hera's steadfast commitment to the values and institutions on which they are founded. We see her at work in schools, hospitals, charities and churches, as well as in matriarchically based business enterprises. Interlingua grew out of the Czech-born Eichner family into a community of 30 nations, working together in the Sussex countryside, in a worldwide translating and interpreting business. For Nelli Eichner 'there was no happiness like shared happiness',[13] in family or in business.

Hestia the gatherer

Hestia, the goddess of the hearth, of the centre to which life returns to the replenished, was honoured in every household. According to Plato, her name means 'the essence of things', and since she is the essence of everything that moves, flows and has life and personality, she herself is the most anonymous, the most impersonal of all the goddesses. It is in this context that Japanese companies, such as Mitsubishi, value communality.

Hestia was the centre on which the city's solid foundation was built, and she was the bedrock of man's being. She is not about striving; she is about being. Her fire warms, kindles and illuminates. She is the gathering point, the source and the centre. As the guardian of our homecoming, she nourishes the depths of our being, leavens our lives and provides a centre in which are contained our disconnected experiences. The original Mitsubishi saw himself as such a guardian of Japan's homecoming, after the war, through the mighty enterprise that he served to create.

Energetic: Ares and Artemis

In its positive vein Ares is represented by Chrysler's saviour, Lee Iacocca.[14] Artemis, on the other hand, is typified by Anita Roddick, the Anglo-Italian of Bodyshop fame.

Ares the activator

Ares is the embodiment of aggression, the Olympian 'action man', the god of war and strife. Thriving on conflict, he rejoices in the delight of the battle. Athena and Ares therefore represent two different aspects of aggression. Whereas Athena fought to defend and protect, fighting with strategy and clear intention, Ares is our primordial rage allowed full sway, our hot-blooded energy. In its positive aspect, unrestrained self-assertiveness turns into creative assertiveness, aggression into courage, and the ambition for power into the quest for achievement. The quest for such a higher law is the manifestation of Ares' higher nature, a passionate instinct for life that persists in the midst of destruction. Thus it was that Lee Iacocca turned Chrysler around.

Artemis the adventurer

Artemis is freedom – wild, untramelled, aloof from all entanglements. She is a huntress, a dancer, the goddess of nature and wildness. Artemis is much more at home with animals, in fact, than with people. She is a primordial teenager.

Today, this goddess of the hunt has become the goddess of sports, aerobics and dancing. Anita Roddick is a particular case in point. She continually combs the world for the naturally based ingredients for her skin and hair care business, The Bodyshop. While her huntress instinct leads her company into rapid, and globally based, business expansion, her orientation towards nature makes Anita a heroine of the Greens all over the world.

Conclusion

The Greek gods, in their full Olympian breadth and depth, represent a formidable array of corporate cultures and managerial personalities. In fact, to encompass them all we had to span the 'businessphere' – north, south, east and west – our heroes and heroines come not only from the US and the UK but also from Italy and Japan.

Similarly, if each of you is to develop your own managerial individuality to the full, you will need to identify not only the kind of manager you most specifically are (know thyself), but also, and ultimately, to develop yourself across all the other godly dimensions. In other words, you will be drawing on the fullness of your European heritage and, in the process, reaching across to Asia and America, and down to Africa.

In the final analysis, then, arete manifests itself in a multiplicity of managerial forms, drawing on and out of, a diversity of human potential. Excellence, European style, is almost the antithesis of its American counterpart, for it is inner- rather than outer-directed, and draws upon a depth and breadth of individuality as opposed to sheer force and impact of immediate personality. As institutions begin to rise to that individual potential, so they become 'learning organizations'.

Moreover, to the extent that you, as an individual manager, are able to fulfil your potential, and in so doing realize the potential of the product or service with which you are caringly involved, so 'quality' results. Learning and individuation, quality and arete, are all interlinked. And, finally, in the interests of clarity and coherence the 14 gods can be reduced to the seven generic types of manager portrayed in table 11.1; personalities with whom we have been concerned throughout this book.

Notes

1 T. Peters and R. Waterman, *In Search of Excellence* (Harper & Row, New York, 1982).
2 T. Peters and N. Austin, *A Passion for Excellence* (Collins, London, 1985).
3 C. M. Bowra, *The Greek Experience* (Bantam, New York, 1957), p. 213.
4 H. D. Kitto, *The Greeks* (Penguin, London, 1950), p. 72.
5 P. Selznick, quoted in Peters, *In Search of Excellence*, p. 282.
6 M. Grant, *Myths of the Greeks and Romans* (Mentor Books, 1962), p. 107.
7 C. Handy, *The Gods of Management* (Pan, London, 1985), p. 10.
8 A. Stassinopoulos, *The Greek Gods* (Weidenfeld, London, 1923), p. 28.
9 Stassinopoulos, *The Greek Gods*, p. 47.
10 Quoted in *The Sunday Times*, May 1988.
11 Stassinopoulos, *The Greek Gods*, p. 196.
12 J. Hillman, *Re-visioning Psychology* (Harper & Row, New York, 1978).
13 R. Lessem, *Intrapreneurship* (Wildwood House, London, 1986), ch. 8.
14 L. Iacocca, *Iacocca* (Bantam, New York, 1980).

12

Building a Holographic Organization

Introduction

Recasting Excellence in the Mould of Arete

I started out in this book by comparing and contrasting the impoverishment of Western-style 'total quality management' with the richness of Europe's scientific and cultural heritage. In effect, the quality of Western civilization, as recently borne out by the liberation of Eastern Europe in the late 1980s, has less to do with Philip Crosby's notion of 'conformance and compliance', and rather more to do with the Greek concept of 'arete'.

Arete conveys a respect for the wholeness or oneness of life, and thus implies a contempt for specialization and for narrowly based efficiency. Rather, arete – or excellence – represents a much higher ideal of efficiency, an efficiency which exists not in one department of life, but in life itself. From that elevated perspective we are able to view 'TQM' in the guise of neither Crosby nor Peters, Deming nor Duran. In fact all these conventional 'quality' gurus lack a global and historical, or a European and cultural, perspective.

Because they have their own historical perspective, the Japanese have been able to culturally recast their work in an Eastern mould. The true quality guru, for Westerners, is Robert Pirsig, for whom quality is not simply conformance. Rather it involves such attributes as unity, flow, proportion and depth. The problem with Pirsig, however, is that he provides us with a philosophy but not with a concept or technique: hence my introduction of the learning organization, duly linked with the rhetorical approach of the Greek sophists.

Total Learning – Quality Management

My underlying premise, then, is that quality lies in conformance to human nature, that learning is a natural extension of human being, and that management is an externalization of learning. Insofar as arete incorporates a duty to oneself, learning is the means to acquire it; insofar as it also encompasses a duty to others, management is a means of applying it. Quality, in that context, forms the bridge between self – the internal – and the external world. Management becomes an extension of human 'being', represented in inner-directed learning (arete) and outer-directed quality (excellence), as is indicated in table 12.1.

The problem is that the neat, linear representation, as indicated in table 12.1, is a gross misrepresentation of reality. Strategy, for example, may be quintessentially an exercise of the imagination, but actually it is often a more conceptual, or mental, exercise. Marketing may have an essentially wilful thrust to it, but it is also highly conceptual in its character. In effect, learning and management, like quality, are essentially *holographic* in nature.

The Holographic Organization

The Paradigm

A hologram is a special type of optical storage system that can best be explained by an example. If you take a holographic photo of, say, a personal computer, and cut out one section of it – the keyboard, for example – you will obtain a picture not of the keyboard but of the whole computer. In other words, each individual part of the picture contains the whole picture in condensed form. *The part is in the whole, and the whole is in each part.*

The technique of holography was first invented in the mid-1950s, by the Hungarian Nobel Prize winner, Denis Gabor. Some 30 years later, the English nobel physicist David Bohm concluded that: 'In the *explicate* or manifest realm of time and space, things and events are indeed separate and discrete. But beneath the surface, as it were, in the *implicate* or frequency realm, all things and events are spacelessly, timelessly, intrinsically, one and undivided [emphasis added].'[1] In other words, the physical universe itself seemed to him – just as the organizational universe does to me – to be a gigantic hologram.

Table 12.1 Management and learning

Human attribute	Learning field	Learning style	Manager's self	Managerial skill	Management knowledge
Imaginative	Holographic	Inspire	Innovative	Create	Corporate strategy
Intuitive	Molecular	Harmonize	Developmental	Facilitate	Organization development
Conceptual	Functional	Deliberate	Analytical	Organize	Finance and accounting
Wilful	Proactive	Energize	Enterprising	Influence	Sales and marketing
Mental	Adaptive	Experiment	Agent of change	Learn	Information management
Social	Responsive	Respond	Animated	Socialize	Personnel management
Physical	Reactive	React	Action-oriented	Direct	Operations management

The implications of all of this for total learning and for quality management are huge. In the first instance, it becomes apparent that all the elements of learning and of management, identified in table 12.1, are explicitly separate but implicitly integrated. In effect, we have the classical and romantic combination that yields Pirsig's overall quality. In the 'explicate' order, for example, the deliberative style of learning is separate from the reactive one, and such a reactive style is separate from operations management. However, in the 'implicate' order they each unfold out of the same unified source.

Within a holographic organizational universe, then, the whole, albeit in condensed form, is contained within each part. The appreciation and manifestation of such a whole, within whatever part, is the essence of quality. Moreover, the more intense the awareness of the whole, within each part, the more total the quality: 'Simplicity means onefoldness; it comes from some simple germ but it might unfold to encompass the complexity of the universe.'[2]

The Unfolding Organization

In essence, then, management and organization are not classically ordered in a linear manner. Simple divisions between marketing and finance, or between 'energized' and 'harmonic' learning, are merely explicate, surface manifestations of a deeper, implicate reality. In such a holographic view of reality, then, the most profound, inseparable reality is the absolute and infinite state of interconnectedness: 'Within this ultimate source all individuals (or organizations) are contained in potential form. Above that individuals are aware of themselves, but also of their connectedness. On the immediate surface individuals (or, again, organizations) consider themselves to be totally separate.'[3] Let me begin on the surface, organizationally speaking, and descend progressively towards the absolute source, relating fields of learning (chapter 4) to levels of organization.

The reactive organization

The *reactive* organization, at its most basic, reacts to individual people and events, in a tangible, immediate and short-term way. Therefore it exhibits a reactive style of managing and learning, and a myopic operational outlook, individually associated with the exuberance of childhood.

The typical *street trader* – offering you whatever he happens to have in stock, just to physically capture your attention – is a reactive case in point. His senses are alert, being invariably fast on his feet, but his thoughts and feelings are comparatively inert. 'Managing by wandering about', incorporating Tom Peter's famous 'bias for action', is an inherent part of this reactive approach to management and organization. Similarly, 'short-termitis' comes from reactive individuals and organizations reacting to surface changes and to tangible phenomena.

The responsive organization

The *responsive* organization, at the next level down, is immediate and short term in outlook, but responds to individuals' feelings rather than to their actions. For example, if a customer stops buying a particular product the reactive organization would immediately offer it, or any available alternative, at a lower price. The responsive one, on the other hand, will first gain a feeling for what the customer likes and dislikes about the product, and then respond accordingly.

A typical such organization is the *family grocery store*, also positioning itself 'close to the customer'. Personal service is its hallmark, and people – whether employees or customers – are treated like personal friends, rather than as either functionalized staff or depersonalized consumers.

Thus the emphasis is, again in Tom Peters terms, on 'productivity through people' rather than upon optimal human relations, or on any other such abstract notion of social responsiveness. Current approaches to 'customer care' and even to TQM often assume such responsive overtones, in the course of taking managers 'back to basics'. People managers and responsive learners gravitate towards this homely form of organization, as does the group-oriented young person.

The adaptive organization

The *adaptive* or 'interactive' organization is able to form and re-form itself, in continual response to specific environment changes. As a temporary, rather than permanent organization, it is frequently project- rather than functionally based, and thrives on 'ad hocracy' as opposed to bureaucracy. Managers of change and experimental learners are therefore best suited to this sort of network-based organization.

Typically small in scale, and *high tech* in nature, such enterprises 'thrive on chaos', in Tom Peters' terms. Populated by footloose and fancy-free knowledge workers, adaptive organizations have permeable boundaries, and therefore are easily able to interact with the outside world. Networks, as opposed to hierarchies, are the order of the day; moreover, change – as opposed to continuity – is considered desirable.

Capable of learning at a rate that is faster than the rate of change, such organizations have no need to engage in particularly long-term thinking. They are also unlikely to be able to grow very large, because of their attachment to the temporary and exploratory identity of youth, and due to the fickle character of their networks.

The proactive organization

As you can now see, the simplified polarity between the 'reactive' and 'proactive' manager or organization represents a vast oversimplification. There are distinctive shades – both responsive and adaptive – inbetween, and further shades of difference to follow.

The proactive organization is, in fact, the one that most strongly exhibits Tom Peters' managerial qualities of 'autonomy and enterprise'. Like its constituent managers, such an organization is demonstrably going places and, now and for the first time, is not primarily short-term in its orientation. Entrepreneurial managers and energized learners, who thrive in such proactive enterprises, seek out prospectively lucrative and far reaching commercial opportunities, in the course of dynamically engaging with the external environment.

In Gifford Pinchot's terms,[4] such *intraprises* are freewheeling, decentralized profit centres, in which self-selecting 'intrapreneurs' are given free reign to pursue their practical imaginations, just like young adults gaining their new-found independence, although bound together in their 'club' by shared communal values.

The functional organization

While Charles Handy regards what I have termed the adaptive organization as 'task-centred', and the proactive enterprise as 'power-centred', the functionally based institution is 'role-centred'.[5] Typically identified as a *bureaucracy*, such a role culture is built upon enduring functional pillars, and is characteristic of large-scale organizations which are built to last. Analytical managers and methodical learners thrive in this kind of organization, which is ordered hierarchically in pyramidical form.

Corporate, regional and nationally based plans, both short- and long-term in nature, are – by intention if not in reality – characteristic of these stable and predictable organizations. Relationships are necessarily compartmentalized and depersonalized. As a result institutions and their formal representatives, rather than individuals in informal groups, are their focal point.

This form of functional organization has, up to now, been the predominant and prevailing form of large-scale organization, both public and private, capitalist and communist. Not surprisingly, such an 'accountable enterprise' has been championed by the Austro-American Peter Drucker rather than by the Anglo-American Tom Peters.

The molecular organization

Whereas the reactive organization is an agglomeration of disconnected people, the responsive organization is a family unit, and the adaptive organization is a network of professionals, the proactive organization is an independent enterprise, albeit often built around an enterprising individual. In other words, such a proactive enterprise, legally represented as a limited company, is the first of the organizational forms to acquire an 'ego' identity, *independent* of the people associated with it.

Moreover, the functional organization transcends this independent identity. Those working within it are *dependent* on outside stake-holders for their ultimate existence. At the same time – whether as an IBM, a Singapore Airlines, or as an Ecole Polytechnique de Lyons – it retains a self-centredness. In other words, there is a clear dividing line between itself and the outside world. People remain employed by the institution, shareholders (in a business contact) hold shares in the organization, and it is ultimately legally constituted, as a corporate whole. What I have called the *molecular* organization is therefore the first institutional form to lose its independent identity completely, and to be subsumed under not a dependent, but through an *interdependent* one.

A genuine *joint venture* is typical of such a molecular organization. In fact, as dealings with institutional suppliers and customers become progressively more long-term and complex, an enduring molecular form of relationship supplants the merely horizontal or vertical ones. This form of inter-organization comes naturally to the developmental manager and to the harmonic learner. Individuals in midlife, in seeking to recognize and subsequently harmonize the different parts of themselves, are potentially receptive to such molecular form. In effect, it results in a transpersonal, trans-organizational and trans-national orientation which supplants the individual, corporate and national ego.

In that context, the humility and 'ego-lessness' of the East is better suited to such molecular organization – witness 'Japanese Inc.' – than the egotism of the West.

The holographic organization

We finally reach down to the ultimate organizational form which underpins this whole book; for whereas the molecular organization involves intense interconnectedness, the *holographic* form transcends even such interdependent form. As Marilyn Ferguson, the American organizational psychologist and futurist has pointed out, in the course of linking ancient wisdom with contemporary brain research: 'In the heaven of Indra there is said to be a network of pearls so arranged that if you look at one you will see all the others reflected in it. In the same way, each object in the world is not merely itself but involves every other object, and in fact is every other object.'[6] In other words, Pirsig finds his Godhead in the circuits of a digital computer, and the organization becomes a gigantic hologram.

In this holographic field of the creative manager (as well as the inspired learner, and the wholly mature individual) learning and managing, operations and finance, knowledge and skill, manager and organization, product and market, institution and environment become, on the one hand, discrete and separate phenomena and, on the other, holographic reflections of each other. In fact, this complementarity between part (classical) and whole (romantic), like that between particle and wave, rock or whirlpool[7] is characteristic of total learning and quality management, just as it is of the new physics.

The Principle of Complementarity

The quantum physicists, as distinguished from the Newtonian classicists, have demonstrated that at the atomic level matter has a dual aspect; it appears as particles and as waves. Light, for example, is emitted and absorbed in the form of 'quanta' or photons, but when these particles of light travel through space they appear as vibrating electric and magnetic fields which show all the characteristic behaviour of waves (see figure 12.1). Similarly, throughout this book, we have alternated between 'particle' and 'wave' orientations, both of which are required for total learning and for quality management.

A particle   A wave

Figure 12.1   Particle–wave duality.

Particles of learning and of innovation, of development and of transformation, are the seven discrete 'horizontal' elements, or states, of the spectrum. Waves of learning and of innovation, of development and of transformation, are represented by the 'vertical' and essentially interconnected flows. These involve both the inner journey, between physical reality and creative imagination, as well as the outer journey, between vision and action.

Alternatively, these complementary forces – 'classical' particles and 'romantic' waves – also make up the two sides of quality. Moreover, in David Bohm's terms, they represent the respectively explicate and implicate orders (see figure 12.2).

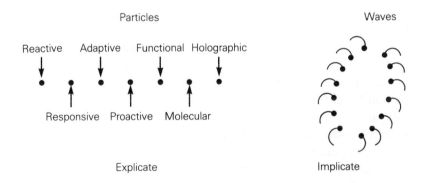

Figure 12.2   The explicate and implicate orders.

Conclusion

The prolific and popular writer on biology and ecology, Lyall Watson,[8] has used an analogy to describe the principle of holography, which will ultimately help us to integrate quality and learning. If, he says, you drop a pebble into a pond, it will produce a series of regular waves that travel outwards in concentric circles. Drop two identical pebbles into the pond at different points and you will get two sets of similar waves that move towards each other. Where the waves meet they will interfere.

If the crest of one coincides with the trough of another, they will cancel each other out and produce an isolated patch of calm water – the same thing as Robert Pirsig's 'peace of mind', which arises when the craftsman, or manager, is so at one with his or her work that true quality results.

In fact, there may be many different combinations of interacting waves, particularly if you increase the number of pebbles dropped from two to seven, equal to the full spectrum. The final result is a complex pattern of ripples, known as the 'interference pattern'.

Light waves, then, behave in exactly the same way as the ripples in the water. When two laser beams touch they produce an interference pattern that can be recorded on a photographic plate. The record, if reflected off an object, will be a hologram. In equivalent terms, it takes communication between any two waves on the learning spectrum – for example, reactive and responsive ones – to produce an interference pattern. Such a pattern, if accommodated by a wholly receptive learning organization (the light-sensitive photographic plate), and subsequently reflected off an object (a product or service), will provide a holographic picture of quality.

When quality and learning become holographically integrated no part can stand in isolation of the whole. The reactive organization becomes a reflection of the unified whole in the same way as the commodity sold by the manager–trader is perceived as an explicate entity of an implicate unity. Duty to oneself, as an individual, is integrated with duty to others, within the organization, as an interference pattern. The sentient way of being and working, to which Shoshana Zuboff alluded, is transformed from a physical to a social context, without losing its original essence.

To that extent the division between managing and learning, or between producer and consumer, is an explicate order divorced from an implicate one, a part disconnected from the whole – and true quality cannot exist.

As we learn and develop, then, as a managerial and organizational species, we need to transform our institutions – from reactive and responsive, or even adaptive, proactive or functional ones – into molecular and ultimately holographic entities. Once we mature in this way the whole notion of quality will change its functional identity – Crosby's 'fitness for purpose' or 'conformance to standard' – to a holographic identity, Pirsig's 'Godhead'. In the process, and as Jagdish Parikh[9] has indicated, we will develop from 'innocent' and professional operators into true 'master managers'. As such, we differentiate and integrate the parts – reactive, responsive, adaptive, proactive, functional, and molecular – within a holographic whole. And whereas the inward manifestation is a process of learning, the outward realization is a product of quality.

Notes

1 K. Wilber, *The Holographic Paradigm* (Shambhala, Colorado, 1982), p. 3.

2 D. Bohm, *ex* Wilber, *The Holographic Paradigm*, p. 59.

3 I. Bentov, *ex* Wilber, *The Holographic Paradigm*, p. 137.

4 G. Pinchot, *Intrapreneuring* (Harper & Row, New York, 1985).

5 C. Handy, *The Gods of Management* (Pan, London, 1982).

6 M. Ferguson, *ex* Wilbur, *The Holographic Paradigm*, p. 25.

7 C. Hampden Turner, *Charting the Corporate Mind* (Basil Blackwell, Oxford, 1990).

8 L. Watson, *Lifetide: the Biology of Consciousness* (Simon & Schuster, New York, 1980).

9 J. Parikh, *Managing Your Self*, (Basil Blackwell, Oxford, 1990).

Appendix A

Management Skills

The conventionally recognized managerial skills of organizing, directing and 'man management', or social skill, can be broken down as follows.

Organizing Skills

Key organizing skills are those of delegation, time management, handling meetings and effective report writing. Possibly the most important single skill in managing is that of delegation.

Delegation

The manager who fails to delegate will inevitably run out of steam, will dampen his subordinates' motivation, and will ultimately fail to get the job done. Problems of delegation characteristically arise when a small, enterpreneurially run organization needs to progress into a larger, more hierarchically controlled form. Characteristically, innovative, enterprising and action managers have more problems with delegation than analytical, developmental or people managers:

Delegation is the name given to the process of deciding-what-to-let-your-subordinates-decide. It's the one ability more than any other that makes managers different from non managers. Managers know the difference between delegating and dumping. Non managers don't. No manager, whatever his level, is humanly capable of making all the decisions. Some he cannot take because he has not the authority. Others are best taken by his subordinates: decisions that are more relevant to their priorities than to his. Finally, some of the most important of a manager's decisions are associated with the freedom he allows his subordinates to do things in their own way.[1]

The skill of delegating, then, is closely connected with your analytical ability to separate part from whole, not only in managerial thought but also in managerial action.

Time management

Next to delegation, effective time management probably occupies pride of place. An efficient manager uses his time deliberately and methodically, ensuring that he sets and follows his priorities correctly[2]:

Managing Your Time
- List seven key objectives for the month
- List four key objectives for the week
- For each day, identify
  - what you must do
  - what you should do
  - what you could do

A word of caution is necessary here. The conventional Western approach to 'time management' is based heavily on an analytical approach to work and to life: it assumes that time is a one-dimensional entity. In effect this is not the case. There is a clear distinction between 'monochronic time', which is divided into linear bits, and 'polychronic' time, which is overlapping and even circular in nature. Whereas Westerners and analytical managers tend towards the former, Easterners and people managers tend towards the latter.

Conducting meetings

Whatever the context, no matter how efficiently you delegate work to others and allocate your own time, you will fail as a manager if you do not communicate effectively, in formal as well as informal settings. Formal communications involve organizing skills, whereas informal communications involve social skills. Conducting meetings is a formal skill that can be acquired through both education and experience[3]:

How to Run a Meeting
For the Chairman
  1. Know your committee (terms, rules, members).
  2. Prepare (compile agenda, plan meeting).
  3. Consult before the meeting (i.e. prepare the agenda).

4. Be firm but fair.
5. Convey sense of urgency/importance.
6. Listen.
7. Seek consensus/agree the action.

For the Member

1. Prepare/know your facts.   4. Be constructive.
2. Don't be late.   5. Don't lose your cool.
3. Accept the chair.   6. Question if in doubt.
   7. Fight your own corner but don't waste time.

In fact, chairing a meeting places a premium on both the formal, analytically based skills to which John Gregory refers, and on the informal – social and facilitative – skills that we are still to uncover.

Finally, the analytical prowess involved in conducting meetings, behaviourally, is mirrored in the cognitive skills involved in report writing.

Report writing

This is another organizational skill that can be acquired, relating, in this case, more to the way you organize information than people. Rosemary Stewart at Oxford, better known for her work on *The Realities of Management*, has nevertheless written precisely on the subject, providing her own checklist and guidelines for effective writing[4]:

LETTER WRITER'S CHECKLIST
• Catch and hold your reader's attention.
• Show your reader why your message is important.
• Show your reader the benefits to them from agreeing/replying.
• Make it easy to read, understand and act on at one reading!

REPORT GUIDELINES
• Plan carefully – think through the entire situation before you start to write.
• Gather all the facts and double check for accuracy.
• Choose an appropriate structure.
• Prepare a detailed outline.
• Anticipate objectives.
• Try to imagine what would convince your reader.
• Beware of exaggeration or bias.
• Edit every paragraph to ensure your meaning is clear.

As in the management of time, formally and analytically, so in the writing of reports, in similarly formal vein, we are following a Western and monochronic model. People managers on the one hand, and Japanese managers on the other, will find it important to frame a formal report within a social context that is less arid and depersonalized than the kind of writing to which Rosemary Stewart refers.

Summary

To the extent that he or she is a master or an artist, a pragmatist or an opportunist, a scientist or craftsperson or actor, the approach of individual managers will differ. Fundamentally, organisational skills – like any others – are never acquired overnight. Would-be organizers have to go through the motions of learning and innovation. We now turn to 'directing' skills.

Directing Skills

There are four subskills involved in 'directing': decision-making and problem-solving, coaching of staff, performance appraisal of subordinates, and counselling. I have deliberately excluded the skill of 'leadership' here because it tends to mean all things to all people.

Decision-making

Some managers view the whole management process as one of decision-making, or solving managerial problems. In 'directing' others, it is certainly necessary for managers to make decisions continually, and effectively, combining attention with intention, and caution with speed. At the same time, to the extent that decision-making and direction setting go together, a blend of analysis and assertion, objectivity and aggression is required.

Decision-making, used interchangeably here with problem-solving, is conventionally viewed as a logical and analytical process, interspersed with a smattering of 'lateral thinking' and behaviourally oriented implementation. Such lateral or 'free' thinking is particularly required when it comes to generating alternative solutions to problems. The behavioural orientation is at a premium only at the implementation stage of decision-making. In table A.1 Keith Jackson, of the Henley

Table A.1 Problem-solving and decision-making.[5]

Stages	Phrases
1. Problem formulation	Detection, identification
2. Problem interpretation	Analysis, description
3. Constructing courses of action	Establishing criteria, generating ideas
4. Decision-making	Evaluation, choice, commitment
5. Implementation	Plan, action, control

Management Centre in England, has set out his standard approach to problem-solving and decision-making in management.

Whereas it is expected that, as a manager, you will sometimes make decisions for others, it is important that decision-making is delegated where appropriate. That may well require coaching. A skilled manager will be adept at coaching his subordinates continually; and Tom Peters regards such coaching as the hallmark of a good manager.

Coaching

Japanese managers spend up to 50 per cent of their time coaching their subordinates; whereas, in the West, while such coaching is acknowledged as a vital part of management on the sportsfield, that view has not traditionally prevailed in business. However, times are changing, and Tom Peters has been prominent in stimulating new attitudes.

In effect, coaching involves a combination of directing and facilitating skills. However, it tends to be seen as an integral part of the hierarchically based, boss–subordinate (leader and led) role, however much Peters may like to see it otherwise. For Peters, in his *A Passion for Excellence*,[6] coaching skills include the capacity to educate, to counsel and to sponsor, effectively and appropriately:

THE GOOD EDUCATOR:
● Articulates consistent performance expectations and objectives.
● Finds a 'learning lab' in task forces and low risk projects.
● Gives balanced, believable, timely feedback.
● Transmits values with integrity.
THE GOOD COUNSELLOR:
● Is easy to talk to.
● Listens well.

- Builds esteem and self-confidence.
- Wants people to do well.

A GOOD SPONSOR:

- Treats people as colleagues.
- Desperately and passionately wants people to succeed.

Whereas coaching is a broadly based skill, performance appraisal is more specific in nature. It is conducted periodically rather than continually.

Performance appraisal

Performance appraisal is sometimes seen to be the hallmark of analytically based management. An objectively conducted, formal review process supplants the highly subjective, informally based judgments of a more personalized management style. The skill involved in such an appraisal therefore lies in being able to combine objectivity and impartiality, with a thorough understanding of the strengths and weaknesses of the individual being appraised. Andrew Stewart,[7] a British occupational psychologist, sets out 14 points on the subject:

1. Agree a time, date and place well in advance.
2. Make sure this place is private (free from interruptions).
3. Set aside ample time – at least two hours.
4. Bring all relevant information about appraisee's performance.
5. Ask the reviewee to review his/her performance point by point.
6. Ask him/her about any problems which might affect performance.
7. Seek out the implications of such on the appraisee.
8. Ask him/her what needs to be done by either of you in order to improve the appraisee's performance.
9. The appraisee should ask about anything he/she feels is affecting his/her performance.
10. Agree the key result areas.
11. The appraisee should suggest and agree future standards.
12. You should suggest the same.
13. Agree future action.
14. Close with a firm date for the next review.

As is the case with running a meeting, performance appraisal has its formal (directive) and informal (social) elements, but the emphasis at this point, as we can see from Andrew Stewart's prescriptions, are on the former rather than the latter.

Counselling

Finally, having conducted such a performance appraisal, it is important for a manager to be able to counsel his subordinates with a view to improved performance. Such 'counselling' involves much more than giving advice, in a crudely directive capacity, but draws more generally on both listening and confrontational skills. At the same time, the overall personal and cultural context has an important part to play (see table A.2). The skill of counselling involves a mixture of directive and facilitating interventions.

Table A.2 Counselling for improved performance[8]

Technique/ style	Purpose	Question
Paraphrasing	This involves rephrasing what the person is saying in order to interpret and clarify factual information for both parties	As I understand it . . . So what you're saying is . . .
Reflecting feelings	This requires careful listening to detect feelings accurate interpretation to put them into words and suitable responses	You feel . . . It seems to you that . . .
Confrontation	This enables the person to identify inconsistences, logical sequences and so on	What would happen if . . .
Silence	This indicates to the person that more is expected and it should be accompanied by various non-verbal signals	Hmm? Ah? Oh? – and so on

Summary

The skilfully directive manager's approach, as should be evident by now, will vary according to his or her personality, and according to the state he or she has reached in skill acquisition and application. It is also important to emphasize that 'directing' skills here are differentiated from the 'influencing' skills to come, and are therefore grounded more in thought and in action than in feeling. Now, by way of contrast, we turn to social skills, which have a strong 'feeling' orientation.

Social Skills

Social, interpersonal or 'man' (an outdated notion if ever there was one) management skills cover the ability to relate to people and to enthuse them – long established social skills – and to tell the right stories and to share values, two sets of skills that have only recently become acknowledged as part of the managerial repertoire, although – in a communal context – they are as old as the hills.

Relating to people

Relating involves the exercise of interpersonal skills in both formal and informal situations, with both individuals and small groups. It requires the skilful expression of thought and action, but more particularly of feeling, in people-centred situations. Peter Honey, well known in the UK for his work on 'interpersonal skills', establishes nine people-related points[9]:

1. Seeking ideas. Asking other people for their ideas.
2. Proposing. Putting forward ideas.
3. Suggesting. Putting forward ideas as questions – how about . . . ?
4. Building. Developing someone else's idea.
5. Disagreeing. Explicitly disagreeing with others.
6. Supporting. Agreeing with what someone else has said.
7. Difficulty stating. Pointing out snags.
8. Seeking clarification or seeking information.
9. Clarifying/explaining/informing.

Interestingly, management trainers and consultants such as Peter Honey, who have taken the time and trouble to articulate their thoughts on 'interpersonal skills', are often more cognitive in orientation than the 'people person' is inclined to be. In fact, such innate people orientation is often more accurately reflected in the selling context than in everyday human relations at work.

Enthusing others

All too often 'interpersonal skills' within an organization are divorced from 'selling skills' without. This division is unfortunate because the two should be closely related. In the sales situation, however, we refer more often to the ability to enthuse customers, rather than – more abstractly – to relate to them, as exemplified by the AIDA – *A*ttention/*I*nterest/*D*esire/*A*ction – maxim[10]:

1. Does the sales talk arouse the attention of the customer at once?
2. Does it awaken his personal interest?
3. Does it create the desire in the customer to buy what is offered, through the conviction that he both wants and needs the article?
4. Does it lead logically to buying action?

Whereas salesmanship, as depicted by Heinz Goldman in his very popular *How to Win Customers*, involves a mixture of innate self- and social interest, 'shared values' – which have recently become the be all and end all of 'corporate culutre' – are more exclusively oriented towards social interest.

Sharing values

In recent years, within the context of corporate culture, the ability to enthuse individuals has been extended towards the capacity to share values, across a whole organization. Such shared values are now seen to be the quintessence of successful organizations, both in Japan and in the US. Interestingly, more attention has been paid to the phenomenon at an organizational level than at the level of managerial skill. Terry Deal and Alan Kennedy, the American corporate culture gurus, provide a good case in point:

Values are the bedrock of any corporate culture. As the essence of a company's philosophy for achieving success, values provide a sense of common direction for all employees and guidelines for their day to day behaviour. These values may be grand in scope ('Progress is our most important product') or narrowly focussed ('Underwriting excellence'). They can capture the imagination ('The first Irish multinational'). They can tell people how to work together ('It takes two to Tandem').[11]

The ability to instil a sense of 'shared values' is now seen as essential to leadership. It differs from relating to, or enthusing, people, in that it calls upon an ability to connect individual need with organizational purpose; in other words, to connect what is everyday and commonplace for the individual and the group with what is unusual and distinctive about the enterprise and its environment.

Storytelling

The capacity to share values is closely related to an ability to tell symbolic stories – tales that enrapture people in the organization. In this context, social and theatrical skills need to be combined; and at the same time the modern manager needs to reach into his ancient heritage, to an age when storytelling was part and parcel of everyday life. Deal and Kennedy refer to this skill as one of managing 'symbolically':

A day in the life of any modern manager is chock-full of little things that don't matter, little things that matter some, and big things that matter a lot. We call the first trivia, the second events, the third dramas. One of the chief skills of a symbolic manager is to distinguish among the three. The culture helps because it defines in large part what is important and what is not. But it is the symbolic manager's native intuition and judgement that help to pick the right moment to make a big deal out of something.

To dramatise trivia is to look like a fool. To overlook drama is to become a victim or villain. To miss an event or miss one's cues when something is fairly important is to look insensitive or, worse yet, stupid. Symbolic managers become adept at separating the rush of corporate life into these different categories. And for events and dramas, they become dramatic experts – actors and directors of recognised repute. They never miss an opportunity to reinforce, dramatise, or involve the central values and beliefs of the culture.[12]

Such an ability to manage symbols is a distinctive skill to which we shall pay even more attention later. In fact, storytelling has many levels to it, from the literal and ordinary, with which we are presently concerned, to the metaphoric and extraordinary – the stuff of inspiration.

Summary

In successfully relating to superiors and subordinates, colleagues and outside stakeholders, enthusing people, instilling a sense of shared values, and telling the sorts of stories that serve to reinforce the corporate culture, the socially skilled manager needs a range of abilities, from innate enthusiasm, and conventionally established interpersonal skills, to the somewhat more mysterious ability to manage symbolically.

Conclusion

Most skill- and even competence-based inventories and courses for managers centre around the established skills of organizing, directing and 'man' managing – three wide-ranging sets of skills. However, at best they only cover less than 50 per cent of the full skill repertoire. So we now turn, in Appendix B, to the emerging managerial skills, of influencing, learning, facilitating and creating.

Notes

1 J. Scott and A. Rocheter, *Effective Management Skills: Managing People* (Sphere, London, 1984).
2 D. Stewart (ed.), *Handbook of Management Skills* (Gower, London, 1987), ch. 2.
3 Stewart, *Handbook of Management Skills*, ch. 20.
4 Stewart, *Handbook of Management Skills*, ch. 4.
5 K. Jackson, *Managerial Problem Solving* (Teach Yourself Books, London, 1982).
6 T. Peters and N. Austin, *A Passion for Excellence* (Collins, London, 1985).
7 Stewart, *Handbook of Management Skills*.
8 Stewart, *Handbook of Management Skills*, ch. 16.
9 Stewart, *Handbook of Management Skills*, ch. 28.
10 H. Goldman, *How to Win Customers* (Pan, London, 1980).
11 T. Deal and A. Kennedy, *Corporate Cultures* (Penguin, London, 1987).
12 Deal and Kennedy, *Corporate Cultures*.

Appendix B

Leadership Skills

Introduction

As, in the course of the 1980s, the rational management establishment has been challenged by not only a 'back to basics' movement (influencing skills), but also by more developmental (learning and facilitating skills) and even inspirational (creative skills) approaches, so the required repertoire of managerial capacities has been expanded. We begin by considering the more instinctive, survival-oriented, influencing skills.

Emergent Skills

Influencing Skills

Influencing skills range from motivating and negotiating to public speaking and even 'intrapreneuring'. In that sense they straddle the divide between long recognized managerial skills, notably public speaking and motivational skills, and those which have been newly defined, most particularly 'intrapreneuring'.

Motivating

The ability to motivate others is – next to delegating – perhaps the most quintessential management skill. It involves not only the provision of an amenable working environment, but also of intrinsic interest, responsibility and recognition. In fact the American occupational psychologist Frederick Herzberg has clearly distinguished between such 'hygiene' and 'motivational' factors at work[1]:

Hygiene factors	Definition/Example
Company policy administration	Availability of clearly defined policies; adequacy of communication; efficiency of organisation
Supervision	Accessibility, competence and personality of the boss
Interpersonal	The relations with supervisors, subordinates and colleagues; the quality of social life at work
Salary	The total rewards package, such as salary, pension, company car
Status	A person's position or rank in relation to others, symbolised by title, parking space, car, size of office, furnishings
Job security	Freedom from insecurity, such as loss of position
Personal life	The effect of a person's work on family
Working conditions	The physical environment in which work is done

These 'hygiene' factors are the 'dissatisfiers' – their absence causes dissatisfaction. However, according to Herzberg they can never, on their own, be a cause of continuing *satisfaction* – that is where the 'motivators' come in:

Motivators	Definition/Example
Achievement	Sense of bringing something to a successful conclusion, completing a job, solving a problem, making a successful sale. The sense of achievement is in proportion to the size of the challenge.
Recognition	Acknowledgement of a person's contribution; appreciation of work by company or colleagues; rewards for merit.
Job interest	Intrinsic appeal of job; variety rather than repetition; holds interest and is not monotonous.
Responsibility	Being allowed to use discretion at work, shown trust by company, having authority to make decisions; accountable for the work of others.
Advancement	Promotion in status or job, or the prospect of it.

Since Herzberg's work in the 1960s more managerial thought has probably been given to the subject of motivation than to any other managerial skill. Nevertheless, Herzberg's approach remains seminal.

Negotiating

Negotiating skills have a harder edge to them than those of motivating people, for they involve both eliciting support and co-operation, and also a form of manipulation. However, in the best of all situations both parties in negotiations are involved in 'win–win' rather than in 'win–lose' outcomes. Bill Scott, one of the burgeoning authorities in the field, sets out his simple scheme for negotiators[2]:

1. Explore shared understanding, interests, priorities, contributions and attitudes.
2. Create interdependent ideas.
3. Shape the deal, involving a knowledge of the background facts and preparation of a supportive climate.
4. Bid up – the higher the level of aspiration, the greater the prospective achievement.
5. Bargain – discover what are the essentials, for the other party, and where he can give.

In recent years many volumes have been written on negotiation, from political, economic, commercial and psychological perspectives. The subject seems to bring together the personal and the institutional, the instinctive and the rational. It also manages to straddle the divide between competitive and co-operative behaviour. In fact, as the subject matter develops we may well find that it becomes as much a facilitating as an influencing skill. But we now turn to the somewhat more prosaic subject of 'public speaking'.

Public speaking

Whereas motivating others, as well as negotiating, usually takes place amongst small groups of people, influencing a large group will inevitably involve some form of public speaking. Moreover, as the media in general, and television in particular, have loomed larger in our managerial lives, so 'self-presentation' has become an ever more important skill. The approach that Brian Sanders (see below) and many others like him take to public speaking is logical, rational and analytical.

The three most important things to remember, in order of importance, are[3]:

1. WHO YOU ARE	your personality, relevant knowledge and experience; you must engage the whole of yourself: voice, eyes, face, arms, hands.
2. HOW YOU SAY IT	increase/enlarge your vocal range; create the right atmosphere.
3. WHAT YOU SAY	requires careful selection and ordering. Everything you say must be relevant.

This can be compared and contrasted with the well known American, Dale Carnegie – of *Winning Friends and Influencing People* fame – who placed a lot of his emphasis on emotional factors. For Carnegie it was primarily a matter of 'psyching yourself up' for the public presentation, and only secondarily a matter of saying the right things in the right way at the right time.

Whereas public speaking, then, is a very specific skill, 'intrapreneuring' is much more generally based – and intrapreneurship probably has that same 'crowd pull' in management circles today that public speaking had in the 1950s.

Intrapreneuring

Although the financial journalist, Norman Macrae, introduced the term in the UK in the late 1970s, it was only by the mid-1980s that intrapreneuring took root, most particularly in the US and Sweden. Influence, then, for the 'intrapreneur', is brought directly to bear upon business creation, within an existing organization.

While the guru of intrapreneuring in the US has been Gifford Pinchot, in Sweden it has been championed by a network of consultants, known as the 'Foresight' Group. In both cases – and unlike the often solitary role of the *entre*preneur – emphasis has been placed on the combination of rugged individualism and teamwork. The individual, exercising his entrepreneurial and influencing skills within an existing organization, must know how to get along with others. At the same time, though, the large organization has to see itself as an 'intraprise' rather than as a bureaucracy, if its intrapreneurs are to be 'set free'.

According to Pinchot, there are four phases in the process of intrapreneurship which serve to reveal its character[4]:

- THE SOLO PHASE – the intrapreneur generally builds up his idea alone to avoid early delays due to ego battles.

- THE NETWORK PHASE – once the basic idea is clear, most intrapreneurs begin to share it with close friends in the company, and a few trusted companies.
- THE BOOTLEG PHASE – an informal team forms around your idea; your home or a restaurant is a good place to meet together.
- THE FORMAL TEAM PHASE – the team gives the 'intrapreneur' the breadth of talent necessary to address all the issues and tasks of a complex start up and to establish the management depth for expansion.

It is similar to entrepreneurship in that it is informal and enterprising but different in that it involves more teamwork and communication.

Summary

Such influencing skills are naturally associated with the enterprising manager, if not also with the agent of change and the technological or organizational innovator. Naturally, the highly developed 'influencer', combining all four sets of the skills to which we have referred, will get further than his or her more narrowly based counterpart.

Learning Skills

So-called 'learning skills', as one part of a managerial whole, range from specific capabilities such as 'rapid reading' to more generalized learning skills – including thinking, information processing, and adaptive skills. These four sets of learning subskills, in themselves, need to be distinguished from the more expansive definition of learning which underpins the whole of this book. More specifically, they are primarily concerned with the cognitive aspect of learning, and less involved with both affective and behavioural aspects. We start, then, with the most specific of these skills – rapid reading.

Rapid reading

This is a discrete skill which can be picked up in a short period of time. A leading advocate of such skill in the UK is the well known Australian consultant, writer and broadcaster, Tony Buzan, according to whom there are some major misconceptions about reading skills[5]:

- Words must be read one at a time. Wrong. We read for meaning rather than for single words.

- The faster reader is not able to appreciate. Wrong. The faster reader will have more time to go over areas of special interest and importance.
- Higher speeds give lower concentration. Wrong. The faster we go the more impetus we gather and the more we concentrate.
- Average reading speeds are natural. Wrong. Such speeds are produced by an incomplete initial training in reading, combined with an inadequate knowledge of how the eye and brain works.

Thinking skills

Thinking skills have been championed, over the past 20 years, by the Anglo-Maltese Edward de Bono, in both primary and adult education. In distinguishing between 'vertical' and 'lateral' thinking he has covered the totality of our thinking processes, both as individuals and as managers. Whereas vertical thinking is self-contained and analytical, lateral thinking is open ended and perceptive[6]:

1. Lateral thinking changes. Vertical thinking chooses. Lateral thinking is generative. There is change for the sake of change. Vertical thinking is selective. It seeks to judge.
2. Vertical thinking uses yes/no. Lateral does not. Vertical thinking is thinking for what is right. Lateral thinking is looking for what is different – the only 'wrong' is the arrogance of rigidity.
3. Vertical thinking uses information for its meaning; lateral thinking uses it for its effect in setting off new ideas. Vertical thinking is analytical, and is interested in where an idea comes from; lateral thinking is provocative, and is interested in where it leads to.
4. In vertical thinking one thing must follow from another; lateral thinking uses jumps. Vertical thinking seeks to establish continuity; lateral thinking thrives on discontinuity.

De Bono has not only written prolifically on the subject of 'thinking', but he also runs an institute for cognitive research, which does a lot of work for primary schools. He was also involved, in the 1970s, with the Venezuelan government, in setting up a ministry in that country to further the thought processes of the population.

Information-processing skills

Whereas thinking skills, in management, have been championed by de Bono alone, information-processing skills have had a number of

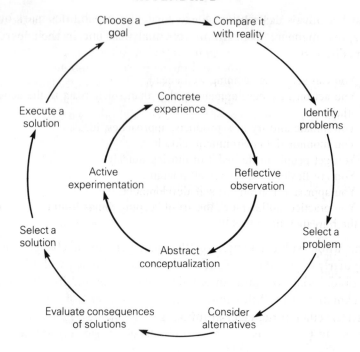

Figure B.1   Kolb's learning cycle.

leading advocates, including Reg Revans in the UK and David Kolb[7] in the US (see figure B.1). Both have likened such skills to scientific method and, thereby, to managerial problem-solving.

Revans' approach is similar to Kolb's in that he substitutes 'test' for 'active experimentation', 'verify' for 'concrete experience', 'survey' for 'reflective observation' and 'hypothesis' for 'abstract conceptualization'. Moreover, Revans has developed an entire management philosophy, centred upon so-called 'action learning'.

Such action learning invites us to continually engage in a process of questioning insight, armed with the learning cycle that he and Kolb prescribe. Such learning, for Revans, should take place amongst 'comrades in adversity', that is with fellow learner–managers, rather than from 'teachers on high'.

Anticipation

Finally, adaptive – or anticipatory – skills are perhaps the most broadly based of all four learning skills. As can be seen from Hickman and Da Silva's description, these particular capabilities mark out the adaptive manager from the merely analytical one in their 'executive versality test'[7]:

1. You can see things coming well ahead.
2. You act on new developments rather than solely react to the actions of others.
3. You initiate and try new products, approaches, ideas.
4. You monitor the environment, closely.
5. You get people in the habit of moving quickly.
6. You are flexible, experimental, tolerant.
7. You approach learning as self-development.
8. You practice 'ad hocracy', the art of keeping things from falling between the bureaucratic cracks.

The whole subject matter of 'the management of change', now so popularly received in management circles, is infused with ideas about flexible, adaptive and interactive management. In that respect Hickman and Da Silva find themselves as a part of a much greater wave of current managerial thinking.

Summary

As I have already indicated, the whole subject of learning, at least in the US and Europe, is being moved into the centre of managerial thought and practice.

We now turn to the quintessential leadership skills, of building or facilitating, and creative skills. In this context it is important to bear in mind that the leader is not the mere 'super manager' but the individual who is able to liberate, and focus, people's energy.

Facilitating Skills

Although facilitating skills may only come truly into their own in the next century, they are certainly becoming increasingly important in management every day. In fact, in many ways it is these developmental (facilitating) abilities that have distinguished Japanese managers and civil servants, from their counterparts around the globe. Facilitating skills range from the specific one of listening, and subsequently recognizing potential in people and things, to that of team-building, in particular, and of building alliances, in general.

Listening skills

Listening skills are important not only in fostering human relationships within the organization, but also without. They require a deeper, empathetic quality than those involved in merely 'relating' to others. With the advent of longer-term, and more intensive relationships between customer and supplier, manufacturer and subcontractor, more intensive listening skills are increasingly being called for.

On a one-to-one basis, listening skills are closely related to powers of observation and, as such, to the practice of meditation, which comes much more naturally to the Japanese than to those of us in the West and the North. Hickman and Da Silva have devised an 'executive sensitivity' test, to help us gauge our listening skills as managers[9]:

1. Do you deal with peoples' long range needs or only with their immediate ones?
2. Do you restrict yourself to superficial relationships or do you really get involved with your people?
3. Are you self focussed when you interact with others, or do you focus entirely on them?
4. Do you assume you already know your subordinates' wishes or are you constantly reviewing them?
5. Do you treat all your employees the same, or do you take account of each of their individual differences?
6. Do you see people the way they used to be, or the way they are becoming?
7. Do you expect people to respond to a situation the way you do, or not?

In the final analysis, good listeners are more likely than not to be adept at recognizing potential in other people.

Recognizing potential

To recognize potential in people or things, products or markets, organizations or environments requires a mixture of skill, exposure, talent and experience. Depth of insight has to be combined with a capacity to interlink socially, technologically and commercially:

In conceiving of a joint venture, the developmental manager unites the potential of one company with another. In order to do this successfully, he must be able to foresee how they might favourably interconnect. He needs to be able to match the other company's needs against his own. Similar principles apply, when spotting a market gap, or sensing a need that is going begging.

The conventional marketing texts gloss over the intuitive wisdom that is involved in 'feeling' for market trends and potential. It is the kind of wisdom and insight that a business broker requires, alongside the person who conceives of a new business. The qualities required are sensitivity and openness, an ability to connect like with unlike, a willingness to be surprised, a fascination for, and with, coincidence, an interest in how things evolve and develop, and a tendency to see the world, including the market place, as shifting, overlapping and ever changing. Chance and response, between them, provide the warp and weft of his business and the pattern of her life. The external chances of life play upon him, and as he responds to them, he shapes his luck.[10]

Amongst other things, an ability to recognize the potential of others, can help a great deal when building teams.

Team-building

This is a task that requires you not only to recognize potential in people and situations, but to realize that potential through appropriate, and complementary groupings of people. Such groupings may exist within departments, within an organization as a whole or, as is increasingly becoming the case, between one organization and another. Margerison[11] in Australia, one of the leading thinkers today in the fields of leadership and group dynamics, sees team-building and team functioning as centred upon the process of 'linking' (see figure B.2).

There is by now a vast management literature on group dynamics, team-building and team management. However, in the context of facilitating skills, your particular emphasis needs to be upon the recognition and development of individual, interpersonal and trans-personal abilities, primarily through the identification and harnessing of opportunities for synergy – hence the importance of Tom Margerison's 'linking' function.

In terms of the spectrum of styles or skills that have been identified here, a blend of all of them would heighten performance.

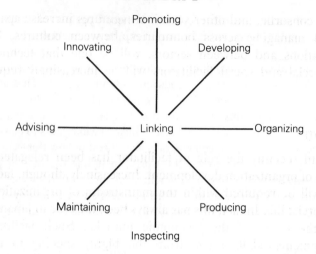

Figure B.2   Team functions.

Building alliances

To build alliances within and across organizations requires a broader managerial perspective than that involved in team-building, which is more limited in scope. Nevertheless, similar skills – relating to the recognition and harnessing of human potential – are involved. The abilities of the facilitator, catalyst or enabler are summarized, in this context, by the Anglo-American management consultant, Nancy Foy. For her, such a person[12]:

- has a well developed sense of design, or aesthetics, as well as being skilled in building 'word pictures' that can be understood across boundaries
- is aware, sensitive to the need for change and development, and alert to where blockages are likely to be, particularly those which might be turned into helpful energy
- is a 'social entrepreneur' in that he takes his percentages, as a trader or broker, more in terms of personal and organisational development than in financial rewards
- is a link between inside and outside, one level or function and another, enriching the connective tissue between different entities
- is a mature outsider, even within his own organisation, and prefers evolution to revolution

The facilitating role that Nancy Foy describes will be at an increasing premium as strategic alliances, co-partnerships, risk-sharing arrangements, consortia, and other such joint ventures increase apace. The role of managing across boundaries, between cultures, between corporations and between sectors, will be one that technological, commercial and social facilitators will be increasingly required to fulfil.

Summary

Up until recently the role of facilitator has been relegated to the fringes of organization development. Increasingly, though, facilitating skills will be required within the mainstream of organizational and commercial life. In fact, this has always been the case in Japan, at least since the onset of the 'economic miracle'. Such facilitating or developmental skills range from the highly specific to the very general.

Finally, we turn to creative skills.

Creative Skills

Creative skills are all too often seen in a very limited, managerial light. Lateral thinking, of the kind referred to under 'thinking skills', is confused with genuine creative action, which requires a combination of thought, feeling and action. In fact, creative skills underpin your ability to envision, inspire, empower and align. First you have to envision.

Envisioning

Very few managers have developed and exercised 'envisioning skills'. For in order to develop a vision for your organization, you need to draw on the fullness of your personal and organizational originality, as the American writers Kiefer and Stroh indicate, and relate it to contemporary circumstances.

An individual manager who holds such a vision is truly compelled: the whole of his or her life is a training ground for the realization of the vision. Work, for such a creative manager, is a true vocation. Everyone and everything he or she comes across has either a part to play in the visionary script, or else stands completely outside of his or her life. In the final analysis, should the actualization of the vision be thwarted, life is virtually no longer worth living.

The manager who has a genuine vision, then, is more likely than not to be able to inspire other people through his or her pervasive and inclusive picture of the future. More specifically, according to Kiefer and Stroh,[13] the visionary capacity involves:

- Creating and communicating a personal and organisational vision to which you are wholeheartedly committed.
- Revitalising and recommiting to the vision in the face of obstacles.
- Understanding an organisation as a complex system whose structure may enable or thwart realisation of the vision.
- Empowering people and being the sort of person whose presence empowers others.
- Developing intuition as a complement to reason.

Inspiring

Envisioning is not something that is created out of nothing. In order to envision the future you need to top your creative imagination. That subconscious source of inspiration has been responsible for the achievements of the world's great leaders and entrepreneurs, as the American writer, Napoleon Hill, discovered in his bestselling book, *Think and Grow Rich*:

The imagination is literally the workshop wherein are fashioned all plans created by man. The imaginative faculty functions in two forms: through, first, synthetic imagination, hunches and inspirations are received by man. It is through a second form of creative imagination that an individual may 'tune in' or communicate with the subconscious mind. The subconscious mind is the 'sending station' of the brain, through which vibrations of thought are broadcast. The creative imagination is the 'receiving net' through which the energies of thought are picked up. Finally, 'autosuggestion' is the medium by which you may put your broadcasting station into operation.[14]

The sorts of inspirational leaders to which Hill referred to in his book were Henry Ford, Thomas Edison and Woodrow Wilson. As we can see their inspiration was fuelled by a combination of refined thoughts, powerful emotions and weighty actions. Some, more than others, were also able to empower others.

Empowering

The notion of empowering people has come into popular management parlance only in recent years. It represents a distinct combination of facilitating and creative skills. As such a manager, within an organization, you not only envision and inspire but also empower others. This notion of making other people powerful, as opposed to merely exercising your own power over others, is now being recognized as an important, emergent skill. The three American O.D. consultants Jaffe, Scott and Omali, in John Adams' book on *Transforming Leadership*, are a case in point:

Of all beliefs that lead to inspired performance, the most essential one is a sense of personal power, which is held by every person within the organisation. The sense of personal power, the belief that one can make a difference, is one of the key elements in inspired performance, and in determining personal health. Power is not the capacity to make others do things, but rather an inner sense of capacity to act and receive reasonable responses from others. Empowered employees feel they have the capacity and support to do their best and to make a contribution. Some people are so self-critical and have such high expectations that they never feel any sense of satisfaction or achievement. Other people feel so distrustful of others that they wouldn't dream of asking for help or expecting a colleague to come through. Such attitudes become prisons, keeping one continually frustrated and isolated.

One theme comes up repeatedly when leaders recall inspired performances. Not only do they feel a sense of personal power, but everyone in the inspired work team feels power as well. This suggests a rule for inspired performance: power is not seen as something one person (the leader) has and others employees do not. Rather, in an inspired team everyone feels power. There is not a sense that if I have power you lose power, but rather a perception that as I gain power, so do we all. Inspired performers report that they feel personal power because they feel valued; that whatever contribution they choose to make will be accepted, and that they can take initiatives and be creative.[15]

Finally, under the guise of creative skills, we have managers who, in the course of empowering and inspiring others, align themselves to some higher power, or vision.

Aligning

To align people, finally, behind a vision, involves merging the vision with theirs, in pursuit of a noble purpose. Noted political and religious leaders, from Gandhi to Martin Luther King, are well known and recent cases in point. Examples of such business leaders are fewer, and further between, although there is certainly evidence of such alignment in many of Henry Ford's writings. In fact Ford – despite his paradoxical nature – saw himself as making the industrial desert bloom, and relieving man from the brute burdens of manual labour on the farms.

This phenomenon of aligning people behind a vision, as Ford did in the past and John Sculley – of Apple – is doing at present, is described by Californian consultant Roger Harrison in his 'Leadership strategy for a new age':

> Alignment occurs when organisation members act as parts of an integrated whole, each finding the opportunity to express his or her true purpose through the organisation's purpose. The individual expands his or her individual purpose to include the organisation's purpose. Organisation alignment behind charismatic leadership must involve the merging of the individual's strength and will with that of the collectivity. In high-performing organisations animated by a noble purpose, this may not feel like much of a sacrifice.
>
> But even high-performing organisations have their inhumanities. They burn people out; they take over their private lives; they ostracise or expel those who do not share their purposes; and they are frequently ruthless in their dealings with those outside the magic circle; competitors, suppliers, the public. It seems to me no accident that many of our most exciting tales of high-performing, closely aligned organisation are either literally or metaphorically 'war stories'. War is the ultimate expression of unbridled will in the pursuit of 'noble' ends.[16]

Summary

These creative skills do not come easily to the average manager, and often it is only in maturity that the individual is able to rise to such heights. However, a start can be made by everyone, should these skills at least be recognized, with a view to their subsequent, and cumulative, development.

Conclusion

We have identified here seven major groups of skills, each of which is strongly differentiated from the other. In other words, the emphasis has been on diversity rather than uniformity. Each of these groups of skills can be acquired and applied in different ways, depending on the kind of skilled manager that you are.

Finally, and with respect to each skill group, every one of you will be at a different stage of development. There will also be some correlation between the kind of individual manager you are, and the skills that come most naturally to you. For example, and as we have seen, the developmental manager would be expected to be a natural facilitator, and the analytical manager a natural organizer.

Notes

1 F. Herzberg et al., Motivation at Work (1968).
2 D. Stewart (ed.), Handbook of Management Skills (Gower, London, 1987), ch. 5.
3 Stewart, Handbook of Management Skills, ch. 8.
4 G. Pinchot, Intrapreneuring (Harper & Row, New York, 1985).
5 Tony Buzan, Use Your Head (BBC, London, 1974).
6 E. de Bono, Lateral Thinking for Management (Penguin, London, 1981).
7 D. Kolb, Experiential Learning (Prentice-Hall, Englewood Cliffs, NJ, 1984).
8 D. Hickman and T. Da Silva, Creating Excellence (Allen & Unwin, London, 1984).
9 Hickman and Da Silva, Creating Excellence.
10 R. Lessem, Intrapreneuring (Wildwood House, London, 1987).
11 R. Margerison and T. McCann, How to Lead a Winning Team (IMCB, 1985).
12 N. Foy, The Missing Link (Foundation for Management Education, London, 1976).
13 J. Adams (ed.), Transforming Work (Miles River Press, Virginia, USA, 1984), ch. 11.
14 N. Hill, Think and Grow Rich (Wilshire, New York, 1954).
15 J. Adams (ed.), Transforming Leadership (Miles River Press, Virginia, USA, 1986), ch. 6.
16 Adams, Transforming Work, ch. 6.

Index

Developmental Management

The following titles have now been published in this exciting and innovative series:

Ronnie Lessem: *Developmental Management* 0 631 16844 3 □
Charles Hampden-Turner: *Charting the Corporate Mind** 0 631 17735 3 □
Yoneji Masuda: *Managing in the Information Society* 0 631 17575 X □
Ivan Alexander: *Foundations of Business* 0 631 17718 3 □
Henry Ford: *Ford on Management** 0 631 17061 8 □
Bernard Lievegoed: *Managing the Developing Organization* 0 631 17025 1 □
Jerry Rhodes:*Conceptual Toolmaking* 0 631 17489 3 □
Jagdish Parikh: *Managing Your Self* 0 631 17764 7 □
John Davis: *Greening Business* 0 631 17202 5 □
Ronnie Lessem: *Total Quality Learning* 0 631 16828 1 □
Pauline Graham: *Integrative Management* 0 631 17391 9 □
Alain Minc: *The Great European Illusion* 0 631 17695 0 □
Albert Koopman: *Transcultural Management* 0 631 17804 X □
Elliott Jaques: *Executive Leadership* 1 55786 257 5 □
Koji Kobayashi: *The Rise of NEC* 1 55786 277 X □
* Not available in the USA   All titles are £18.95 each

You can order through your local bookseller or, in case of difficulty, direct from the publisher using this order form. Please indicate the quantity of books you require in the boxes above and complete the details form below. NB. The publisher would be willing to negotiate a discount for orders of more than 20 copies of one title.

Payment
Please add £2.50 to payment to cover p&p.
□ Please charge my Mastercard/Visa/American Express account
card number □□□□□□□□□□□□□□□□
Expiry date _____
Signature _____
(credit card orders must be signed to be valid)
□ I enclose a cheque for £_____ made payable to **Marston Book Services Ltd**
(PLEASE PRINT)
Name _____
Address _____

_____ Postcode _____
Tel No _____
Signature _____ Date _____

Please return the completed form with remittance to:
Department DM, Basil Blackwell Ltd
108 Cowley Road, Oxford OX4 1JF, UK
or telephone your credit card order on 0865 791155.

Goods will be despatched within 14 days of receipt of order. Data supplied may be used to inform you about other Basil Blackwell publications in relevant fields.
Registered in England No. 180277 Basil Blackwell Ltd.